AF677356

Principles of Suretyship Volume I

Principles of Suretyship

Volume I

JOHN B. FITZGERALD
Surety Consultant

RAY H. BRITT, LL.B., CPCU, AIM
Fidelity and Surety Claim Consultant

DANIEL D. WALDORF
Vice President and Surety Director
Alexander & Alexander, Inc.

Coordinating Author
LOWELL S. YOUNG, M.B.A., CPCU, CLU
Director of Curriculum
Insurance Institute of America

First Edition • 1991

INSURANCE INSTITUTE OF AMERICA
720 Providence Road, Malvern, Pennsylvania 19355-0770

First Edition • December 1991

Library of Congress Catalog Number 91-73928
International Standard Book Number 0-89462-066-5

Printed in the United States of America

Foreword

The American Institute for Chartered Property Casualty Underwriters and the Insurance Institute of America are independent, nonprofit, educational organizations serving the needs of the property and liability insurance business. The Institutes develop a wide range of programs—curricula, study materials, and examinations—in response to the educational requirements of various elements of the business.

The American Institute confers the Chartered Property Casualty Underwriter (CPCU®) professional designation on those who meet the Institute's experience, ethics, and examination requirements.

The Insurance Institute of America offers associate designations and certificate programs in the following technical and managerial disciplines:

Accredited Adviser in Insurance (AAI®)
Associate in Claims (AIC)
Associate in Underwriting (AU)
Associate in Risk Management (ARM)
Associate in Loss Control Management (ALCM®)
Associate in Premium Auditing (APA®)
Associate in Management (AIM)
Associate in Research and Planning (ARP®)
Associate in Insurance Accounting and Finance (AIAF)
Associate in Automation Management (AAM®)
Associate in Marine Insurance Management (AMIM®)
Associate in Reinsurance (ARe)
Associate in Fidelity and Surety Bonding (AFSB)
Certificate in General Insurance
Certificate in Supervisory Management
Certificate in Introduction to Claims
Certificate in Introduction to Property and Liability Insurance

The Institutes began publishing textbooks in 1976 to help students meet the national examination standards. Since that time, we have produced more than seventy-five individual textbook volumes. Despite the vast differences in the subjects and purposes of these volumes, they all have much in common. First, each book is specifically designed to increase knowledge and develop skills that can improve job performance and help students achieve the educational objectives of the course for which it is assigned. Second, all of the manuscripts of our texts are widely reviewed prior to publication, by both insurance business practitioners and members of the academic community. In addition, all of our texts and course guides reflect the work of Institute staff members. These writing or editing duties are seen as an integral part of their professional responsibilities, and no one earns a royalty based on the sale of our texts. We have proceeded in this way to avoid even the appearance of any conflict of interests. Finally, the revisions of our texts often incorporate improvements suggested by students and course leaders.

We welcome criticisms of and suggestions for improving our publications. It is only with such constructive comments that we can hope to improve the quality of our study materials. Please direct any comments you may have on this text to the Curriculum Department of the Institutes.

Norman A. Baglini, Ph.D., CPCU, CLU
President and Chief Executive Officer

Preface

Principles of Suretyship (AFSB 151) is designed to be one of five courses and examinations, the successful completion of which will lead to an Associate in Fidelity and Surety Bonding (AFSB) designation. Principles of Suretyship provides a foundation for the study of suretyship by explaining the general principles, financial analysis, and terminology applicable to all types of bonds. The additional four courses and national examinations required to earn the AFSB designation are AFSB 152 (Contract Surety), AFSB 153 (Fidelity and Noncontract Surety), CPCU 6 (The Legal Environment of Insurance), and CPCU 8 (Accounting and Finance).

The two-volume text, *Principles of Suretyship*, was a labor of love by many expert active and retired industry specialists. The three primary authors have over 100 years of surety experience among them. They are John B. Fitzgerald, retired President of CIGNA Bond Services, Philadelphia; Ray H. Britt, LL.B.,CPCU, AIM, retired Superintendent, Fidelity and Surety Division of the Claim Department and Assistant Secretary, United States Fidelity and Guaranty Company, Baltimore; and Daniel D. Waldorf, Vice President and Surety Director, Alexander & Alexander, Inc., Dallas.

The contributing authors, recognized individually on a separate page following this preface, added much of value to this text. As the affiliations shown on the contributing authors' page indicate, they all have a rich background in suretyship.

The initial motivation for developing the Associate in Fidelity and Surety Bonding (AFSB) designation program evolved from the joint efforts of the National Association of Surety Bond Producers (NASBP) and the Surety Association of America (SAA). These organizations perceived the need for an organized, coordinated curriculum to assist in the development of those whose job duties or professional interests involved fidelity and surety bonding. Academic achievement awards for outstanding AFSB completers will be sponsored by these two organizations and the National Association of Independent Sureties (NAIS) and the American Surety Association (TASA).

The following individuals were particularly instrumental in the impetus to develop this program: Theodore J. Adams, CPCU, Director of the NASBP; J. Martin Huber, Executive Vice President of the NASBP; Lloyd Provost, President of the SAA; Dennis E. Wine, Vice President of Surety at the SAA; and the late Bruce T. Wallace, former Executive Vice President of the NASBP.

Thanks should go to S. Wesley Porter, Jr., CPCU, Director of Educational Services in the Field Services Department of the Institutes. He developed the initial outlines for the proposed fidelity and surety courses. These outlines were expanded and refined during several meetings of fidelity and surety experts, which were held at the Institute and in cities throughout the country. The assistance of those involved in these meetings was much appreciated and helped to give a clearer focus for the authors of the text.

The response of the fidelity and surety segment of the property-liability industry has been gratifying. Many have spent time and effort in reviewing manuscripts from authors. The following have reviewed most or all of the chapters: Douglas R. Bowen, CPCU, AIM, United States Fidelity and Guaranty Co.; Roland T. Chiaradio, The Aetna Casualty & Surety Co.; John B. Fitzgerald, retired, CIGNA Bond Services; Robert N. Fox, retired, Western Surety Co.; John L. Hannum, Insurance Company of the West; David L. Hixenbaugh, CPCU, Employers Mutual Casualty Company; Willard R. Holley, retired, United States Fidelity and Guaranty Co.; Richard C. Lewis, retired, Fidelity and Deposit Co.; Douglas J. Paterson, Safeco Insurance Companies; Lynn M. Schubert, American Insurance Association; Jane E. Sjoman, CPCU, Continental Guaranty & Credit Corp.; Donald E. Vaile, J.D., retired, United States Fidelity and Guaranty Co.; Dennis E. Wine, The Surety Association of America. Special thanks goes to them.

Others have reviewed one or more chapters: Theodore J. Adams, CPCU, T. J. Adams & Associates; Herbert M. Benton, J.D., CPA, Herbert M. Benton & Co.; Frank C. Bonner, Jr., CPCU, American Re-Insurance Co.; David E. Bordon, J.D., Sedgwick, Detert, Moran & Arnold; Marcia C. Brejda, CPCU, CPIW; Ray H. Britt, CPCU, retired, United States Fidelity and Guaranty Co.; Joseph L. Burke, CPCU, Fidelity and Deposit Company of Maryland; Duncan L. Clore, J.D., Strasburger and Price; Frank Conly, North American Reinsurance Corp.; James A. Daily, United States Fidelity and Guaranty Co.; E. Harned Davis, Insurance Company of the West; James D. Dixon,

Chubb Group of Insurance Companies; Clarence E. Duvall, retired, Fidelity and Deposit Company of Maryland; James V. Folmer, Pennsylvania National Mutual Casualty Insurance Co.; John C. Garde, Fidelity and Deposit Company of Maryland; Robert E. Giveans, CIGNA Bond Services; Denton R. Hammond, CPA, VanderBloemen/Hammond Associates; J. Martin Huber, Executive Vice President, National Association of Surety Bond Producers; Donald G. Jewitt, J.D., CIGNA Property and Casualty Companies; William Jungreis, MBA, CPCU, CIGNA Bond Services; Richard D. Justa, Sentry Insurance—A Mutual Company; David Litzkow, St. Paul Fire and Marine Insurance Co.; John A. Lombardi, Fidelity and Deposit Company of Maryland; Marion J. Long, Merchants Bonding Company; Ray Lorah, Reliance United Pacific Surety Managers; Raymond MacNeil, Reliance United Pacific Surety Managers; John J. Mangan, CPCU, ARM, CIGNA Bond Services; David McCreery, Contractors Bond Line; Robert C. McGuire, CPCU, ITT Hartford; Ronald M. Metcho, CPCU, ARM, R. A. Saul Agency, Inc.; Thomas C. Moore, CIGNA Bond Services; Dennis Palmer, Fidelity and Deposit Company of Maryland; Theodore G. Parks, CPCU, United States Fidelity and Guaranty Co.; John J. Petro, LL.B., McNamara and McNamara; John T. Posey, CPCU, CLU; Hugh F. Rocks, CIGNA Bond Services; Roger M. Rossiter, CPCU, Employers Reinsurance Corp.; Keith Sears, retired, The Travelers Group; Richard S. Skewes, General Reinsurance Corp.; Michael M. Tracy, J.D., Hess, Egan, Hagerty & L'Hommedieu; Michael W. Vann, CPCU, CLU, United States Fidelity and Guaranty Co.; Rob V. Weldy, J.D., The Surety Association of America; William H. Woods, J.D., McNamara and McNamara. Their efforts are also appreciated.

Teresa Davis Thamer, CPA, assisted in developing and evaluating some of the accounting statements presented.

Although many members of the Curriculum and Publications Departments of the Institute shared the task of turning these manuscripts into a finished book, special mention should be made of Karen Porter, J.D., Assistant Director of Curriculum, without whose help the project would not have been completed successfully.

Ultimate responsibility for the project rests with the Curriculum Department of the Insurance Institute of America, which welcomes comments and suggestions for further improvements in this text.

Lowell S. Young, CPCU, CLU

Contributing Authors

The Insurance Institute of America acknowledges with deep appreciation the help of the following contributing authors:

Stephen Dullard, CPCU
Assistant Contract Manager
CNA Insurance Companies

Denton R. Hammond, CPA
Partner
VanderBloemen Hammond Associates

Howard T. Johnson
Vice President
Employers Reinsurance Corporation

Richard C. Lewis
Surety Consultant

Roger M. Rossiter, CPCU
Assistant Vice President
Employers Reinsurance Corporation

Warren L. Souders, Jr., CPA
Assistant Contract Manager
CNA Insurance Companies

Table of Contents

CHAPTER 1

Overview of Suretyship

Suretyship plays an important role in handling the loss exposures facing individuals, organizations, and governments. This chapter defines and gives a history of suretyship, explains the use of bonds, describes the personnel and underwriting considerations involved in suretyship, and its relationship to other forms of insurance, and forecasts the role of suretyship in the future.

ROLE OF SURETYSHIP AND THE USE OF BONDS

The role of any risk-transfer mechanism in the economy is to prevent financial hardship resulting from events beyond the control of the person or entity affected. In suretyship, the events are almost always under the control of the bonded person, or *principal*. A *surety bond* protects an *obligee*, who is the party to whom a principal owes an obligation. It is a written instrument requiring that two parties pay a third party a sum of money if an obligation is not fulfilled. The principal is the party primarily responsible for the obligation on the bond, and the principal almost always controls events that may bring about a loss. The obligee is the beneficiary of the bond and is the party to whom the principal is obligated. The *surety* is the party who guarantees fulfillment of the principal's obligation to the obligee.

The following are typical examples of losses to which governments, businesses, and individuals are exposed as a result of a principal's failure to perform obligations that may be secured by bonds.

1. The assets of a child's, insane person's, or deceased person's estate are stolen, dissipated, or negligently invested by a person in a position of trust with responsibility for those funds.
2. A construction contractor fails to complete projects undertaken for a variety of reasons:

a. The owners or employees of the business steal current contract proceeds or receipts from the projects.
b. The contractor has not submitted adequate bids on one or more projects and cannot complete them or pay obligations incurred to date in the performance of those projects.
c. The contractor has invested surplus funds in nonliquid assets such as land, boats, or paintings, or the contractor is under-capitalized and therefore cannot pay unforeseen costs incurred in the projects.

3. A public official receives public funds and cannot account for them because of misappropriation or failure to protect them from theft by employees or others.
4. Duplicate securities, issued to an owner who alleges the certificates were lost, stolen, or destroyed, are presented to a transfer agent by a person in legal possession of the certificates, which are drawn, issued, or endorsed to that person's order.
5. A business fails to pay fees, taxes, or penalties to a state or local government or engages in unethical conduct to the detriment of customers or to the public.
6. The federal government loses revenue when importers or customs brokers fail to pay duties, fines, and penalties.

Governments, businesses, and individuals, seeking ways to transfer such risks of loss, have created the demand for fidelity and surety bonds. The following are the major categories of bonds:

1. Contract bonds (construction contracts)
2. Fidelity bonds (bonds providing coverage to employers for employees' dishonest acts)
3. Noncontract bonds (all other bonds, including public official, license and permit, and fiduciary bonds; judicial bonds in civil proceedings; and financial guarantee bonds)

In a typical contract bond situation, the project owner wants to build a structure or improve land. In a construction contract bond a contractor and a bonding company assure the project owner that the contractor will perform all obligations under the contract on time, within budget, and according to specifications.

Fidelity bonds are a response to people in positions of trust who can cause losses to others by dishonest acts such as theft, larceny, embezzlement, or breach of trust. Employers often transfer this risk of loss to another entity, which provides a fidelity bond to reimburse an employer for losses caused by employees' dishonest acts.

Noncontract bonds involve all other situations in which sureties guarantee performance of obligations, few, if any of which, arise from contract.

Bonds Required by Law

Federal, state, and local governments, as well as courts, have created a market for fidelity and surety bonds through statutes (written laws), regulations, ordinances, and rules of court. For example, to protect public funds, legislatures have enacted laws that require the following:

1. As a general rule, contractors entering into contracts with public bodies for improvements to real property must post two guarantees—one conditioned upon faithful performance of the contract, and the other upon payment of obligations incurred in the performance of the contract. Occasionally, both the performance and payment obligation may be included in a combination performance and payment bond.
2. Public officials must post bonds, conditioned upon their faithful performance of duties, to qualify for office.
3. Fiduciaries or other entities in positions of trust appointed by courts to administer funds must post bonds conditioned upon their faithful performance of duties.
4. Businesses and individuals, to qualify for licenses or permits, must post bonds to guarantee performance of the obligations required by the licenses or permits.

Third-Party Beneficiaries. In addition to public bodies, businesses and individuals benefit from legislation. Some of the required bonds have provisions that result in benefits to third parties. Third parties who benefit from contracts, including bonds, are called *third-party beneficiaries*.

For example, one bond that benefits third parties guarantees payment for labor and materials on construction projects. The federal and all state governments require this bond of contractors agreeing to perform public works. This bond protects against a contractor's failure to pay certain subcontractors, laborers, and material suppliers whose services and supplies are essential for performance of the contract. Without this bond, unpaid subcontractors, laborers, and material suppliers of public works contractors have no recourse against anyone other than the contractor or subcontractor to whom they supplied the labor or material. They do not have mechanic lien rights against public property, nor do they have any other right to collect from the public body. Therefore, as indicated above, laws require that public bodies obtain from a public works contractor a bond with the payment obligation. This bond assures both the public body and subcontractors, laborers, and material suppliers that the contractor's obligations to them will be paid.

Other types of bonds that may benefit third parties are those required of fiduciaries, licensees, and public officials. A third party injured by a public official's act has a right of action against the official and the surety on the official's bond. This right of action also may be available to a third-party beneficiary in the case of a wrongful action committed by a *fiduciary,* who is any person in a position of trust. Third-party beneficiaries neither create a market for surety bonds nor pay a premium for the protection they receive.

Financial Institutions. A financial institution should have fidelity coverage on all of its employees and crime coverage to protect it from losses resulting from crimes and fraud committed by outside parties. Laws require that financial institutions purchase financial institution bonds. Thus, both self-interest and government action have created the market for fidelity and crime coverages.

Bonds Required by the Private Sector

The private sector also has created a market for surety bonds. Business entities and individuals need many different types of bonds as protection from loss. Despite this need, the private sector underutilizes bonds but would probably use them to a greater extent if individuals knew more about their value.

The largest potential market for bonds in the private sector is private construction projects. There, contractors would be bonded by owners and subcontractors by general contractors and construction managers in private work. Despite the protection offered by such an arrangement, many in the private sector believe that any contractor who can obtain a surety bond does not need the guaranty in the first place. Additionally, some in both the private and public sectors believe that bonds are a wasted expense because they fear that sureties might not pay claims. This belief is erroneous, as evidenced by the fact that, in the 1980s, sureties paid over 50 percent of premium dollars received in loss and loss adjustment expenses. Therefore, while public entities use bonds more extensively, the history of suretyship attests to their significance in both the public and private sectors.

HISTORY OF SURETYSHIP

Suretyship has a long history, as evidenced by biblical references to the surety relationship. Even in ancient times, it was clear that care was necessary in a surety obligation, or the surety was liable to pay on behalf of the principal whose character, capacity, or financial ability was often unknown. Ancient Roman ordinances required surety for the construction of buildings, walls, and highways.

Personal suretyship developed along with western civilization in Europe, and it developed even further with the establishment of the United States. This section discusses the law and personal suretyship, as well as the development of corporate suretyship.

The Law and Personal Suretyship

Although personal suretyship among private individuals is an age-old practice, it still exists today, but to a much more limited extent than in the past. As the law of suretyship developed over the years, courts and legislatures sought to protect private individuals who became sureties for others without compensation.

English Common Law. English *common law* became the foundation for American law. The common law included all statutory and case law of England and the American colonies before the American revolution, including unwritten customs and tradition from ancient times. *Statutory law* is written law created by legislative bodies. *Case law* develops out of court decisions in particular cases, which establish precedents for future cases. A *precedent* is a decision by a court that serves as an example, or authority, for a later, similar case. The common law is important in decisions regarding suretyship and governs many issues in this area.

Statute of Frauds. In 1677 the English Parliament passed the Statute of Frauds in order to eliminate abuses in the enforceability of verbal contracts arising from acts of fraud and perjury. The Statute of Frauds required that, in order to be enforceable, certain contracts must be in writing and signed by the persons making the contract. Among the contracts covered by the statute was any promise to answer for another person's debts or defaults. Most American states have adopted statutes similar to the Statute of Frauds.

Since bonds are promises to answer for another person's debts or defaults, they must be in writing and signed by the sureties. Likewise, any changes in surety contracts must be supported by written memoranda, addenda, or riders attached to the bonds and signed by the sureties.

Legal Treatment of Personal Sureties. Court decisions and statutes have developed and refined the common law over the years. The law remains favorable to individuals who become sureties and who receive no compensation for the risks they take. Where statutes still permit personal sureties on statutory bonds, most of them require that appropriate authorities carefully assess an individual's qualifications according to the statutes involved. Typically, an individual must establish a net worth in real estate either equal to twice the penal sum of the bond or acceptable to the regulatory body or obligee. A *penal sum* is the maximum amount a surety must pay if a principal does not fulfill the obligation.

The legal treatment of individual sureties formed the background for corporations that assumed the debts or defaults of others in exchange for premiums during the nineteenth century. The legal environment changed as corporate suretyship became more popular. Courts and legislatures were reluctant to give for-profit corporate sureties the favorable treatment they had given to individual sureties, who often were trying to help friends or relatives. Corporate sureties are experts and professionals. Therefore, the law holds them to a higher degree of responsibility than it requires for individual sureties.

Decline of Personal Suretyship. As corporate suretyship grew, personal suretyship declined. Most people who became personal sureties did so as a favor to friends or relatives. Defaults of principals in these situations were costly monetarily and interpersonally. Friends and relatives often became bitter enemies.

A typical suretyship situation in agrarian America illustrates how and why personal suretyship declined. A farmer needs a cow but does not have the funds to purchase it. The farmer goes to her brother and asks him to guarantee that he will vouch for her obligation to buy the cow on credit. The farmer still is principally obligated to the seller, but the brother guarantees that he will pay for the cow in the event of his sister's default. In turn, he can collect from his sister-farmer in the event of her default. In a modern-day situation, the farmer might ask her brother to cosign for her on buying a tractor or some other piece of farm equipment.

In these situations, the principal's default carries not only the risk of bad feelings, but also the risk that the surety might not have sufficient funds to back up the obligation. The farmer's brother could, for example, stand as surety with the sincere belief that the farmer will pay and that standing as surety is only a formality. When the default occurs, the brother finds that he does not have the money owed. The result is that the person who sold the cow to the farmer is left with neither the cow nor the money, suffering a serious net loss with no one to go after but two insolvents.

This example shows that personal suretyship declined in part because society could not continue to bear the costs of the personal suretyship system because it is too often untrustworthy, leaving creditors with no recourse. Personal sureties, having all the protection of the law favorable to sureties, could delay and perhaps even avoid payment. If personal sureties were not responsible financially, creditors had little chance of recovery from two insolvent debtors, the principal and the surety. One observer noted the following:

> The inherent weakness of personal surety was the frequent failure of the bondsman to make good because of insolvency, debts or other causes. The economic unsoundness of personal surety was testified to by the federal government in 1894, when it officially recognized corporate suretyship with the disclosure that it alone had $35,000,000 in uncollectible claims against the insolvent individual bondsmen.[1]

The Development of Corporate Suretyship

As the American economy became more industrialized, and therefore more complex, the amounts of money sureties had to guarantee became too large for personal sureties to handle. Corporate suretyship was the answer for guaranteeing the very large amounts of money involved in the day-to-day business of the newly industrialized country. This section discusses the development of corporate suretyship from its inception to its present role as a complement to insurance.

Early Corporate Suretyship. Following the Civil War, and particularly during the Reconstruction period, American commerce and industry developed rapidly. As a result of the growing number and complexity of financial/commercial relationships, the law governing these relationships became more necessary and sophisticated. There was a need for something more stable and permanent than the age-old system of personal guarantees. In the late nineteenth century, corporate suretyship emerged in the United States as a response to this need. With strength, specialized experience, and strong financial resources, corporate sureties replaced personal sureties.

The first known American company to write surety bonds was the Fidelity and Casualty Company of New York. In 1880, the company started in the fidelity field, providing coverage for dishonest acts of employees, and then expanded the following year into all types of surety bonds. At the close of the nineteenth century, most major East Coast insurance companies, with home offices in Hartford, Boston, New York, Philadelphia, and Baltimore, had expanded their general insurance writings to include surety bonds, which complemented their other lines of business. As the country grew and prospered throughout the twentieth century, many new regional insurance and surety companies formed. Today, many insurance companies write fidelity and surety bonds, as well as property and liability lines of coverage.

Corporate Sureties Today. Property and liability insurers have entered the business of writing fidelity and surety bonds, and fidelity and surety companies have entered the business of writing property and liability insurance. Today, for the most part, multi-line property and liability insurers serve the market for fidelity and surety bonds in the United States.

There is keen competition among companies in the fidelity and surety industry. Exhibit 1-1 shows 1990 net premiums written for the fidelity and surety lines of business for the top twelve companies in each category and in both categories combined. The exhibit also shows that seven companies had over $100,000,000 of combined fidelity and surety net premiums written. Most of the companies listed in the exhibit are major property and liability underwriters, while some specialize in fidelity or surety underwriting.

In the multi-line companies, fidelity and surety is usually a small operation compared with the property and liability operations of the company. Generally, there are fewer people involved in the production, underwriting, and claim operations of these lines. Annual written premiums for these lines are substantially less than the premiums of other forms of insurance. However, the profit for these lines, as a percentage of earned premiums, tends to be larger.

Exhibit 1-2 shows that in 1990 fidelity accounted for slightly less than half of 1 percent of the property-casualty (property-liability) business, while surety accounted for slightly more than 1 percent of the industry's net premiums written. Exhibit 1-2 also shows the relative size of fidelity net premiums compared with those for surety. In 1990 fidelity had less than half (37 percent) of the net premiums written for surety. Fidelity had $899 million of net premiums written, while surety had $2.458 billion. From 1981 to 1990 the net premiums for both fidelity and surety increased 2.4 and 2.5 times respectively, while total property-liability net premiums written increased 2.2 times.

Complementary Relationship of Suretyship and Insurance. Corporate suretyship and insurance are complementary lines of business that have many common financial and reporting procedures. The legal and underwriting characteristics of each line of business are more closely related to each other than either would be to other financial service industries. The consolidation of financial and capital resources of both lines in a single corporate operation make a company more financially credible, enabling it to make sound commitments on individual surety bonds. These companies usually have a broader market potential because some customers require insurance as well as surety bonds. The various states recognize the connection between suretyship and insurance by requiring that insurance departments regulate surety companies.

Corporate sureties evaluate risks to determine which principals merit their backing, thus allowing them to assure obligees that they will compensate them if principals default. Federal, state, and local governments recognize the benefits of accepting corporate sureties

Exhibit 1-1
1990 Net Premiums Written (Millions of Dollars)
by Company or Group

Fidelity		Surety		Fidelity and Surety Combined	
1. Chubb	166	1. Aetna	109	1. AIG	196
2. AIG	131	2. St. Paul	95	2. Chubb	189
3. CUNA Mutual	98	3. USF&G	94	3. Aetna	189
4. Aetna	79	4. Fidelity & Deposit	88	4. St. Paul	151
5. St. Paul	55	5. Continental	84	5. Fidelity & Deposit	136
6. Fidelity & Deposit	47	6. CNA	77	6. Continental	119
7. Continental	35	7. Reliance	74	7. USF&G	114
8. Hartford Ins.	32	8. Fireman's Fund	66	8. CUNA Mutual	98
9. Reliance	22	9. AIG	64	9. Reliance	96
10. Western Surety	22	10. Swiss Reins.	62	10. CNA	81
11. USF&G	20	11. Hartford	47	11. Hartford	79
12. Ohio Casualty	14	12. Amwest	44	12. Fireman's Fund	66

Adapted from *Best's Aggregates and Averages, Property-Casualty*, 1991 Edition (Oldwick, NJ: A.M. Best Company), pp. 181-183.

Exhibit 1-2
Net Premiums Written (Millions of Dollars)

Year	Total Property-Casualty Industry	Fidelity	Percent of Total	Surety	Percent of Total
1981	99,276	381	0.38	970	0.98
1982	103,968	360	0.35	1,094	1.05
1983	108,983	377	0.35	1,272	1.17
1984	118,166	432	0.37	1,565	1.32
1985	144,186	588	0.41	2,264	1.57
1986	176,552	801	0.45	1,890	1.07
1987	193,246	1,009	0.52	2,023	1.05
1988	202,015	980	0.49	2,066	1.02
1989	208,388	928	0.45	2,275	1.09
1990	217,825	899	0.41	2,458	1.13
Total	$1,572,605	$6,753	0.43	$17,879	1.14
1990/1981 =	2.2	2.4		2.5	

Adapted from *Best's Aggregates & Averages, Property-Casualty*, 1991 Edition (Oldwick, NJ: A.M. Best Company), pp. 136, 137, and 151. © A.M. Best Company—used with permission.

instead of personal sureties and have enacted laws permitting or requiring that corporate sureties write bonds required by statutes.

SURETY PERSONNEL

The corporate surety's evaluation of applications of would-be principals is an involved process, usually starting with the producer and ending with the underwriter. Each step of the process requires a special understanding of the particular field of suretyship and a keen awareness of the factors required to qualify as a person or entity as principal on a bond. This section explains the functions of the personnel involved in the process of writing surety bonds.

Producers

Traditionally, the agent is the first-line producer of surety bonds. Most agents, or producers, have powers of attorney from the sureties they represent. A *power of attorney* is an instrument authorizing another to act as one's agent or attorney. Producers' authority, if any, to execute bonds is limited either by the terms of the power of attorney or by another agreement between the producer and the company. For bonds that producers may not execute, their recommendations as to the client's qualification for surety credit is a condition to the underwriting process.

Producers have a responsibility to the surety not to abuse their authority. They should develop fully and present fairly and accurately all the data on which they base their recommendations and on which the underwriters will make their decisions. Producers must share their knowledge of the applicant with the underwriter, obtaining all the information requested by the underwriter in the application form and by other information, if necessary. They also must decide whether to recommend the applicant to the underwriter for the bond or coverage requested.

Some independent insurance producers specialize in producing contract surety business. Many of them belong to the National Association of Surety Bond Producers (NASBP). These producers' primary focus is producing contractor surety bonds and servicing the insurance and bonding needs of their contractor clients. They also serve the vital function of educating the general public, legislative bodies, contractor associations, and others about the benefits of surety bonds.

Underwriters

Underwriters have a responsibility to the producer and to the producer's client to assess the data presented in order to determine if the data supplied are sufficient to make an underwriting decision. They then must decide whether to approve the bond or coverage for which application has been made. (Chapter 4 examines surety underwriting.)

In order to fulfill their various duties, underwriters have many considerations and functions, including, among other things, the responsibility for the bond forms the surety company uses and the surety company's application forms and forms for indemnity, subordination, collateral, and other agreements.

Underwriters also determine the premium for the risk and whether the company should undertake the risk. They determine what conditions the applicant should meet before the company undertakes the risk, who should indemnify the surety, and whether to require collateral before undertaking the risk.

The Surety Association of America (SAA) collects data on premiums written and earned and losses incurred on the various fidelity and surety lines. These data have been used recently to calculate loss costs that the SAA member companies may use to determine the premiums necessary for specific risks. Each surety company must decide what expenses it needs to charge above and beyond the loss costs. (Chapters 9 and 10 examine surety ratemaking.)

Claim Representatives

Claim representatives of surety companies sort through the often conflicting information provided by obligees, third-party claimants, principals, and indemnitors. They frequently must make decisions and act in ways that affect the financial well-being of one or more of those parties. The effects can be beneficial to some and detrimental to others. They sometimes may be assisted by outside counsel or, in the case of construction-contract losses, by professional engineers. (Chapter 12 treats the claims process in greater detail.)

Sound claim practices include, but are not limited to, the following:

1. Determination of the facts
2. Evaluation of the facts
3. Review of the law and its application to the facts
4. Documentation of decisions and actions in order to demonstrate the process through which claim representatives made decisions or took action

Claim representatives must know the surety's claim philosophy and faithfully carry it out. Sureties are aware of their role in the economy and society. Their first duty is to the parties who rely on the protection of surety bonds. Their second duty is to the principals and indemnitors for whose business, personal necessity, or convenience they provide bonds.

The roles of producers, underwriters, and claim representatives in a fidelity and surety operation are very distinct. People should be trained fully in their roles, and one person should not attempt to perform all three functions because special skills are needed for each. The nature of the relationship that develops between producers and underwriters, on the one hand, and producers and their principals, on the other hand, is such that it is unwise for either a producer or an underwriter to attempt to resolve a claim situation even when it appears to be very simple.

SURETYSHIP, INSURANCE, AND BANKING

Some aspects of suretyship are most like other forms of insurance, but suretyship also shares some common features with banking. This section explains both the common features and unique characteristics of suretyship, insurance, and banking.

Suretyship and Insurance

Corporate suretyship has become an important component of the insurance business although it differs in some ways from other forms of insurance. Insurance commissioners regulate the business of suretyship along with other lines of insurance. The following are common elements of suretyship and other forms of insurance:

- Assumption of risk by a professional risk-taker
- Receipt of a premium by a risk-taker
- Protection against financial loss
- Contract in which the risk is defined

The risk of loss in property and liability insurance is usually the accidental occurrence of events such as fire and windstorm, or the occurrence of a crime such as theft. The risk of loss in bonding arrangements is the failure of persons or entities to perform obligations they have assumed. The following are examples of such obligations:

- To be honest employees
- To perform fiduciary obligations faithfully
- To perform official duties faithfully
- To perform a contract and comply with all its terms and conditions
- To pay obligations incurred in the performance of a contract
- To meet all of the conditions of an ordinance or statute in the performance of a licensed trade or business

Insurance is designed to protect the insured against the financial consequences of adverse events. All insureds in a group pay premiums into a funding pool to cover individual losses as they occur, transferring the risk of loss to the group. The key to this risk pooling is that losses are anticipated.

Suretyship, on the other hand, is designed to protect the obligee from exposures to loss. Suretyship achieves this objective by prequalifying prospective principals on the basis of their credit strength, ability to perform, and character. The economic risk of bond default stays with the bonded party, who must reimburse the surety for any loss the surety must pay. The hope of all parties is that there will be no failure in performance and, therefore, no loss.

Suretyship and Banking

Suretyship is essentially an extension of credit by a surety to the principal and, as such, is somewhat similar to banking. A bank charges interest and expects borrowers to repay loans. The bank does not expect to suffer any losses as a result of the loan, but if there is a default it has the right to pursue the defaulting borrower for repayment of the loan. The bank gives the borrower the benefit of the bank's money. Similarly, a surety gives a principal the benefit of the surety's credit standing and expects the principal to perform the obligation. In case of default, the surety, like a bank, has the right to restitution.

Suretyship is a financial relationship and deals with matters that are defined in monetary terms. Although bank credit fulfills many financial needs and has a prequalification process similar to suretyship, suretyship goes beyond bank credit, particularly because it guarantees performance as well as monetary obligations. Therefore, a surety's guarantee involves much more than an extension of credit.

THE NATURE OF SURETYSHIP

Suretyship creates a special relationship between parties to the agreement, and it is most important to understand who the parties are and what their obligations are to each other. This course will use the same terminology for these parties throughout, and it is essential to learn the basic terms at this time.

Three-Party Relationship

A surety bond is a written instrument in which two parties, the principal and the surety, become obligated to a third party for the payment of a sum of money, not to exceed the bond amount, if the obligation is not fulfilled. The three parties to the typical surety bond are defined below:

1. The *principal* is primarily responsible for the fulfillment of the obligation set forth in the bond and must perform some act under certain conditions or respond in money damages.
2. The *obligee* is the beneficiary under the terms of the bond. If the obligation is not fulfilled, the principal and the surety are liable to the obligee for damages. However, the limit of the surety's liability to the obligee is the amount of the bond.
3. The *surety* is the party who joins with the principal for the purpose of guaranteeing to the obligee the fulfillment of the principal's obligation.

A surety bond, or contract of suretyship, has unique characteristics. It does not stand alone, but rests on an underlying contract or obligation. A person buys a bond because of an agreement with another person who requires a guarantee that a contract or obligation will be fulfilled. The relationship between the two parties is shown below.

A B

Contract/Obligation

The contract (or other obligation which may or may not be a formal contract) can be between any two parties: contractor-owner, mayor-city, or guardian-court. In each case, B wants some assurance that A will perform as agreed. So A provides this by securing and offering a bond through which A becomes the principal, and B becomes the obligee. The party who provides the bond is the surety. The original contract or obligation becomes the basis for the guarantee that the surety provides. The illustration below shows the relationship between the bond and the underlying agreement.

Surety

(A) Principal  (B) Obligee

Contract/Obligation

For example, Owner, a fast-food chain, wants to build a new outlet and engages Contractor to construct a building. The building contract is between Owner and Contractor:

Contractor Owner

Building Contract

Owner, however, has suffered in the past because of defaulting contractors. Owner wants assurance that, if Contractor defaults, Owner will not lose money and the project will be completed in a timely and efficient manner with the desired quality of work. Contractor therefore goes to Surety to obtain assurances that will satisfy Owner. The resulting three-party contractual situation is shown below.

Surety

Contractor  Owner

Building Contract

Contractor is still primarily liable to Owner. Surety either will pay moneys due or ensure performance of the contract, whichever is necessary to satisfy Contractor's obligation to Owner. However, Contractor's obligation does not end because Surety sees that the terms of the contract between Contractor and Owner are fulfilled. In the event of a default, Contractor must still indemnify Surety, and Surety is entitled by law to pursue Contractor to recover its loss. This notion is explained more fully in the following section on joint and several liability.

Joint and Several Liability

A surety bond is not a one-party obligation. In fact, most bonds are joint and several liability instruments. This means that the obligee may seek recovery from either the principal or the surety, or from both. Each of the parties is equally liable for the entire obligation. In the case of bankruptcy, the court may release the principal and decide that the surety is liable for the entire obligation. If the principal defaults, and the surety steps in and fulfills the obligation, the law provides that the surety "stands in the shoes" of the obligee and inherits all the rights which the obligee had with respect to the principal. The principal does not evade any obligations by virtue of the surety's backing.

The surety always has a right to reimbursement from the principal (even if the principal is unable to pay) if the surety is sued individually. The exception is the surety who steps in and pays obligations that are not legally those of the principal. In a sense, the surety's guarantee gives the principal only a business opportunity that might not be available otherwise. Beyond this, the principal must meet all obligations incurred or answer to the surety alone or to both the obligee and the surety. The real protection in the arrangement is to the obligee, not the principal.

A surety bond remains in effect until the underlying agreement ceases, either because it has been performed or because it has been canceled. The surety's liability can end in a matter of days, or it can remain in force for years, depending on the law and the basic agreement. Most surety bonds cannot be canceled by sureties once the obligations have been undertaken. Because the principal generally cannot "retire" from a promise, neither can the surety. Failure of the principal to pay the premium to the surety does not excuse the surety from its obligation to the obligee.

A Contract of Indemnity

A surety contract is a contract of indemnity, or an agreement to provide compensation in the event of a loss. The loss could be a few dollars or the entire bond amount. The surety bond will respond up to the limits of liability (the *bond penalty*), but it will pay no more than the amount of the obligee's actual loss unless the bond is a *forfeiture bond*.

Forfeiture is one method of terminating a surety bond. It is also one of the harshest measures that can exist for the principal. Most sureties do not look with favor at writing forfeiture bonds, and it is impossible to obtain reinsurance for forfeiture bonds. Most surety bonds are not forfeiture bonds, and bonds with forfeiture clauses are usually financial guarantee bonds. The forfeiture clause provides the surety with no alternative to immediate forfeiture of the bond amount regardless of the extent of the obligee's loss.

For example, a state may require that an owner obtain an "oil well plugging bond" with a forfeiture provision. This bond requires that, once the well runs dry, the owner must plug the well and generally clean up the premises. Forfeiture in these situations is a very undesirable alternative where, for example, the face amount of the bond is $8,000, but the clean-up cost is only $2,000.

UNDERWRITING CONSIDERATIONS

An existing contract between the principal and obligee always precedes a surety contract. The surety bond, an additional contract between the principal, the surety, and the obligee, guarantees the principal's compliance with the terms of the original contract. It is the principal, not the surety, who is primarily responsible for fulfilling contract work and other obligations. If the principal defaults, the surety may make payment in lieu of completing the work or may engage others to complete it.

Under common law, however, it is the principal's duty to indemnify the surety for any loss suffered as a result of default. If the surety underwriter has attended to the most important considerations in writing the bond, it is likely that the principal can indemnify the surety. Therefore, the surety only rarely should suffer a loss since it is the surety underwriter's job to ascertain that the principal can perform contractual obligations or, if the principal fails to perform, to indemnify the obligee from the principal's net worth for that failure. The considerations that should be reviewed by the surety underwriter include the diversity of obligations specified in the original contract, the principal's ability to perform, and the nature of the principal's performance. (Chapter 4 includes a detailed discussion of the other, more specific underwriting factors.)

Diversity of Obligations

Surety obligations are more or less diverse, according to the degree of exposure to loss. This exposure in bonding situations varies so greatly that the various surety obligations must be studied separately. For instance, the surety underwriter may have to guarantee that buildings will be constructed to the owner's satisfaction (in full compliance with plans and specifications as set forth under the contract), that grass will grow by a guaranteed date, that snow will be plowed within a certain time after it has fallen, and that suppliers and subcontractors will receive payment.

Some bonds with a low loss frequency and with small face amounts require little underwriting and are therefore more freely written. Other bonds, particularly some types of contract bonds such as efficiency guarantees, may not be written freely for even the best potential clients because the nature of the obligation is often highly speculative.

The importance of the surety in fulfilling the role of risk-bearer shifts considerably from the first type of obligation to the second. In the case of the "freely written" bonds, the surety merely may be endorsing a candidate for consideration. In the other case, the surety may find it necessary to change the nature of the obligation to protect itself and the principal. The obligee, of course, is intent upon securing protection from any and all possible failures of the principal. A situation may arise in which the surety, in order to do its job of guaranteeing the principal's action, must help the principal establish the ground rules—which may mean altering the contract and changing the obligation.

Principal's Ability to Perform

A fundamental principle of suretyship is the principal's continued obligation to the obligee. Although the surety guarantees the principal's performance, the principal is never excused from obligations under an original contract. Therefore, inherent in every bonding situation is a principal's ability to perform. The surety provides the assurance to the obligee that the principal will perform based on the findings of the surety's investigation. The investigation includes a review of the principal's financial capacity, its past experience, and its resources other than money that are needed to fulfill the obligation.

A financial guarantee differs from performance and fidelity guarantees in that it requires not only ability and honesty, but also payment of a sum to meet the contractual obligation. Although most financial guarantee bonds are for fixed amounts known when the bond is written, some bonds provide variable amounts; others have an open penalty in which the only limit is the extent to which the surety may obligate itself legally.

Nature of Principal's Performance

Sureties do not write bonds with ambiguous limits as freely as they write those in which the limits are clear. This is true in all surety lines.

In contract bonds, this principle of clear limits is significant in terms of performance as well. If the bond obligation is to perform the contract in accordance with the plans and specifications provided by the owner, the bond is more readily written than if the bond obligation is ambiguous about time and performance criteria or results. To guarantee efficient operation of an item is a riskier task than to guarantee that the item will be delivered. Consider the difference in exposure to loss in the following two examples of job descriptions:

1. Remodel laundry building heating and air conditioning systems and provide that the air temperature will remain at 70°F under all conditions.
2. Construct two-story addition to county courthouse as per specifications architects and engineers have prepared.

The first job is much smaller in size but has a higher risk of failure and requires a stronger financial strength than the latter.

PRINCIPAL'S GUARANTEE TO SURETY

Given the extent of the surety's obligation, it is clear why underwriters find it important to have applications or indemnity agreements signed. While the best way to avoid a default is for the surety to prequalify the principal and to work closely with the principal to solve performance problems along the way, there is always the chance that the principal will default. In this case, the surety can by law sue the principal, but the process is expensive and time-consuming. With a signed agreement, however, the surety has the best chance of being indemnified by the principal without bringing suit.

Indemnity Agreements

In an indemnity agreement the principal agrees to reimburse, or indemnify, the surety if the surety must pay for the principal's default. A standard practice in corporate suretyship is to obtain a contract of indemnity, commonly in the form of a bond application, from any person or entity applying for a bond. In addition, if the applicant for the bond is a corporation, partnership, or association, the persons who have a major financial interest in the corporation, partnership, or association may be required to execute a contract of indemnity. Spouses and others with a major financial interest in applicants which are corporations, partnerships, or associations also may be required to execute the contract of indemnity.

The indemnity agreement underwriters typically use allows the surety certain specific rights. For example, in the event of a claim on a contract bond, the surety may, among other actions, do the following:

- Call for cash collateral
- Take control of the project and equipment
- Receive assignment of the balance of contract funds

In lieu of an individual application for each bond, the contract of indemnity may be a *general indemnity agreement* or a general application for bonds. The surety relies on the promises of those who execute the bond when it becomes surety for any of the principals named in it. Therefore, those who execute the bond become indemnitors of the surety on all bonds executed, or to be executed (in the case of a general indemnity agreement) by the surety in behalf of any principal named in it. Usually, a general indemnity agreement is required of a principal when several bonds of a similar type are needed, such as a line of contract bonds or a line of license and permit bonds.

Collateral

Some surety bonds are extremely risky because chances for claims are likely and chances for loss are very high. A surety should reject these bonds. If, however, the surety chooses to write a risky bond, it should insist that the principal post adequate *collateral* as security for the risk.

Collateral should be cash or an asset that can be converted quickly and easily into cash. The surety may hold either a certificate of deposit that is in the principal's name, but assigned to the surety, or negotiable bonds or stock certificates with guaranteed stock powers for the surety attached. Instead of holding a principal's assets, a surety may elect to hold an irrevocable standby letter of credit issued by a commercial bank for the principal, but with the surety named as the beneficiary.

Security Interests in Property

Security interests in personal property, such as equipment, furniture, or commodities, and real estate mortgages may be assets of considerable value. However, they may not be converted to cash easily or quickly to meet an obligee's immediate demand. If the collateral is an interest in personal property, the surety must file the security agreement with the appropriate court to *perfect the security interest*, or give the surety a priority interest over others who may have interests in the same property. A general indemnity agreement can qualify as a security agreement. When a principal posts collateral, the surety and the principal must agree to conditions for posting and for eventually returning the collateral to the principal. Sureties use *collateral agreement forms* for this purpose.

LEGAL REMEDIES

The obligee is entitled to only one performance of an obligation secured by a contract of suretyship. The principal, rather than the surety, should perform this obligation. From this concept, several legal and equitable remedies for sureties have evolved.

When the surety has paid on behalf of the principal, the principal must repay, or *indemnify*, the surety for the amount of loss. *Exoneration* is the surety's right to compel a principal to perform when the surety receives notice of the principal's default. The surety can have the obligation performed by the exhaustion of the principal's resources instead of using its own resources. *Quia timet* is a remedy for a surety having reason to believe that a principal will default and allows the surety to sue the principal to prevent the surety's loss. *Subrogation* is the surety's right to enforce a third party's rights against the principal. The surety must have made a payment to the third party in order to exercise subrogation rights. Chapter 12 elaborates more fully on the claims process.

REINSURANCE AND COSURETIES

The surety business, like other forms of insurance, has methods for transferring and sharing, or not retaining, excessive risk. Sureties transfer portions of the risk to reinsurers or share the risk with one or more cosureties.

Reinsurance

Insurance is a contractual arrangement under which one party, the insurer, assumes all or part of the risk that otherwise would fall upon the other party, the insured. *Reinsurance* is a contractual arrangement under which one insurer, called the *primary insurer*, transfers to another insurer, known as the *reinsurer*, all or part of the risks that the primary insurer has assumed under one or more of its insurance contracts. Reinsurers also reinsure some of their assumed risks. Sureties reinsure their risks in much the same way that property and liability insurers reinsure.

Cosureties

When two or more sureties execute the same bond with the principal, they are called cosureties. The cosureties and the principal are jointly and severally liable to the obligee. The obligee may collect the full loss from any of the cosureties up to the penal sum of the bond. If the cosureties limit their respective liabilities in the bond, the maximum amount the obligee may collect from any one of them is the extent of its limited liability.

Each cosurety underwrites the risk, collects its own premiums, does its own claim investigation, and adjusts its own claims. A cosurety that has paid a claim has a right to *contribution*, or reimbursement, from the other cosureties. Most corporate sureties enter into a separate cosurety agreement with each of the cosureties. This agreement defines each cosurety's share of the risk. One of the cosureties is designated as the controlling cosurety for the purpose of collecting the premium, investigating defaults, and adjusting losses. After the controlling cosurety pays a loss or expense, it collects an agreed upon share of the loss or expense from the other cosureties.

SURETYSHIP IN THE 1980s AND 1990s

The 1980s were turbulent years in the financial history of the United States. Along with other businesses, the surety business felt the impact of economic problems. This section discusses the economics of the 1980s, the position of the surety business during that time, and the future of suretyship.

The 1980s and the American Economy

Several factors provide evidence for the financial problems of the 1980s. Exhibit 1-3 shows that the business failure rate for 1989, for example, was 65 per 10,000, compared with 27.8 ten years earlier and 37.3 twenty years earlier. The rate of business failures for the five years from 1983 to 1987, however, was at a record level failure rate for the entire period, ranging from 102 to 120 per 10,000 listed enterprises.

Additional evidence of economic difficulty is the number of bankruptcies that occurred. In 1980 there were nearly 278,000 total bankruptcies pending nationwide. This figure grew each year to more than 1.03 million by the end of 1990, three and one-half times the number in 1980.

Exhibit 1-4 shows the volatility of interest rates during this period. In 1961 the prime interest rate charged by banks was 4.5 percent. This figure climbed to 7.91 percent in 1970 and to a record 18.87 percent by 1981. The prime rate continued in double digits until 1985, when it descended to 9.93 percent. It increased to 10.87 percent in 1989 and continued at the high rate of 10.01 for the year 1990.

Exhibit 1-3
Business Failures (Rate per 10,000 Listed Enterprises)

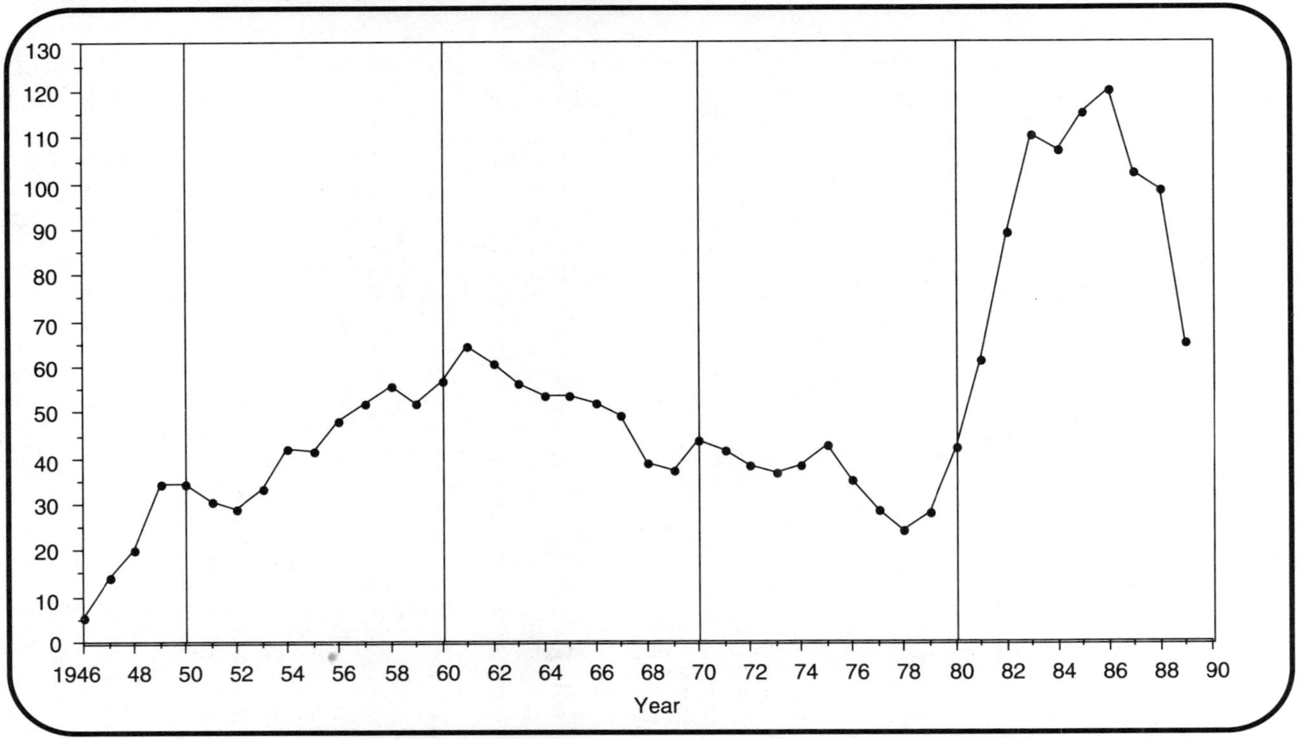

Adapted from *Statistical Abstract of the United States, 1990* (U.S. Department of Commerce, Bureau of the Census, Table No. 876) and *The Failure Record Through 1989* (Dun & Bradstreet Corporation).

Exhibit 1-4

Prime Interest Rate (Percent per Annum)

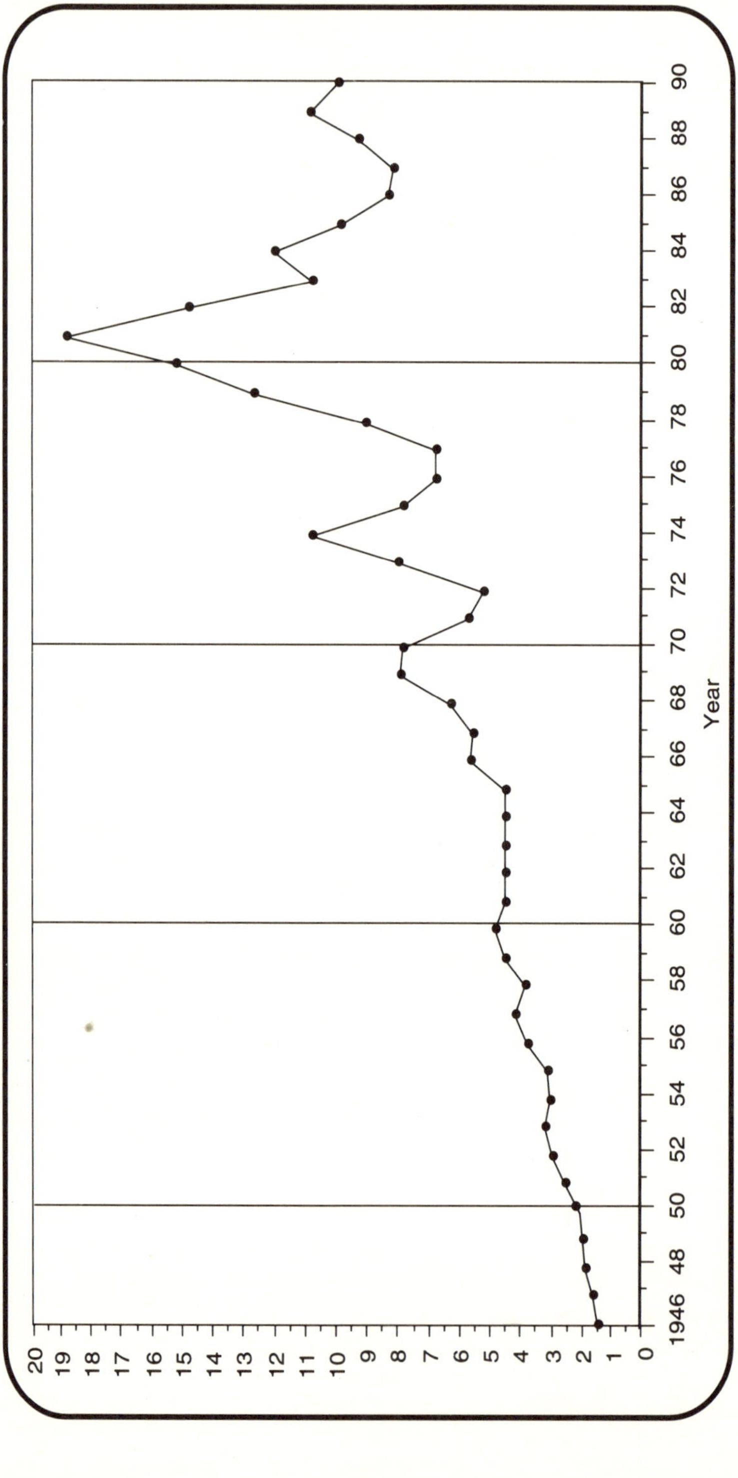

Adapted from *Economic Report of the President*, Transmitted to Congress February 1991, Superintendent of Documents, U.S. Government Printing Office, Washington, D.C., Table B-71.

Exhibit 1-5
Total Overall Operating Ratio for Property-Liability Industry (1981 to 1990)

	Loss and Loss Adjustment Expenses Incurred*		Underwriting Expenses Incurred**		Dividends to Policy-holders*		Combined Ratio After Dividends		Net Investment Gain & Other Income*		Overall Operating Ratio
Fidelity	53.4	+	32.9	+	0.1	=	86.3	–	9.1	=	77.2
Surety	50.5	+	48.0	+	0.5	=	99.1	–	12.1	=	86.9
Total Property-Liability Industry	81.5	+	26.3	+	1.5	=	109.4	–	9.7	=	99.7

* Ratios to Premiums Earned
** Ratios to Premiums Written

Adapted from *Best's Aggregate & Averages, Property-Casualty*, 1991 Edition (Oldwick, NJ: A.M. Best Company), pp. 136, 137. © A.M. Best Company–used with permission.

Insurance Industry Performance in the 1980s. Profitability in the insurance industry can be judged by using the combined ratio and the overall operating ratio. The *combined ratio* is a measure of profitability. It is calculated on a trade basis by adding loss and loss adjustment expenses as a percent of premiums earned to underwriting expenses as a percent of premiums written. If the ratio is over 100 percent, there is loss. The higher the ratio over 100 percent, the greater the loss. The lower the ratio under 100 percent, the more profitable the company. Dividends as a percent of premiums earned also can be added to determine a combined ratio after dividends. Exhibit 1-5 shows these ratios for the fidelity and surety portions of the property-liability industry and the total property-liability industry for the decade 1981-1990.

The *overall operating ratio* is calculated when primarily investment income as a percent of premiums earned is added to the combined ratio. As Exhibit 1-5 indicates, the property-liability industry, as a whole, ended up just about flat, with an overall operating ratio of 99.7. For the decade, surety had a respectable overall operating ratio of 86.9, and the fidelity sector had an even better ratio of 77.2.

Exhibit 1-5 also reveals that the underwriting expenses as a percent of premiums written are much higher for surety (48.0 percent) and somewhat higher for fidelity (32.9 percent) than for the total property-liability business (26.3 percent). These expenses reflect that there is more effort required to qualify and analyze many surety bond applications (particularly contract surety when significant financial and accounting information is examined and considered in detail before issuing bonds) than is required for underwriting property-liability insurance in general. The same is true for fidelity, but to a lesser degree. Although the property-liability business expects pure losses as a course of doing business, surety and fidelity segments are somewhat more selective in underwriting, and therefore the loss and loss adjustment expenses are somewhat lower as a percent of premiums earned.

Exhibit 1-6 shows that the totals for the decade for the overall operating ratio are the same as those shown in Exhibit 1-5. However, there can be significant variability from year to year in the total property-liability business, as well as in the fidelity and surety components of the business.

The years 1982 through 1985 were particularly unprofitable for the property-liability business. The years 1982 through 1984 were unprofitable for the fidelity segment of the industry. The years 1985 through 1987 were unprofitable for the surety segment of the business.

Fortunately, for those companies heavily involved in fidelity and surety, the unprofitable years for fidelity did not correspond to the unprofitable years of surety. In this respect, the two sectors of the business cushioned each other through their unprofitable years.

Surety and Fidelity Performance in the 1980s. The Surety Association of America (SAA) distributes annual countrywide loss experience summaries for both the fidelity and surety classifications.

Exhibit 1-7 shows fidelity experience from 1978 to 1989 for the following components: total financial institutions, blanket; total mercantile fidelity, blanket; total governmental entities, blanket; total individual or schedule fidelity; and total forgery.

The major component of fidelity, total financial institutions, accounted for about 64 percent of total fidelity in 1989. At the same time, mercantile fidelity accounted for about 31 percent of total fidelity, the rest of the categories accounting for about 5 percent. (AFSB 153 will examine these categories.)

Exhibit 1-8 shows the SAA's Countrywide Twelve-Year (1978-1989) Surety Experience for Total Surety. The contract portion of the surety business for the twelve-year period ranged from a high of 69.3 percent in 1980 to a low of 54.9 percent in 1986. In 1989 contract surety accounted for 63 percent of the surety business. Noncontract surety business for the twelve-year period from 1978 to 1989 was lowest, 30.7 percent, in 1980 and reached a high of 45.1 percent in 1986. In 1989 noncontract surety accounted for 37 percent of the business. (The contract portion of the surety business is examined in greater detail in AFSB 152, and the noncontract portion, in AFSB 153.)

Exhibit 1-6
Overall Operating Ratio

Year	Total Property-Casualty Industry	Fidelity	Surety
1981	97.6	89.4	81.7
1982	100.5	103.2	84.6
1983	102.3	111.9	81.6
1984	107.4	106.2	87.7
1985	106.3	83.9	102.2
1986	99.1	68.0	107.6
1987	95.6	63.9	100.6
1988	95.7	64.1	82.8
1989	99.0	61.1	79.3
1990	99.0	83.8	72.4
Totals	99.7	77.2	86.9

Adapted from *Best's Aggregate & Averages, Property-Casualty,* 1991 Edition (Oldwick, NJ: A.M. Best Company), pp. 136, 137. © Copyright A.M. Best Company–used with permission.

Suretyship's Future

There are numerous reasons for the disastrous results in the fidelity business from 1982 through 1984 and in the surety business from 1985 through 1987. Numerous suggestions also might be made about how to avoid these results in the future. A simple explanation for the problems in fidelity and surety might be the following:

- The insurance industry cycles had significant effects on fidelity-surety underwriting, as well as on the other property and liability lines.
- Economic and legal climates and conditions had adverse effects on the frequency and severity of losses.

Some experts in the industry, however, see the problems as more complex, often involving internal problems such as relaxed underwriting standards and the need for more fully trained personnel. Speakers for the surety business see the following as major issues facing the business in the 1990s:[2]

- Maintenance of underwriting standards
- Onerous bond forms and contract documents
- Inadequate rates
- Inability to attract new capital
- Inadequate return on equity

Exhibit 1-7
Fidelity Direct Earned Premiums

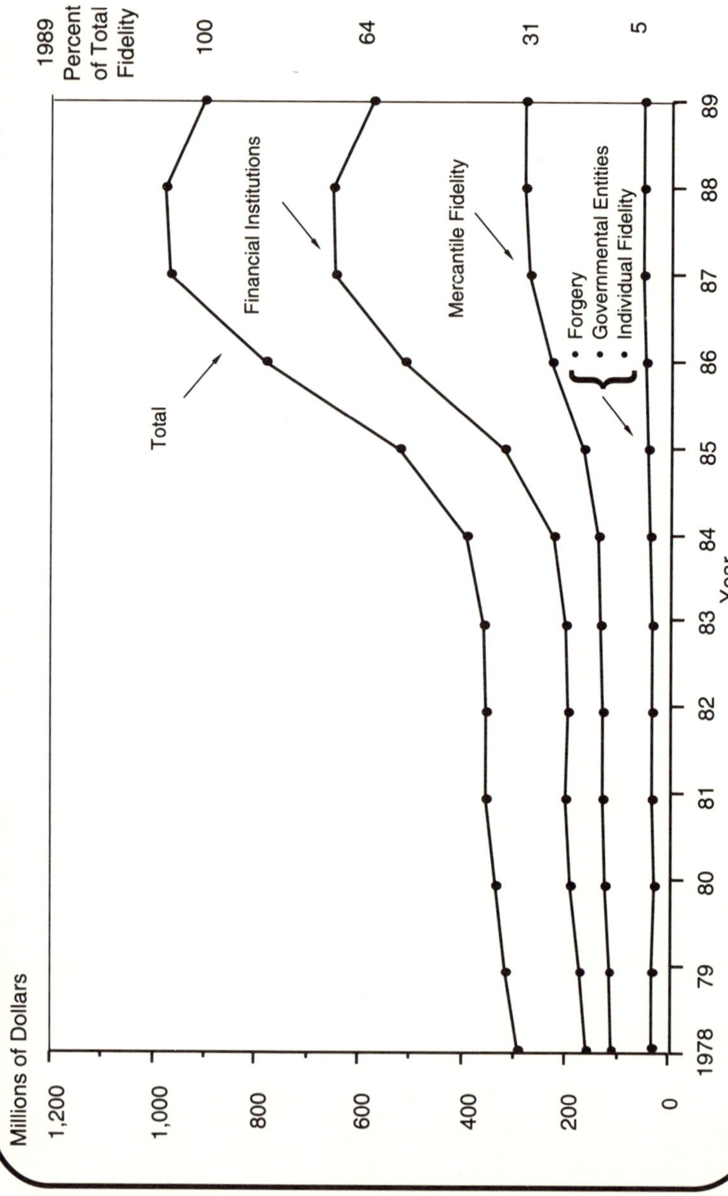

Adapted from Surety Association of America Countrywide Twelve Year 1978-1989 Fidelity Experience, Iselin, NJ.

Exhibit 1-8
Contract and Noncontract Surety (Percent of Total Surety)

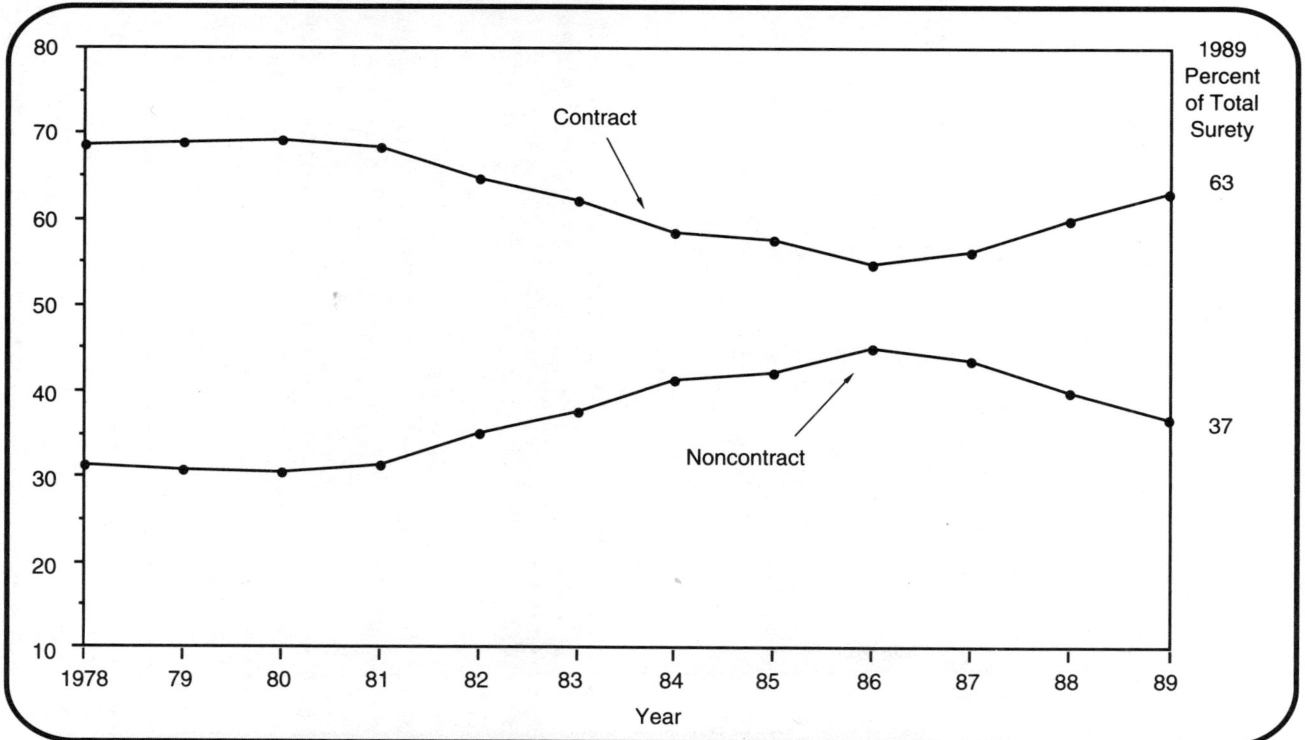

Adapted from the Surety Association of America Countrywide Twelve Year 1978-1989 Surety Experience, Iselin, NJ.

- Misunderstanding of the product because of overselling by agents
- Superfund and hazardous waste cleanup projects
- New tax laws
- Litigiousness of American society

In light of these issues, sureties should continue to do the following:

- Offer a good product that provides coverage for insurable risks at a reasonable price (fidelity)
- Be thorough and careful in the underwriting of the risks assumed (fidelity and surety)
- Resolve claims promptly and fairly through sound claim practices.

Suretyship, including the fidelity line, is an increasingly complex area of expertise. Technological and other developments in the past few years have increased the need for sophisticated producers, underwriters, and claim personnel. Executives in the industry believe that there is a need for better training of new recruits to the surety industry.

SUMMARY

Surety plays a significant and extensive role in American life, and it has done so for many years. Today, the surety and fidelity businesses are conducted for the most part by insurance companies.

Like a property insurance contract, a surety contract is a contract of indemnity. The three parties to this contract are the principal, the obligee, and the surety. The surety joins with the principal and guarantees the obligee that the obligation assumed by the principal will be fulfilled. Essentially, the surety agrees to provide compensation up to the amount of the obligee's loss, not to exceed the bond amount, should the principal default on an obligation. However, because surety bonds are joint and several obligations, each of the parties to the bond is equally liable for the entire obligation. As a result, the surety always has a right to reimbursement from the principal even if the surety is sued individually.

Suretyship also is related to banking in that it is a mechanism for extending credit. Like a bank loan for a credit applicant, a surety agreement provides a business opportunity to a bonded party. And, like an applicant for credit, a prospective bond principal on a bond is carefully reviewed. In the surety business, this review is conducted by the surety underwriter, who receives both financial and performance information about the prospective principal from the surety producer, or agent. Other key personnel in the bond business include claim representatives who, in the event of a principal's default, review the case to resolve any disputes that arise in connection with a claim.

The market for bonds is created partly by law, which requires bonds for individuals and organizations who perform certain business activities. Bonds generally are required of contractors who perform public works; of public officials, fiduciaries, or others who administer either public or private funds; and of businesses and individuals to qualify for licenses or permits. In addition, financial institutions should have fidelity coverage on employees. The private sector also has created a market for bonds, the largest of which is for private construction projects.

While all bonds, for public or private work, assure the obligee that the terms of the original contract with the principal will be fulfilled, some surety bonds may require collateral and others do not. Collateral can be cash or some other relatively liquid asset. Some sureties accept security interests in personal property and real estate mortgages as collateral. In addition to requiring collateral, sureties also protect their interests by executing bonds with cosureties and by transferring portions of their risks to reinsurers.

Although it is clear that there has always been a need for suretyship, the surety and fidelity businesses suffered in the 1980s. There is reason, however, to be optimistic about the future of the surety and fidelity fields. Many experts cite the need for strict underwriting standards and better training of personnel to improve the business' financial performance. Experts also agree that a "back to basics" approach will help to ensure a bright future for suretyship.

Chapter Notes

1. Albert Remmen, *The Contract Bond Book* (Cincinnati, OH: The National Underwriter Company, 1987), p. 3.
2. Extracted from "State of the Surety Industry, 1990," J. Martin Huber, *Suretyscope*, Spring 1990, pp. 25-34.

CHAPTER 2

Types of Bonds

Surety and fidelity are the two basic categories of bonds. Surety bonds are generally grouped into two classes, contract and noncontract bonds, which are commonly divided as follows:

- Contract bonds
  - Bid bonds
  - Performance bonds
  - Payment bonds
  - Maintenance bonds
  - Advance payment bonds
  - Supply bonds
- Noncontract bonds
  - Judicial bonds
  - License and Permit bonds
  - Miscellaneous bonds
  - Public official bonds (blanket public official bonds are classified as fidelity bonds)
  - New financial guarantee bonds (which now have their own NAIC line code)

There are commonly three sources of employee dishonesty insured under fidelity bond coverages: commercial risks, financial risks, and public official risks. Burglary, theft, and forgery coverage can be added to each to create a crime package.

There are literally hundreds of forms in use in contract, judicial, public official, license, permit, and crime bonds as well as traditional financial guaranty obligations (commonly included under license, permit, and miscellaneous bonds). A traditional financial guarantee bond is conditioned for the payment of money, whether or not the exact amount is known or stated, and with no other alternative. One list for all types of license and permit bonds alone numbers eleven hundred.

The *Agent's Bonding Guide* contains a quick reference chart of over two hundred and fifty kinds of bonds, from abatement of tax bonds to bonds required of winemakers.[1] The chart also includes a key as to the locations in the bond rating manual for appropriate rates. It indicates who furnishes particular bonds and lists twenty-five categories for the degree of hazard involved in each bond type. Another reference lists approximately four hundred kinds of license bonds, from those for adjusters to those for yacht brokers.[2]

A *surety bond* is a written agreement providing for monetary compensation or satisfactory completion of an obligation by the surety should the principal fail to perform specified acts within a stated period of time. It is a three-party agreement whereby the surety is bound, with the principal, to the obligee.

This chapter introduces the many types of bonds available from corporate surety companies under the surety (contract and noncontract) and fidelity bond classifications. It also discusses the valuable role each bond serves in today's economic environment.

CONTRACT BONDS

A *contract bond* secures the performance of obligations under a written contract. Contracts may be for construction of a building, delivery of mail, the guarantee of efficiency of an electrical system, or a supply of oil to a municipality. A bond often required by both private and public agreements is the supply bond. It guarantees faithful performance of a contract to furnish supplies or materials. In the event of a default by the supplier, the surety is obligated to indemnify the purchaser obligee for the loss.

Contract surety is the most prevalent kind of suretyship, and many in the industry consider it the most attractive bond, as well as the most potentially hazardous. It is available to protect building project obligees (construction project owners) against financial loss resulting from the failure or default of construction contractors, who have the duty to perform their contracts. Exhibit 2-1 is an example of a contract bond form.

A contract surety bond obligation is one under which the surety joins with the construction contractor to ensure that the contractor will perform the contract in accordance with its terms, conditions, and specifications on time and at the agreed upon price. If not, the additional cost to complete the project will be available to the owner up to the penal sum of the bond.

Exhibit 2-1
Contract Bond

ABC Insurance Company

CALIFORNIA PERFORMANCE BOND
PUBLIC WORK

Premium: ______________________ Bond No.: __________________________

KNOW ALL PERSONS BY THESE PRESENTS:

That we,

as Principal, and ABC Insurance Company, a corporation organized under the laws of the State of _________ and duly authorized under the laws of the State of _________ to become sole surety on bonds and undertakings, as Surety, are held and firmly bound unto

as Obligee,

in the penal sum of DOLLARS

($), lawful money of the United States of America, to be paid to the said Obligee, successors or assigns; for which payment, well and truly to be made, we bind ourselves, our heirs, executors, successors, administrators and assigns, jointly and severally, firmly by these presents.

NOW, THEREFORE, whereas the said Principal has entered into a contract of even date herewith with the said Obligee to do and perform the following work, to-wit:

as is more specifically set forth in said contract, to which contract reference is hereby made;

THE CONDITION OF THIS OBLIGATION is such, that, if the said Principal, his, her, or its heirs, executors, successors, administrators and assigns, shall well and truly do the said work, and fulfill each and every of the covenants, conditions and requirements of the said contract in accordance with the plans and specifications, then the above obligation to be void, otherwise to remain in full force and virtue.

No right of action shall accrue under this bond to or for the use of any person other than the Obligee named herein.

Sealed with our seals and dates this day of ,19

____

____
Principal

ABC Insurance Company

By _______________________________

____

Construction Contract Bonds

The following are the five major types of construction contract bonds:

1. The *bid bond* guarantees that the bidder, or proposer, will actually enter into the contract at the proposed price and provide the required performance and payment bond.
2. The *performance bond* indemnifies the owner for financial loss caused by the contractor's failure to perform the contract in accordance with all the terms and conditions of the contract.
3. The *payment bond* guarantees that the surety will pay for certain labor, material, and supply bills and subcontractors associated with the project if the contractor fails to pay these costs. Although some obligees require bonds that cover all tiers of claimants, only the first and second tiers of claimants are generally covered under the bond.
4. A *maintenance bond* may be required upon completion of the construction project to protect against defective workmanship and materials.
5. The *advance payment bond* may be required to guarantee repayment or liquidation by the principal of moneys advanced by the obligee in connection with a construction or supply bond or other type of contract.

While construction contract bonds guarantee to the owners that contractors will perform the contracts on time and pay labor and material bills incurred on the job, they also provide owners with the additional security of knowing that contractors have satisfied sureties' comprehensive prequalification reviews.

At the same time, bonds benefit lenders, architects, engineers, attorneys, and risk managers. They provide lenders with assurance that, if the contractors are paid, projects that secure loans will be finished in accordance with contractual terms free of liens. Performance and payment bonds provide confidence that, at least in the surety's opinion, the contractor has the ability to finish the project according to plans and specifications. For owners' attorneys, bonds provide the security of knowing that clients will be protected should contractors fail to perform. Bonds provide the satisfaction for risk managers of knowing that owners are protected against one of the major perils of building—contractor failure.

Government Requirements

Surety companies, which are state licensed, write construction bonds on federal, state, or municipal projects that usually award work through open, competitive, and sealed bid proposals. These bonds make it possible for the governmental owner to accept a low bid and to gain the advantage of competitive bidding. An increasing number of private project owners require performance and payment bonds from primary contractors on negotiated contracts. Primary contractors frequently require their subcontractors to provide these bonds for the protection of the primary contractors. Sureties, when writing primary contractors' bonds, may require bonding for subcontracts over a certain dollar amount.

The corporate surety industry plays a vital role in providing bonds for contractors on private projects and for government builders of the national infrastructure, which includes highways, bridges, dams, power lines, factories, and office buildings.

NONCONTRACT BONDS

This section will examine (1) license and permit bonds, (2) judicial bonds in civil proceedings, (3) miscellaneous bonds, (4) public official bonds, and (5) federal noncontract surety bonds.

License and Permit Bonds

The most important function of *license and permit bonds* is the protection they afford the general public and governmental bodies. They strengthen the laws, ordinances, and regulations designed to protect public health and safety. These bonds safeguard the public against financial loss caused by the misfeasance or malfeasance of licensees. They may also guarantee the payment of taxes due to state or local governments. *Misfeasance* is the improper and unlawful execution of an act that is in itself lawful and proper; *malfeasance* is the execution of an unlawful act that one should not do at all. Exhibit 2-2 shows a sampling of the various occupations and activities that require license and permit bonds, and Exhibit 2-3 is an example of a license bond form.

In order to operate in the American market economy, many business enterprises must have the following:

1. A license or permit from a governmental body, either municipal, state, or federal, to conduct operations or to exercise a special privilege
2. A corporate surety bond to guarantee compliance with licensing requirements

In examining license and permit bonds, the purposes, frequency, and categories of license and permit bonds will be discussed, as well as license bond forms.

Exhibit 2-2
Coding Index—License and Permit Bonds

Worded Description	Class
Livestock Insurance Companies	408
Milk Dealers	426
Bricklayers	440
Garbage Collectors	440
Window Cleaners	440
Radio & Television Antenna Installers	441
House Moving Contractors	444
Curb Contractors	445
Awning Erectors	446
Outdoor Advertising	446
Aerial Spraying	447
Entomological Services	447
Fumigators	447
Seismic Exploration	449
Dredge Mining Protection	450
Tobacco Products Distributors	452
Slot Machine Taxes	454
Bail Bond Agents	456
Securities Agents	462
Mobile Home Dealers—Used	465
Abandoned Service Stations	468
Automobile Registration Services	468
Citrus Fruit Commission Merchants	470
Seed Sellers	470
Cotton Samplers	471
Book Solicitors	473
Hat Cleaners	474
Charity Entertainments	475
Cosmetology Schools	476
Polygraph Examiners	477
Children Adoption Agencies	478
Cemetery Care	480
Crankcase Lubricating Oil Distributors	481
Liquefied Petroleum Gas	483
Liquor—Warehousemen	491
Artificial Color Processors	499
Birdnesting	499
Clam Diggers	499
Health Clubs	499
Hog Cholera Serum Dealers	499
Ice Dealers	499
Immigrants Lodging Places	499
Nursery Stock Dealers	499
Pistol Toting	499
Prepaid Legal Service Plans	499
Rough Fish Removal	499
Yacht and Ship Brokers	499
Indian Reservation Businesses—Bonds of Traders	499
Turnpike Tolls	598

Exhibit 2-3
License Bond Form

PLUMBER'S BOND

KNOW ALL PERSONS BY THESE PRESENTS That we, ____________ as Principal, and ________________, as Surety, are held and firmly bound unto the Mayor and Council of ____________, a municipal corporation existing under the laws of the State of ____________, in the full and just sum of ________ Dollars, for which payment well and truly to be made, the said Principal binds him or herself, his or her heirs, executors, and administrators, firmly by these presents.

WHEREAS, the said Principal has made, or is about to make, application to be a licensed plumber, to engage in the business of plumbing, and to lay sewer, gas pipe, water mains, etc., within the corporate limits of the City of ____________, which license has been or is about to be granted in accordance with law:

NOW, THEREFORE, the condition of this obligation is such, that if the said Principal shall for the period ending June 30, 19____, well and faithfully, and in a workerlike manner, perform the above mentioned work, and shall indemnify and save harmless the said Mayor and Council of ________________, from any and all arising in connection therewith from the negligence or carelessness of the said Principal, his or her agents, servants, or employees, in doing said work, then this obligation to be void; otherwise to be and remain in full force and virtue.

SIGNED, sealed and dated this __________ day of __________, 19___.

____
Principal

____
Surety

Adapted from: *Fundamentals of Bonding, A Manual on Fidelity/Surety*, Dr. Franklin L. Moore, CPCU (The Rough Notes Co.: Indianapolis, IN, 1989).

Purposes. The purposes that license and permit bonds fulfill result from the demand created by public interest requirements.

Public Interest Requirements. License or permit bonds are required when the public interest demands regulation of certain types of businesses for the protection of citizens and property. The issuance of a license or permit is a special privilege conditioned upon the licensee's following a standard of conduct outlined in the applicable law, ordinance, or regulation. These standards of conduct are usually designed to prevent abuse of the privilege. License and permit bonds generate the highest premium volume in the noncontract surety business.

The licensee's obligation generally is to comply with the statutes, ordinances, or regulations required by governmental bodies. Most levels of government recognize these license and permit bonds as indispensable to the enforcement of protective laws. There are over 80,000 governmental units in the United States administering laws, including local entities such as school districts, that require these bonds.

Fulfillment of Needs. The needs that license and permit bonds fulfill are so diverse that it is possible to mention only a few here:

1. *Indemnification*—A bond may indemnify a public body against loss or damage to its property. In some instances the indemnity extends to third-party private persons and properties and may also protect revenues by guaranteeing tax payments that laws or ordinances require.
2. *Qualification*—By requiring a bond, a public body can save the time and expense necessary for exhaustive investigations to determine the licensee's financial and character qualifications.
3. *Convenience*—The bond is a practical convenience for a licensee because it eliminates the need for a cash deposit to guarantee compliance with the law.

Frequency. Many types of license bonds are required annually, although some are required for short periods in connection with special privileges. Most license and permit bonds are *continuous*, meaning that they remain in full force and effect until canceled. In terms of surety risk, continuous bonds are more desirable and cost-efficient to write and maintain because they automatically renew from year to year.

In most communities, plumbers, electricians, and others file annual bonds. Building and road contractors, in addition to the usual performance and payment bonds, must often file short-term bonds for special types of work, such as blasting operations, street obstruction, opening of sewers, and other work subject to regulation. Many firms must give license bonds to guarantee proper installation and maintenance of signs and underground storage tanks or vaults. These are continuous bonds.

Categories. In describing how license and permit bonds can be categorized, they will be examined, first, in broad classifications and, second, by the type of guarantees they fulfill. The two categories of license bonds will then be discussed.

Broad Classifications. License and permit bonds are divided into two broad classifications:

1. Bonds that indemnify the governmental body named as obligee for loss or damage resulting from the failure of the principal to comply with the law, ordinance, or regulation, including the

payment of any tax covered by the bond.

2. Bonds that give third parties a right of action in their own names to recover losses or damages. (The third parties are any parties other than the named obligee.) The losses or damages may result from the principal's default of obligations under the law, ordinance, or regulation requiring the bond.

Types of Guarantee. License and permit bonds are also divided into five common types according to the nature of the guarantees involved:

1. Compliance guarantees—regulatory
2. Indemnity guarantees—public safety with third-party liability
3. Good faith guarantees—public protection with third-party liability
4. Credit guarantees—public protection with third-party liability
5. Financial guarantees—tax, lease, workers compensation, and forfeiture

Two Categories of License Bonds. License bonds fall into two general categories, according to the inherent hazards or the specific purpose of the bond:

1. *Code observance bonds* are categorized as normal hazards or special hazards.
   a. *Normal hazards,* which are more commonly called *compliance* or *conformance bonds,* guarantee that the licensee will work or conduct business in compliance with applicable codes, statutes, or ordinances. Included in this group of licensees are drainlayers, electricians, oil burner installers, pawnbrokers, plumbers, sewer tappers, sign hangers, and small loan companies.
   b. *Special hazards* involve an unusual degree of exposure because of peculiarities in the licensees' or applicants' businesses. A surety company may therefore want to know that underlying insurance is in place. Applicants must be experienced and financially responsible, and often include abstracters, auctioneers, blasting and explosive handlers, securities dealers, employment agencies, house movers, demolition experts, motor vehicle dealers, and real estate brokers.
2. *Tax payment and money remittance bonds* are financial guarantees for the licensee's payment of taxes, or for payment for products received from others. As a rule, surety companies restrict these bonds to experienced and financially responsible

applicants, including collection agencies, commission merchants, gasoline dealers, and milk dealers. They also secure tax payment for amusement facilities, sales, sporting events, and liquor, beer, and wine taxes. These undertakings are federal, state, and local guarantees. One of the largest categories of license bonds is for sales taxes levied on merchandise.

License Bond Forms. Most license bonds are simple in form. The licensee and the surety are bound firmly to the municipality, or other governmental unit, as obligee for a specified amount. If the licensee faithfully discharges legal responsibilities, the obligation becomes null and void. Otherwise, it continues in force to indemnify for any default by the licensee.

License bonds serve multiple purposes, and requirements for them are constantly broadening under new laws and ordinances in response to the need for additional safeguards in today's rapidly changing social environment.

Judicial Bonds in Civil Proceedings

Judicial bonds in civil proceedings fall into two categories, *court bonds* and *fiduciary bonds*, each of which includes many bond forms. After license and permit bonds, court and fiduciary bonds have the highest premium volume in the noncontract surety business.

Court Bonds. Court bonds are required of parties to a lawsuit (litigants) who seek privileges or remedies that the law allows only upon posting a bond. They protect a party in litigation from possible loss suffered as a result of the court's granting a privilege to the other party. In some proceedings the opposing party may have the right to file a "counter" bond to negate the effect of the first request, or a subsequent decision by a court may determine that a party who obtained a privilege or remedy was not entitled to it. Court bonds fall into the two categories of litigants: *plaintiffs' bonds* and *defendants' bonds*. The degree of legal hazard is generally much greater for defendants; and, consequently, the surety's underwriting requirements are much stricter for defendant bonds.

A plaintiff commences a lawsuit. Because the plaintiff voluntarily begins litigation by choice, the plaintiff's bond is sometimes referred to as a *voluntary court bond*. The defendant, on the other hand, is the party against whom the plaintiff complains and must assume a defensive position. A defendant's bond is therefore called a *compulsory court bond*.

For example, prior to court proceedings, Jones, in a lawsuit against Brown, requests the return of property in Brown's possession, contending that it legally belongs to her. A court bond can protect Brown's right to the property should the court later decide that she has a right that is superior to Jones' claim. These bonds protect the interests of the opposing litigant or of another interested party. In all cases, the law prescribes the bond coverage, and only a bond complying with legal requirements is acceptable.

Court bonds, or litigant bonds, are noncancelable, and liability continues until the principal's obligation is discharged or the applicable statute of limitations has expired. The bonds in this classification fall into three groups: civil proceedings, admiralty, and release of civil proceedings.

Bonds in Civil Proceedings. *Bonds in civil proceedings*, also called *litigant bonds,* are required in a cause of action at law. A *civil action* is, generally, any lawsuit that is not a criminal prosecution. For underwriting purposes sureties usually divide these bonds into plaintiffs' bonds and defendants' bonds.

Plaintiffs' Bonds. This section discusses several plaintiffs' court bonds, including attachment bonds, appeal bonds, bonds on order of civil arrest, court cost bonds, release of attachment bonds, injunction bonds, temporary restraining order bonds, bonds to discharge mechanics' liens, replevin bonds, and claim and delivery bonds.

Attachment is a legal term for the taking or seizing of another person's property under court order and bringing it into the court's custody to secure an ultimate judgment awarding damages in a lawsuit. As it refers to plaintiffs' bonds, attachment is the plaintiff's taking of the defendant's property into custody with the court's approval before trial as security for the payment of any judgment that the plaintiff may recover in the action. A *plaintiff's attachment bond* provides indemnity to a defendant if the attachment proves to be wrongful. This damage can occur when a court decides that the law did not warrant an attachment or when a plaintiff fails to win a judgment against the defendant. Ordinarily, a court allows attachment of property where the plaintiff shows a legal ground for it.

Examples of how a plaintiff's attachment bond works are situations in which defendants are residents of other states, are about to leave the states where the lawsuits are filed, or are about to remove or conceal the property in question. The plaintiffs in these situations need some guarantee that the property in question will be accessible if they win the suit. Before the trial and with the court's approval, a plaintiff may take the property in question into custody as security for the payment of an eventual judgment against the defendant. The plaintiff posts an attachment bond to guarantee the return of the property to the defendant and the payment of all court costs and damages should the plaintiff lose the case. The court may later decide that there was no legal ground for attachment, or the plaintiff may fail to obtain a judgment against the defendant. Many states will not permit an attachment before judgment.

When a plaintiff loses in a trial court and appeals to a higher court, a *plaintiff's appeal bond* is necessary if the trial court's decision merely denies the plaintiff the remedy sought, such as damages. It is generally necessary for the plaintiff to post bond only for the payment of appeal costs. If, however, the court's decision gives the defendant affirmative relief, such as damages or an order in the defendant's favor, a bond to stay execution (delay action) of the court's decision may be necessary. An appeal bond can be of high risk if not collateralized or if it is written for a principal with meager financial means, while a bond for the original lawsuit brought in the lower court is of a lower risk.

A plaintiff who initiates another person's arrest may have to provide a *bond on order of civil arrest*. Civil arrest is available to any wronged individual who seeks retribution permitted by law, such as for nonpayment of alimony or child support. The bond usually guarantees payment of the costs and any damages that the defendant may incur if a court finally decides that the arrest ought not to have been made. These bonds are also called "bail" or "appearance" bonds. Most surety companies avoid them, except in connection with misdemeanors and traffic violations, and usually require collateral if they do issue them.

Among the various forms of judicial bonds are *court cost bonds*, which secure payment of such items as fees of the clerk of the court and the sheriff. A *release of attachment bond* is required for the return or redelivery of property in compliance with a court order. In some states it may guarantee payment of a judgment. Exhibit 2-4 is an example of a bond securing court costs.

An *injunction bond* is required when a court gives an order conditioned upon the plaintiff's furnishing such a bond. An injunction is a court order that requires a defendant to do or refrain from doing something. The injunction is in force pending the final outcome of the case, when the court determines the plaintiff's and the defendant's rights. The bond indemnifies the defendant against loss should the court finally decide that the injunction was inappropriate.

Similar to an injunction bond is that for a *temporary restraining order* (T.R.O.), in which a plaintiff requests that the court require a defendant to refrain from a specified action temporarily. The difference between a T.R.O. and an injunction is that the T.R.O. has a much shorter duration.

A plaintiff property owner supplies a *bond to discharge a mechanic's lien* pending final court determination of the owner's liability. A mechanic's lien is a lien against real estate for payment due for labor or materials for the construction of a building or other improvement upon the property. A general contractor may also provide this bond to remove any liens resulting from a contractual agreement with the

Exhibit 2-4
Bond Securing Court Costs

ABC Insurance Company

____________________ Plaintiff against Defendant ____________________	**SECURITY FOR COSTS.**

Whereas, The above named ....
...., non-resident of the State of
.... has commenced an action in the ....
Court of the .... against the above-named
defendant .... and the
said ....
being entitled to security for costs under the provisions of the Civil Practice Act.

Now, Therefore, the ABC Insurance Company, a Pennsylvania corporation, having an office and usual place of business at ....
.... does pursuant to the said provisions, hereby undertake that it will pay on demand to the said defendant, all costs which may be awarded to the said defendant, in said action not exceeding the sum of .... dollars.
Dated at .... this .... day of ...., 19 ....

ABC Insurance Company

By ....
Attorney-in-Fact

project owner.

A plaintiff supplies a *plaintiff replevin bond* in an action to recover possession of specific articles of personal property. Personal property is any property except real estate. The bond guarantees the return of the property, if a court orders a return, and the payment of all costs and damages a court awards to a defendant. Replevin bonds are frequently required in suits over conditional sales contracts involving the sales of articles or goods on the installment plan. The seller retains legal title to the property until the buyer has finished payments.

The *claim and delivery bond* is similar to the replevin bond and secures the recovery of specific personal property wrongfully taken and detained.

Defendants' Bonds. Many defendants' bonds are "counter to" plaintiffs' bonds. For example, a *release of attachment bond* nullifies a plaintiff's attachment bond. A defendant may post a *counter-replevin bond* to protect against a plaintiff's replevin (return of property) attempt. A *dissolve injunction bond* suspends the operation of an injunction. By posting a *release of garnishment bond*, a defendant can lift restrictions a plaintiff places on property.

To appeal a case to a higher court, a defendant must usually provide a *defendant's appeal bond*, which halts the action on the lower court's order until the higher court reaches a decision. If the higher court affirms the original court's decision against the defendant, the bond ensures that the defendant will comply with that final decision.

At times a defendant who has been sued in a state court has the right to request that the case be transferred, or removed, to a federal court in the same locality for trial. A *removal bond* must usually accompany this request to guarantee the payment of all costs related to the removal should the court determine that the removal was inappropriate.

Bonds in Admiralty Proceedings. *Bonds in admiralty proceedings* are fundamentally court bonds because the United States District Courts, which are the federal system's trial courts, generally hear all admiralty and maritime cases. In admiralty, an action may be brought against a ship. For example, the United States Marshal may seize a ship and hold it as security for a claim. The owner may have the ship released by posting a bond or other approved security for the claim.

The complaint in a civil action against a ship is called a *libel*, and the one who brings the action is called the *libellant*. In an action against a ship, the libellant may have to post bond for payment of all costs, including court costs and the costs of seizure and holding.

When a warrant for the seizure of a ship is issued, a U.S. marshal must impound the ship until all damages are satisfied. The marshal will discharge the ship if the damages sought have been paid, or if an admiralty bond is received from the shipowner to guarantee compliance with the court's decision in the action. The marshal is expected to move promptly lest the ship leave port and, possibly, the court's jurisdiction.

Release of Civil Proceedings Bond. The *release of civil proceedings bond*, or *bail bond*, is a defendant's bond that is required in most states to gain release from incarceration in order to participate in a pending civil action. A civil action is, generally, any lawsuit that is not a criminal prosecution. Where a person is under arrest but is also involved in a civil action, the person may be released upon posting a bond. An example is that of a person arrested for not paying alimony. This bond requires that the person stay in the specified jurisdiction of the court and appear upon the court's order. If the person breaches the bond, the entire bond penalty is due and payable as a forfeiture. Major sureties do not usually provide this bond, but most insurance companies provide bail bonds for their insurance clients who are detained as a result of serious automobile accidents.

Fiduciary Bonds. A *fiduciary* is a person appointed to handle the affairs of another who cannot handle his or her own affairs. Because of this role, the fiduciary occupies a special position of trust and confidence.

The sole purpose of the *fiduciary bond* is to protect all who have an interest in an estate or a property from any loss that a fiduciary may cause by improper acts. Parties with an interest in an estate can include "infants" (children), incompetents, creditors, heirs, or other beneficiaries. Losses may result from dishonesty or from failure to perform faithfully the duties that the law requires. Because the *probate court* is responsible for the appointment and control of fiduciaries, fiduciary bonds are also called *probate bonds*.

Fiduciary obligations have long been viewed as hazardous. Sureties, however, do not consider properly underwritten, short-term fiduciary bonds as hazardous and write them freely but carefully. The protection of all interested persons generally requires that fiduciaries file surety bonds guaranteeing the faithful performance of their duties.

Following are summaries of various fiduciary coverages:

1. *Administrators, trustees, or executors under wills*—An administrator (male) or administratrix (female) is a fiduciary appointed by a probate court to manage and distribute the estate of a person who died without leaving a will. An executor (male) or executrix (female) or trustee is one named in a will to distribute and settle the estate of a testator (the person who leaves a will). Exhibit 2-5 is an example of an administration bond.

2. *Guardians of minors*—Courts appoint fiduciaries to administer minors' estates.

3. *Guardians, committees, or conservators of estates of incompetents*—Courts appoint these fiduciaries to handle affairs of persons who, because of mental or physical immobility, cannot handle their own affairs and have been declared incompetent.

4. *Receivers and others appointed by the courts in fiduciary capacity*—Courts appoint these fiduciaries to take possession and control of property that is the subject of litigation (foreclosure or partition) and to dispose of it at the court's direction. In

Exhibit 2-5
Administration Bond

ABC Insurance Company

Bond No. ....
File No. ....

ADMINISTRATION BOND
STATE OF NEW YORK

SURROGATE'S COURT: COUNTY OF

KNOW ALL PERSONS BY THESE PRESENTS, That we ....
....
as Principal, and ABC Insurance Company, a Corporation having an office and place of business at .... in the County of ...., City of ...., State of New York, as Surety, are held and firmly bound unto the PEOPLE OF THE STATE OF NEW YORK for the security and benefit of the persons now or hereafter interested in the estate of the deceased named below in the sum of .... DOLLARS lawful money of the United States of America, for the payment of which, well and truly to be made, we bind ourselves, our heirs, executors, administrators, successors and assigns, jointly and severally, firmly by these presents.

Signed, sealed and dated the .... day of ...., 19 .... .

THE CONDITION OF THIS OBLIGATION IS SUCH, That if the above fiduciary ....
....
shall faithfully discharge the trust reposed .... as .... administrat.... of all and singular the goods, chattels and credits of .... deceased late of the County of .... and obey all lawful decrees and orders touching the administration of the assets committed to ....
including but not limited to decrees or orders directing repayment of amounts allowed as advances on commissions and render a verified account of ....
administration whenever required to do so by the Court then this obligation shall be void; otherwise it shall remain in full force and effect.

..................................(SEAL).
..................................(SEAL).

ABC Insurance Company

By ....
Attorney-in-Fact

STATE OF ....
COUNTY OF .... SS.:

On this .... day of ...., before me personally appeared .... to me known and known to me to be .... the individual .... described in and who executed the foregoing instrument .... and acknowledged to me that ....
executed the same.

foreclosure proceedings, the receiver usually serves as a property manager up to the time of sale.

5. *Receivers in bankruptcy*—Bankruptcy courts appoint receivers to collect the assets of bankrupt estates under court supervision and to hold them pending the election of trustees in bankruptcy.
6. *Trustees in bankruptcy*—Trustees manage property for the benefit of bankrupt estates and their creditors.
7. *Assignee for the benefit of creditors*—The assignee is a fiduciary appointed in a state insolvency court for the benefit of a select group of creditors. These bonds are generally hazardous where the insolvent is forced into federal bankruptcy court, and the federal court holds the state court assignee responsible for acts that are contrary to the federal bankruptcy law.
8. *Commissioners for sale of real estate*—A fiduciary appointed to sell property and divide the proceeds according to a court order is a commissioner for the sale of real estate.

Fiduciary bonds are essentially fidelity instruments in that the major element of risk to trust estates and to surety companies lies in the possible dishonesty of fiduciaries.

A fiduciary bond applicant must be honest, persistent, devoted, and zealous in assembling trust or estate assets. Ignorance of the law does not absolve a fiduciary from liability, and retention of an attorney is usually necessary. The fiduciary must compensate an estate whether default results from dishonesty or from ignorance.

Anyone who has a beneficial interest in an estate or property may seek indemnity under a bond for loss resulting from the principal's failure to fulfill legally required obligations.

Categories. The three categories of fiduciary bonds are as follows:

1. *Bonds filed in probate courts*, which include bonds of administrators or personal representatives and executors of estates of deceased persons, trustees under wills, or guardians of minors; and guardians, committees, or conservators of incompetents' estates
2. *Bonds filed in equity courts*, including bonds of receivers in state or federal courts, assignees for the benefit of creditors, and trustees and commissioners for the sale of real estate
3. *Bonds filed in United States District Courts under the Federal Bankruptcy Act*, including receivers and trustees in various types of bankruptcy proceedings

Duties. When the fiduciary and the surety execute a bond, a continuing responsibility for the faithful administration of the estate's assets or other property begins. This responsibility does not terminate until the fiduciary gives an accounting to the court and the court has entered a discharge order on the records or the beneficiaries of the estate sign a release. This responsibility may last for only a year or two, as in the case of an administrator of an estate not governed by a will or of an executor of a will, or twenty-five years or more, as in the case of guardians of incompetents or trustees involving trusts that cover the lifetime of one or more persons.

An administrator or executor of a deceased person's estate may incur liability for such things as failure to liquidate assets in conformance with the law. A guardian could cause losses by making investments that do not meet the requirements of the law. The eventualities for which the fiduciary and the surety are responsible could occur in spite of the fiduciary's best intentions through an honest mistake or ignorance of the law. It is advisable for the fiduciary to seek the advice of an attorney who specializes in probate law. All surety underwriters recommend counsel with an attorney and, depending on the circumstances, may make it a condition for writing the bond. It is not unusual, however, for intentional mishandling of fiduciary responsibilities to cause losses in spite of expert legal advice. These possibilities are inherent in the nature of the fiduciary bond business.

Miscellaneous Bonds

Many bonds do not fit neatly into major categories. While not as numerous as license and permit bonds, the extensive *miscellaneous bond* list includes some bonds that also fit into other classifications. Only the more important types of miscellaneous bonds are included here.

The law requires many bonds, and these bonds must be conditioned as required by statute, ordinance, or regulation. The law requires others with conditions imposed at the discretion of approving authorities. Others may be purely voluntary bonds or undertakings with conditions that only the obligee prescribes.

Surety companies divide these bonds into three groups: (1) bonds required by the federal government; (2) bonds required by states, counties, municipalities, or political bodies other than the federal government; and (3) bonds required by individuals, firms, corporations, associations, or other legal entities. The Surety Association of America (SAA) provides all member companies with a rate manual structured in this manner, and all companies, whether they are members of the SAA or just use SAA rates, have rate manuals organized on the same basis.

Forms. Bond forms are not standardized and may vary with the obligee. Flexibility on the part of surety companies is necessary to meet the requirements of diverse laws, ordinances, and regulations, as well as the specific needs of various obligees. Nevertheless, where bonds are necessary to comply with the terms of a statute, ordinance, or regulation, they will be construed to provide the protection the law imposes on the principals and the sureties regardless of what the bond provides on its face.

Terms. The term or period that the bond covers must correspond with the term or period the law requires (statutory bonds) or with what the obligee requires (nonstatutory bonds). In either case, the right to file a claim under the bond for losses sustained while the bond is in force continues for various periods as the bond or the law requires.

Bonds Required by Federal Government. There are circumstances requiring bonds to guarantee payment of federal income taxes due or claimed to be due. The federal government accepts these bonds only if sureties write them on the appropriate U.S. Treasury Department form. These bonds are direct financial guarantees, and surety companies customarily require collateral (usually 100 percent of the penalty of the bond in cash or in another form readily convertible into cash). U.S. government securities are preferred; but, like any market security, 100 to 125 percent of the liability assumed may be required to cover fluctuations in the market price of the security. The principal bond forms used are the following:

1. Estate tax bonds
2. Bonds for credit claimed for foreign taxes accrued and not paid
3. Bonds for extension of time for payment of deficiency tax
4. Bonds for extension of time for payment of tax
5. Bonds for release of federal tax liens
6. Bonds to stay assessments pending appeal

Miscellaneous Indemnity Bonds. A *refunding bond,* required from the distributees of the estate of a person absent from the jurisdiction, is one form of a miscellaneous indemnity bond. Bonds of this kind may be necessary for a distribution of property by a receiver. This distribution can occur when a trustee is appointed under a special state statute providing for the management and disposition of an absentee's estate or where letters of administration have been granted on the assumption of death arising from a person's disappearance. A court issues letters of administration (1) appointing an administrator, and (2) citing specific steps to be followed by the administrator in the collection, recording, accounting, and distribution of the missing person's estate. The distributee's receipt of funds from a missing person's estate requires a bond to guarantee the return of the distribution should the missing person later return.

Bonds Required by Other Legal Entities. Miscellaneous bonds not grouped under obvious classifications are generally hazardous risks. These bonds are guarantees protecting the public from loss resulting from action or inaction in violation of statutes, regulations, or ordinances. They include any bonds that guarantee payment of a specified amount of money or a sum of money calculated to be due using formulas or procedures contained in state statutes or ordinances. Many of them have been neither time- nor volume-tested and require extra effort by the surety to evaluate the principal and its obligation. These bonds may guarantee lengthy and technical contracts between the obligee and the principal that require great effort to analyze and interpret.

An example of this type of bond is the *student bond*, which guarantees the return of borrowed property, bill payment, and indemnification of a college against damage to property. Another example is a bond required when a subcontractor must guarantee the return of machinery to the contractor who leased it.

Financial Guarantee Bonds. One of the most interesting types of bonds in the miscellaneous category is the traditional *financial guarantee bond*. These bonds guarantee the payment of money, whether or not the exact sum is known or stated, and give no alternative. An example is a *lease bond* for railroads, steamships, express companies, airlines, and other transportation companies. Lease bonds also extend to public service corporations that have plants in operation and own and operate public franchises. These bonds may guarantee rent payment and performance of other obligations contained in leases.

Lost Instrument or Securities Bonds. When a person loses a document, certificate, or instrument, the issuer will not usually deliver a duplicate until the owner of the lost instrument furnishes an indemnity bond. These bonds, called *lost instrument* or *lost securities bonds*, guarantee that, should the original lost document be found, it will be returned to the surety or obligee for proper disposal. The bond protects the issuer "forever." If no one presents a claim within a statutory time period, the surety closes the file. The surety, however, may still be liable if a claim arises.

For rating and underwriting purposes, lost securities bonds fall into two groups, fixed and open penalty bonds. The amount and type of bond required in each situation is specified by the obligee. A *fixed penalty bond* has a penalty stated in the bond. *Open penalty bonds* are those that (1) have no penalty stated in the bond, (2) have a penalty stated in the bond that is over two times the face value of the instrument, (3) have an instrument without a face value, or (4) have an amount that is over two times the market quotation. They are also bonds that, by covenant, give the obligee the right to demand new bonds in different or greater amounts. This situation arises when the security of the first bond appears insufficient to the obligee. A *lost instrument bond* for stocks and bonds is the most common example of an open penalty bond. The obligee specifies the amount and type of bond required in each situation. Exhibit 2-6 is an example of an open penalty bond.

Lost instrument bonds are usually easy to issue to individuals of known reliability, even when their financial status is not strong. The two important underwriting considerations are that (1) the lost instrument is not likely to reappear and (2) the owner did not endorse it.

Other Miscellaneous Indemnity Bonds. A relatively new line of financial guarantee bonds, sometimes referred to as credit enhancement bonds, guarantees the payment of principal and interest on investment instruments. Bonds also have been used to secure continued investment in a scheme or payment of deferred premiums. These bonds enhance equity or defer obligations, and many consider them to be financial guaranty "insurance."

Depository bonds, *workers compensation self-insured bonds*, and the other new financial guarantee bonds are extremely hazardous because they are intrinsically tied to the economic conditions of the marketplace. When the economy is doing well, and the surety underwriting cycle is at its zenith, some insurance companies aggressively seek additional premium income from these bonds. This trend often appears when the property and liability insurance lines are not doing well. At those times, some sureties make financial guarantee bonds readily available to increase the company's market share rapidly. Market conditions, market share, and operating cycles, however, should never be the reason for writing hazardous bonds more freely.

Insurance companies have assumed different positions with regard to participation in financial guarantee bonds of this type. Many companies do not write them. Others write them in the surety department, but only with very stringent guidelines. Still others have created separate departments to write them under stringent underwriting guidelines and with close financial management supervision.

Bank Depository Bonds. In the 1930s sureties succumbed to the temptation to write "lucrative" *bank depository bonds*, which guaranteed repayment of moneys deposited in a bank in the event of the bank's failure or insolvency. While this is practically a nonexistent line of business today, it was a common line of business at the time. During the 1930s losses from bank failures because of the Great Depression

Exhibit 2-6
Open Penalty Bond

ABC Insurance Company

Open Penalty
Lost Securities Bond

KNOW ALL PERSONS BY THESE PRESENTS, That we, ...
as principal, and ABC Insurance Company, a corporation having its office and principal place of business in ....
as surety, are held and firmly bound unto ....
....
....
their respective successors and assigns (hereinafter called Obligee(s)), in an aggregate sum, lawful money of the United States, sufficient to indemnify the Obligee(s) in case of a default under the conditions of this bond as hereinafter set forth, not exceeding, however, the maximum for which the Surety may lawfully obligate itself in respect to any single risk, to be paid to the Obligee(s), their respective successors and assigns, as their interests may appear, for which payment well and truly to be made we, the Principal and the Surety, bind ourselves, our heirs, executors, administrators, successors, and assigns firmly by these presents.

Signed, sealed and dated this .... day of ...., 19 ..... .

WHEREAS, the aforesaid Principal and Surety represent that the Principal is the sole owner of
....
....
....
and that said instrument or instruments have been lost, mislaid, stolen or destroyed, so that the same cannot be found or produced; and

WHEREAS, the Obligee(s) have been requested to issue duplicate instrument or instruments in place of the original or pay unto or credit the principal's account with the value thereof upon being indemnified against loss by reason of so doing, and

WHEREAS, on the faith of the foregoing representations and in consideration of this bond of indemnity, the Obligee(s) have complied or agreed to comply with said request.

NOW, THEREFORE, THE CONDITIONS OF THIS OBLIGATION ARE, that if the Principal, the heirs, legal representatives, successors or assigns of the Principal, or any of them, shall in case the mislaid, lost, stolen or destroyed original or originals be found or come into the hands or power of any of them, or to the hands, custody or power of any person, deliver or cause the same to be delivered unto the Obligee(s) in order to be cancelled, and shall also at all times indemnify and save harmless the Obligee(s) from and against any and all claims, actions and suits whether groundless or otherwise, and from and against any and all liabilities, losses, damages, costs, charges, counsel fees and other expenses of every nature and character by reason of the said mislaid, lost, stolen or destroyed original or originals and/or the issuance of a duplicate or duplicates in lieu thereof or the paying or crediting of the face amount of the original or originals without surrender thereof whether or not caused by, based upon, or arising out of inadvertence, accident, oversight or neglect on the part of the Obligee(s) or their respective officers, agents, clerks, and employees and/or omission or failure to inquire into, contest or litigate the right of any applicant to receive any payment, credit, transfer, registration, exchange or delivery in respect of the original or originals and/or the duplicate or duplicates issued in lieu thereof, and/or caused by, based upon or arising out of any other matter or thing whatsoever, then this obligation shall be void; otherwise shall remain in full force and effect.

PROVIDED, HOWEVER, that this bond is executed upon the following express conditions:

1. That the Surety shall be liable only for the actual financial loss suffered by the Obligee(s) by reason of issuing duplicate of the above-described instrument or instruments to the person entitled thereto as shown by the books of the Obligee(s) or paying unto or crediting such person's account with the value thereof and only up to the amount hereof.

2. That the Obligee(s) shall immediately notify the surety of any claim of ownership or interest in said original instrument or instruments made by any individual, firm or corporation.

....
PRINCIPAL

ABC Insurance Company

BY: ....

ATTEST: ....

---

were so great that many sureties became insolvent as a result. This history is often cited by seasoned underwriters to support the proposition that extreme caution is necessary to survive a period of negative market conditions with a share of highly hazardous financial guarantee bonds. Following the Great Depression, during which many banks failed, the federal government established insurance programs to guarantee the payment of many deposits. Presently the use of depository bonds is negligible.

Workers Compensation Self-Insured Bonds. *Workers compensation self-insured bonds* are guarantees given by employers who self-insure their workers compensation obligations. They also cover employer retentions of part of the risk, which can be significant. Should the self-insured corporation become insolvent and unable to pay the workers compensation claims, the surety continues payments for as long as the claims are outstanding or until the claimants die. Bond rates are usually only a fraction of the workers compensation insurance policy rates.

The bond premiums are paid until the bond obligation is satisfied or until the self-insured company regains solvency. Some state regulations require that the bonds be written on an annual basis, making them cumulative obligations. Hence, a $5 million bond written for six one-year terms becomes a $30 million obligation to cover all claims that may have arisen during the bond terms. Most of these bonds are written for only better managed and financially strong companies.

Public Official Bonds

A *public official bond* guarantees the faithful performance of duties by a public official who is in a position of trust, as well as an honest accounting of all public funds handled by the official. The bond must comply with the statutes and, for this reason, carries whatever liability the statutes require.

The two general kinds of public official bonds are *statutory* and *common law bonds*. The chief distinction between a statutory bond and a common law bond is that the obligee (the public) of a statutory bond is entitled to all the remedies and processes that the law grants. This bond contrasts to the common law, or voluntary, bond, which is an ordinary contract. Another way to explain the difference is to use the county sheriff as an example. The sheriff is elected and required by law to furnish a statutory bond. If, however, the sheriff wants his deputies bonded, this is a voluntary decision. The deputies would therefore furnish common law bonds.

The election of a public official is only the first step in the chain of events that qualify an official for the performance of required duties. As a general rule, the official is not qualified to function in the capacity of the elected official until the official takes the oath of office and the bond meets the necessary legal requirements. The surety bond, therefore, becomes a prerequisite for assuming office and is a guarantee of the good faith performance required by law.

There are similarities between the public official bond and the oath of office. The typical official bond is phrased as follows:

> Now, therefore, the condition of this bond is such that if the above bounden principal shall faithfully perform the duties of his said office or position as required by law, then this obligation to be null and void; otherwise to remain in full effect.

The typical *oath of office* is similarly phrased:

> ...I will faithfully discharge the duties of the office of ____________ according to the best of my ability and in strict accordance with the laws.

It is not difficult to understand the necessity for a public official bond. Officers whose duties are to receive and dispense money, invest public funds, or seize and dispose of property; to arrest or detain persons; or otherwise come into conflict with the rights of citizens must generally furnish bonds to protect those interested in, or those injured by, the exercise of such powers.

The complete nature and purpose of these bonds is not so readily apparent, and they are often confused with other forms of liability insurance policies. Under liability insurance policies, which are two-party agreements, losses are paid directly to the insured. Under the public official bond, losses are not paid to the principal named in the bond, but to the obligee (the electorate). The guarantee of a public official bond is that the public will not suffer loss, up to the amount of the bond, because of the failure of the bonded official to perform the duties of office honestly and faithfully. Exhibit 2-7 shows a typical public official bond.

The bond term usually coincides with the public official's term of office. The penalty amount of the bond is most commonly a sum equal to the largest amount of cash, checks, and securities under the official's control at any one time. This amount does not always protect the public against aggregate "hidden" losses that accumulate over a period of years.

All public official bonds required by statute, and written for officials having custody of public funds, protect the public in case of an official's failure "to account for and to turn over" those funds regardless of the cause of loss. Losses from fire, accident, burglary, robbery, or forgery are chargeable to the official, who may provide security against the loss through proper insurance policies.

The law usually holds the official responsible for all activities of subordinates in the office. It is important for the official to protect against losses that may be caused by subordinates, such as dishonesty losses from employee theft and forgery. Insurance policies, such as coverage for physical damage or destruction by fire to money, securities, or other property, also may contribute to broader coverage.

Public official insurance to protect the official from dishonesty and other crime losses is now provided under the new simplified crime policy subsequently discussed in this chapter. Under this policy, burglary, robbery, theft, and forgery coverage may be added to form a crime package.

Public employee dishonesty coverage Forms O or P can cover loss from employee dishonesty. Form O covers loss in any one occurrence to the limit of the policy involving one or more employees, whether the result of a single act or a series of acts. Form P covers loss in any one occurrence to the policy limits caused by each employee, whether the result of a single act or a series of acts. When faithful performance of duty is endorsed to coverage Forms O or P, a depository failure exclusion is an automatic part of that endorsement.

A public official may be liable for a loss of funds caused by a depository bank's failure in which the official has deposited the funds. The official is liable, absent strict compliance with the statute governing the deposit of those funds. The public body usually designates the depository bank or banks for the safekeeping of public funds. The public official is relieved of the responsibility for the depository failure if the funds are deposited in accordance with the public body's designation. If public bodies did not follow this procedure, most sureties would refuse to write public official bonds.

Exhibit 2-7
Typical Public Official Bond Form

KNOW ALL PERSONS BY THESE PRESENTS, That we John Jones as Principal, and the John Doe Surety Company, a corporation, as Surety are held and firmly bound unto (state, county or political sub-division of which public official is an officer) in the penal sum of $............. Dollars, lawful money of the United States of America, for the payment of which, well and truly made, *said principal binds himself, his heirs, executors, administrators and assigns*, and said surety binds itself, its successors and assigns, jointly and severally, firmly by these presents.

WHEREAS, the said principal has been elected or appointed to the office of.................................. and is required to furnish a bond for the faithful performance of the duties of said office.

NOW THEREFORE, the conditions of this obligation is such that if the above bounden principal shall faithful perform the duties of his said office or position as required by law, and shall pay over to the persons authorized by law to receive all monies that may come into his hands during the said term without fraud or delay, and at the expiration of said term, or in case of his resignation or removal from office, shall turn over to his successor all records and property which have come into his hands, then his obligation to be null and void; otherwise to remain in full force and effect.

Adapted from: *Fundamentals of Bonding, A Manual on Fidelity/Surety*, Dr. Franklin L. Moore, CPCU (The Rough Notes Co.: Indianapolis, IN, 1989).

Federal Noncontract Bonds

Federal noncontract surety bonds are generally grouped into three categories: immigrants' bonds; excise, or Internal Revenue, bonds; and customs bonds. The forms are printed, numbered, appropriately titled, and generally available from the pertinent department of the U.S. government.

Immigrants' Bonds. The *immigrants' bond* is a class of federal bonds covering aliens entering the United States. These bonds secure aliens' compliance with all immigration laws and regulations, including appearance in hearings. The bonds are issued for principals such as patients, students, professional entertainers, athletes, tourists, and others lawfully entering the country. Others are bonds given by hospitals authorized to receive alien patients, by employers importing alien workers for work in this country, and by transportation companies for payment of fines or sums imposed on them under immigration laws and regulations.

The federal government prepares immigrants' bond forms and may require them on individual or blanket forms. An individual bond form covers the alien named in the bond, a blanket bond form covers a number of aliens, or those on a list that is part of the bond.

Some of these bonds run for indefinite terms, others run for definite terms but may be extended for additional periods. The latter occurs when the government grants an alien permission to remain in the country for a longer period than that anticipated at the time the original bond is executed.

The alien's failure to comply with all of the bond's conditions and failure to stay in the country at the end of the authorized period subjects the bond to forfeiture and payment of the penal sum. The blanket bond is subject to the forfeiture of a pro rata sum equal to the number of aliens involved in the failure to depart.

A bond guaranteeing the payment of fines imposed under the Immigration Act is a term bond that guarantees the payment of fines or sums imposed upon a shipping company transporting aliens into this country who are ineligible for admission because of quota limitations, health, or other circumstances.

Where an alien is held for deportation, the alien's release may be obtained pending a hearing by filing a bond guaranteeing that the alien will be delivered for deportation to the Immigration and Naturalization Services upon request.

The U.S. Attorney General is vested with discretionary power to obtain a bond guaranteeing that aliens entering the United States will not become public charges or inmates of public institutions while in the United States.

Excise Bonds. *Excise bonds* protect public revenue under an arrangement by which the U. S. government ensures that it will get its money by requiring that handlers of taxable commodities furnish bonds guaranteeing compliance with regulations and payment of taxes. They include guarantees for the payment of duties, taxes, fees, and other revenue sources and for the enforcement of penal statutes. Excise bonds are drawn and printed by the pertinent governmental department with the approval of the U.S. Attorney General.

Manufacturers, distillers, processors, brewers, winemakers, and dealers or carriers of products for which a federal permit may be required are all subject to taxation under the Internal Revenue Code and tax rules and regulations.

Bonds required of these businesses guarantee that they will comply fully with applicable laws and regulations and pay all taxes, fines, or other charges due the government. In some instances the bond is subject to forfeiture in its entirety for a principal's failure to comply with the law. There are approximately thirty variations of these bonds, and all are issued on the government's own forms furnished by the Internal Revenue Service. Below are some examples:

- The *distilled spirits bond* is provided by distillers, rectifiers, or bonded warehousemen to guarantee compliance with laws relating to the manufacture, storage, and transportation of distilled spirits.
- The *industrial alcohol bond* covers the manufacture of alcohol and the operation of a bonded warehouse for the storage of alcohol. The manufacturer must furnish this bond to guarantee that it will not use denatured alcohol for illegal purposes.
- The *tobacco manufacturers bond* guarantees federal taxes on tobacco and ensures that the tobacco manufacturer will abide by all regulations relating to the manufacture of tobacco products, including the payment of all taxes due.

Customs Bonds. The Customs Service of the U.S. Department of the Treasury regulates the importation of commodities into the country. It is a Customs official's job to ensure that the taxed merchandise remains under Customs control, usually in a bonded warehouse, until the duty is paid or a bond secures payment of the duty.

The customs bond may be issued on a single transaction form or on a continuous form. The U.S. Department of the Treasury provides a single customs bond form adaptable for all types of transactions, and the surety designates in the form the type of transaction to be covered. The statutory language for the appropriate transaction is incorporated by reference, and the penal sum, or limit of liability, is entered in the form at the time of execution. Exhibit 2-8 shows U.S. Customs Bond Form 301.

FIDELITY BONDS AND CRIME INSURANCE

Fidelity bonds protect employers against dishonest acts of employees. Crime insurance protects the insured's property against burglary, robbery, or theft. Fidelity bonds and crime insurance have been combined to form the new, simplified commercial crime policy. Each of these coverages is described in this section.

Traditionally, fidelity bonds were simply referred to as "bonds" because there were three parties to the fidelity contract: the employer (obligee), the employee (principal), and the bond company or insurer (surety). In this respect the fidelity arrangement resembled other surety arrangements. Recently, however, fidelity bonds have been termed "employee dishonesty insurance" because fidelity and forgery bonds and various crime coverages are included by a rider in the property and liability package insurance policies. Initially, fidelity bonds were written on an individual basis, and not all insurance companies wrote fidelity bonds.

Employee dishonesty losses are seldom publicized because employers believe that information about such failures of trust is a negative reflection on the firm and its management. This lack of publicity about dishonesty losses may be one reason employers have inadequate limits or no fidelity coverage at all to protect the firm's assets. Since all firms who have employees have fidelity exposures, consideration should be given to coverage and limits that are both affordable and adequate to protect the firm's assets.

Buyers of employee dishonesty and crime coverages usually wish to purchase more than one form of coverage, such as employee dishonesty plus theft of money and securities by outsiders, or loss due to forgery of checks issued by the insured. In response to this demand, combination crime policies, or *package policies*, have developed. A package policy combines a number of individual property and liability insurance coverages into a single insurance policy.

One goal of package policies generally is to standardize the format of property and liability insurance contracts. A uniform policy format eliminates redundancies and overlaps in coverage, making it easier for all parties to locate information. Each line of insurance now has one set of forms and endorsements, plus one set of manual rules, that apply to both monoline and commercial package policies. In the years prior to development of the simplified combined fidelity bond and crime insurance policy, various lines of insurance policies were developed in a haphazard fashion, creating confusion in consumers' minds. Today's coverage forms are more understandable to the typical commercial insured. The need for crime insurance arose from the fact that commercial business personal property and inland marine insurance exclude the crimes covered in fidelity bonds and crime insurance.

Coverage

Many buyers of combination employee dishonesty and crime insurance policies purchase the five most common insuring agreements:

- Employee dishonesty
- Loss inside the premises (money and securities)
- Loss outside the premises (money and securities)
- Money orders and counterfeit currency
- Depositor's forgery (checks)

Employee dishonesty insurance is usually written as part of the simplified *Commercial Crime Policy*, which covers loss resulting from any dishonest act of a bonded employee that causes the insured a loss and provides the employee or another person or entity with a financial

Exhibit 2-8
U.S. Customs Bond Form 301

Approved through 4/30/87
OMB No. 1515-0144

DEPARTMENT OF THE TREASURY
UNITED STATES CUSTOMS SERVICE

CUSTOMS BOND

19 CFR Part 113

CUSTOMS USE ONLY	BOND NUMBER[1] (Assigned by Customs)
	FILE REFERENCE

In order to secure payment of any duty, tax or charge and compliance with law or regulation as a result of activity covered by any condition referenced below, we, the below named principal(s) and surety(ies), bind ourselves to the United States in the amount or amounts, as set forth below. | Execution Date

SECTION I—Select Single Transaction OR Continuous Bond (not both) and fill in the applicable blank spaces.

☐ SINGLE TRANSACTION BOND	Identification of transaction secured by this bond (e.g., entry no., seizure no., etc.)	Date of transaction	Transaction district & port code
☐ CONTINUOUS BOND	Effective date	This bond remains in force for one year beginning with the effective date and for each succeeding annual period, or until terminated. This bond constitutes a separate bond for each period in the amounts listed below for liabilities that accrue in each period. The intention to terminate this bond must be conveyed within the time period and manner prescribed in the Customs Regulations.	

SECTION II— This bond includes the following agreements.[2] (Check one box only, except that, 1a may be checked independently or with 1, and 3a may be checked independently or with 3. Line out all other parts of this section that are not used.)

Activity Code	Activity Name and Customs Regulations in which conditions codified	Limit of Liability	Activity Code	Activity Name and Customs Regulations in which conditions codified	Limit of Liability
☐ 1	Importer or broker....113.62		☐ 5	Public Gauger....113.67	
☐ 1a	Drawback Payment Refunds.... 113.65		☐ 6	Wool & Fur Products Labeling Acts Importation (Single Entry Only)....113.68	
☐ 2	Custodian of bonded merchandise....113.63 (Includes bonded carriers, freight forwarders, cartmen and lightermen, all classes of warehouses, container station operators)		☐ 7	Bill of Lading (Single Entry Only)....113.69	
☐ 3	International Carrier....113.64		☐ 8	Detention of Copyrighted Material (Single Entry Only)....113.70	
☐ 3a	Instruments of International Traffic.113.66		☐ 9	Neutrality (Single Entry Only)....113.71	
☐ 4	Foreign Trade Zone Operator....113.73		☐ 10	Court Costs for Condemned Goods (Single Entry Only)....113.72	

SECTION III— List below all tradenames or unincorporated divisions that will be permitted to obligate this bond in the principal's name including their Customs Identification Number(s).[3] (If more space is needed, use Section III(Continuation) on back of form.)

Importer Number	Importer Name	Importer Number	Importer Name

Total number of importer names listed in Section III:

Principal and surety agree that any charge against the bond under any of the listed names is as though it was made by the principal(s).

Principal and surety agree that they are bound to the same extent as if they executed a separate bond covering each set of conditions incorporated by reference to the Customs Regulations into this bond.

If the surety fails to appoint an agent under Title 6, United States Code, Section 7, surety consents to service on the Clerk of any United States District Court or the U.S. Court of International Trade, where suit is brought on this bond. That clerk is to send notice of the service to the surety at:

Mailing Address Requested by the Surety

PRINCIPAL[4]	Name and Address	Importer No.[3] SIGNATURE[5]	SEAL
PRINCIPAL[4]	Name and Address	Importer No.[3] SIGNATURE[5]	SEAL
SURETY[4,6]	Name and Address[6]	Surety No.[7] SIGNATURE[5]	SEAL
SURETY[4,6]	Name and Address[6]	Surety No.[7] SIGNATURE[5]	SEAL

SURETY AGENTS	Name[8]	Identification No.[9]	Name[8]	Identification No.[9]

PART 1— U.S. CUSTOMS

Customs Form 301 (111883)

benefit. The employee may steal alone or in collusion with other employees or nonemployees. The loss may involve money, merchandise, or any other property, real or personal.

It is important to emphasize that the employee dishonesty insurance part of the simplified commercial crime policy is not an "all-risks" coverage. Loss must result from the bonded employee's dishonesty, and the bond does not cover an act or error unless it involves dishonesty. "Employee dishonesty" is defined as follows in the Employee Dishonesty Coverage Form A:

> . . . dishonest acts committed by an "employee", whether identified or not, acting alone or in collusion with other persons, except you as a partner, with the manifest intent to:
>
> (1) Cause you to sustain loss; and also
>
> (2) Obtain financial benefit (other than employee benefits earned in the normal course of employment, including: salaries, commissions, fees, bonuses, promotions, awards, profit sharing or pensions) for:
>
> (a) The "employee"; or
>
> (b) Any person or organization intended by the "employee" to receive that benefit.[3]

Employee dishonesty insurance is currently part of a package crime policy that allows an insured to select the crime coverages needed to insure its business or governmental operation. The definition above was drafted by the SAA for the bankers blanket bond to overcome the broadened interpretation courts had placed on previous language.

Employee dishonesty insurance, as a general rule, covers acts of employees who are subject to the insured's direction, whose salaries or wages are paid by the insured, and for whom the insured withholds income tax. Most policies specifically define "employee."

Employee dishonesty insurance for public employees, as previously discussed in this chapter, can be extended to cover not only fidelity exposures but also faithful performance of duty. Since some statutes prescribe faithful performance of duty for public employees, most insurers provide the coverage when reasonable security procedures and controls are in place. Faithful performance extends beyond dishonesty coverage, requiring that the duties of the position be performed in a way that precludes any loss to the public body. Any loss to the public body caused by the official, resulting from performance of duty contrary to statutory prescriptions, will activate the faithful performance clause.

Policy Forms

The Commercial Crime Policy provides various crime coverages for mercantile or governmental entities. It is easy to read and may be tailored to fit the insured's needs by attaching only those coverage forms that are desired. (The Commercial Crime Policy replaces the earlier *Comprehensive 3-D Forms*, the *Blanket Crime Policy*, and *Commercial Blanket Bonds*.) There are eighteen coverage forms available in the Commercial Crime Program, each of which provides coverage for a particular set of hazards:

- *Form A—Employee Dishonesty (Blanket)*—This form protects the insured against loss of money, securities, and other property caused by the dishonesty of one or more employees, up to the limit of insurance.
- *Form A—Employees Dishonesty (Schedule)*—This form protects the insured against loss of money, securities, and other property loss caused by the dishonesty of any person named or engaged to perform the duties of positions shown in the schedule.
- *Form B—Forgery or Alteration*—This form protects the insured against loss caused by forgery or alteration of instruments such as checks, drafts, or promissory notes that are made or drawn by the insured or its agent.
- *Form C—Theft, Disappearance, and Destruction*—This form provides protection against loss of money or securities by "any act of stealing" by nonemployees, disappearance of money and securities, and loss of money and securities by any peril that destroys money or securities.
- *Form D—Robbery and Safe Burglary*—This form pays for loss of, and loss from damage to, covered property resulting directly from the covered causes of loss.
- *Form E—Premises Burglary*—This form provides coverage for loss of property, other than money and securities, caused by actual or attempted burglary or robbery of a premises guard.
- *Form F—Computer Fraud*—This form provides coverage for loss of, and loss from damage to, money, securities, and property other than money and securities by computer fraud. Computer fraud includes property theft, that is, using a computer to fraudulently transfer that property from inside the premises to a person or place outside the premises.
- *Form G—Extortion*—This form insures against loss of money, securities, and any property other than money and securities, that results directly from extortion. It covers loss away from the premises as a result of a threat to a person or a relative of the person threatened.

- *Form H—Premises Theft and Robbery Outside the Premises*—This form covers theft of inside or outside property, other than money and securities, while it is in the care, custody, and control of a messenger.
- *Form I—Lessees of Safe Deposit Boxes*—This form covers securities and property loss from the insured's safe deposit box.
- *Form J—Securities Deposited With Others*—This form provides coverage for insureds who place their securities in the custody of a designated third party, such as a governmental body or stockbroker.
- *Form K—Liability for Guests' Property—Safe Deposit Coverage*—This form is used for lodging facility insureds to provide legal liability coverage arising from loss of guests' property while in a safe deposit box.
- *Form L—Liability for Guests' Property*—This form is available for lodging facility insureds and provides legal liability coverage for loss or destruction of guests' property while the property is inside the premises of a lodging facility.
- *Form M—Safe Depository Legal Liability*—For insureds other than financial institutions, this form is available to cover the legal liability of the depository for loss of customers' property while inside the depository premises.
- *Form N—Safe Depository Direct Loss*—For insureds other than financial institutions, this form covers the loss of customers' property (excluding money) resulting from robbery, burglary, destruction, or damage while the property is inside the depository premises.
- *Form O—Public Employees' Dishonesty (Per Loss Basis)*—This form covers loss in any one occurrence to the limit of insurance, involving one or more employees, whether the result of a single act or a series of acts.
- *Form P—Public Employees' Dishonesty (Per Employee Basis)*—This form covers loss in any one occurrence to the limit of insurance caused by each employee, whether the result of a single act or a series of acts.
- *Form Q—Safe Burglary and Robbery*—For commercial and governmental insureds, this form is an alternative to Coverage Form C and provides coverage for the loss of money and securities resulting only from specified perils.

FINANCIAL INSTITUTION BONDS

Financial institution bonds are written specifically for financial institutions, including commercial and savings banks, savings and loan associations, credit unions, stockbrokers, finance companies, and insurance companies. These bonds insure against loss of property resulting from employee dishonesty, burglary, robbery, larceny, misplacement, mysterious unexplainable disappearance, forgery, and certain other perils. Specifically, financial institution bonds provide indemnity against loss of money, securities, bullion, precious metals and articles made from them, jewelry, gems, semiprecious and precious stones, and specified papers and documents.

Bonds for financial institutions may be issued on surety companies' own forms or, as is usually the case, on standard SAA forms. Standard riders may alter or amend the SAA forms. Each standard bond form bears a number or a title, such as Financial Institution Bond Standard Form No. 24.

The employee dishonesty agreement in the bond covers dishonest or fraudulent acts committed by an employee, acting alone or with others, to obtain financial benefit. The employee must have intent to cause a loss to the insured. Insuring agreements differ among these bonds. Following are other agreements:

1. The *On-Premises Insuring Agreement* covers loss of property, as defined, through robbery, burglary, damage, destruction, theft, or larceny in an office on the premises of the insured. Losses can occur while the property is within any covered office of the insured that is described in the bond. It also covers any loss of or damage to the interior of any of the insured offices or furnishings, fixtures, equipment, safes, and vaults through specified perils, except loss or damage by fire.
2. The *In-Transit Insuring Agreement* covers loss of property while in transit and in the custody of a designated messenger.
3. Extortion—*Threats to Persons Insuring Agreement* covers loss of property surrendered away from an office of the insured as the result of a threat communicated to the insured to do bodily harm to a director, trustee, employee, or partner of the insured or their relatives, within the territories covered for extortion.
4. Extortion—*Threats to Property Insuring Agreement* covers loss of property surrendered away from an office of the insured as the result of a threat communicated to the insured to do damage to the premises or property of the insured within the

Exhibit 2-9
Financial Institution Bond

FINANCIAL INSTITUTION BOND
Standard Form No. 24, Revised to January, 1986

Bond No.

(Herein called Underwriter)

DECLARATIONS

Item 1. Name of Insured (herein called Insured):

Principal Address:

Item 2. Bond Period: from 12:01 a.m. on ______________ to 12:01 a.m. on __________
(Month, Day, Year) (Month, Day, Year)

Item 3. The Aggregate Liability of the Underwriter during the Bond Period shall be
$

Item 4. Subject to Sections 4 and 11 hereof,
the Single Loss Limit of Liability is **$**
and the Single Loss Deductible is **$**

Provided, however, that if any amounts are inserted below opposite specified Insuring Agreements or Coverage, those amounts shall be controlling. Any amount set forth below shall be part of and not in addition to amounts set forth above. (If an Insuring Agreement or Coverage is to be deleted, insert "Not Covered.")

Amount applicable to:	Single Loss Limit of Liability	Single loss Deductible
Insuring Agreement (D)—FORGERY OR ALTERATION	$	$
Insuring Agreement (E)—SECURITIES	$	$
Optional Insuring Agreements and Coverages:	$	$

If "Not Covered" is inserted above opposite any specified Insuring Agreement or Coverage, such Insuring Agreement or Coverage and any other reference thereto in this bond shall be deemed to be deleted therefrom.

Item 5. The liability of the Underwriter is subject to the terms of the following riders attached hereto:

Item 6. The Insured by the acceptance of this bond gives notice to the Underwriter terminating or canceling prior bond(s) or policy(ies) No.(s)
such termination or cancellation to be effective as of the time this bond becomes effective.

TSB 5018d

Printed in U.S.A.

FI-25 Revised December, 1990

territories covered for extortion.

5. *Forgery or Alteration Insuring Agreement* covers loss resulting directly from forgery or alteration of, on, or in any instrument specified in the insuring agreement.
6. *Securities Insurance Agreement* covers loss resulting directly from the insured having, in good faith, for its own account or for the account of others, acquired, sold, or delivered, or given value, extended credit or assumed liability, on the faith of any original instrument specified in the insuring agreement that proves to bear a forged signature or that has been altered, lost, or stolen.
7. *Counterfeit Currency Insuring Agreement* covers loss through receipt by the insured, in good faith, of any counterfeited or altered paper currencies or coin of the United States or Canada.

One of the most important bond forms issued is the *Standard Form No. 24*. In January 1986 the SAA revised the Bankers Blanket Bond, Standard Form No. 24, changing its name from "Bankers Blanket Bond" to "Financial Institution Bond." (See Exhibit 2-9.)

Eligible insureds for Financial Institution Bond Standard Form No. 24 include the following:

1. National banks, state commercial banks, and trust companies
2. American agencies of foreign banks, cooperative credit associations of Nebraska, industrial banks, and Morris Plan Banks
3. Title insurance companies
4. Federal banking agencies such as Federal Reserve Banks, Federal Deposit Insurance Corporation, Federal Home Loan Banks, and Federal Land Banks

There are other financial institution bond forms specifically designed, named, and numbered to cover particular classes of financial institutions, including stockbrokers, finance companies, credit unions, and insurance companies.

SUMMARY

There are almost as many types of bonds as there are commercial or legal arrangements. The volume of business that corporate bond companies transact, the services they render to the public, and the amount of credit and security extended to all branches of commercial enterprise prove or are evidence that corporate suretyship is one of the most essential and challenging areas of the insurance business.

Surety and fidelity are the two basic categories of bonds. A surety bond is a three-party written agreement providing for monetary compensation or satisfactory completion of an obligation by the surety should the principal fail to perform specified acts within a stated period of time. Surety bonds use basic forms and are required by governmental bodies and laws, as well as by accepted business practice. Fidelity bonds, on the other hand, are more complex. These bonds cover an employer for a loss resulting from an employee's dishonest acts.

Surety bonds generally fall into seven categories: contract, license and permit, judicial bonds in civil proceedings, miscellaneous, public official, and federal noncontract.

The *contract bond* guarantees the performance of an underlying written contract and the payment of bills arising under the contract. Bid, performance, payment, and maintenance bonds are the four most common kinds of contract bonds.

License and permit bonds meet public interest demands for regulation of certain types of businesses for the protection of citizens and public or private property. Plumbers, real estate brokers, auctioneers, grain warehouse operators, sign-hangers, sidewalk and curb builders, and excavation and street obstruction contractors must post permit bonds.

Judicial bonds in civil proceedings include *court* and *fiduciary bonds*. Court, or litigant, bonds protect the rights of opposing parties in lawsuits. Federal courts require *admiralty bonds* in actions against ships. *Release of civil proceedings bonds*, commonly called *bail bonds*, gain release from incarceration of people who also are involved in civil actions. *Fiduciary bonds* are required of administrators, executors, guardians, committees, trustees, and other fiduciaries appointed by probate courts to manage the estates of others. These bonds guarantee faithful performance of duty in accordance with the laws applicable to a trust. They are frequently called "probate bonds" because they are customarily filed with a probate court. Bonds are written for executors named in wills that require bonds. Those having an interest in an estate may include "infants" (children), incompetents, creditors, heirs, or other beneficiaries.

Miscellaneous bonds are bonds that do not fall within other classifications. The law requires some of these bonds, with discretionary conditions established by approving authorities; others are purely voluntary bonds with conditions prescribed by an obligee. They may be bonds required by the federal government; by states, counties, or other political subdivisions; or by persons, firms, corporations, associations, or other legal entities.

Miscellaneous indemnity bonds include "new" financial guarantee bonds, such as the limited partnership bonds and others that enhance investment schemes. They are hazardous undertakings because they are affected by economic conditions.

Public official bonds guarantee the faithful performance of duty by a public official in a position of trust and also provide for an honest accounting of all public funds under an official's control.

Federal noncontract bonds are divided into three general classifications: immigrant bonds, excise bonds, and customs bonds. *Immigrant bonds* secure aliens' compliance with immigration laws and regulations. *Excise bonds* protect public revenues and include guarantees for the payment of duties, taxes, and fees and for the enforcement of penal statutes. *Customs bonds* guarantee payment of the duty on merchandise brought into the country and all other customs obligations, including fines, penalties, or forfeitures.

There are three forms of fidelity bond coverages:

1. Employee dishonesty for commercial risks
2. Employee dishonesty for financial institutions
3. Employee dishonesty for public officials

Burglary, theft, and forgery coverages may be added to each of the preceding to create a crime package for the protection of the obligee. This coverage insures against property loss that might result from the dishonesty of employees, forgery, theft, disappearance or destruction, robbery or safe burglary, other burglary, and extortion.

The new, simplified commercial crime policy offers protection to mercantile establishments and public bodies. Standard forms cover financial institutions, and riders alter or amend them. These policies are very broad in coverage and provide obligees with coverage for almost every kind of loss in the crime area.

Chapter Notes

1. Franklin L. Moore, *Agent's Bonding Guide* (Indianapolis, IN: Rough Notes Company, 1982), pp. 228-252.
2. Franklin L. Moore, *Fundamentals of Bonding* (Indianapolis, IN: Rough Notes Company, 1989), pp. 167-169.
3. Employee Dishonesty Coverage Form A—Blanket, Surety Association of America.

CHAPTER 3

Bond Production

A reliable source of surety credit is vital to contractors engaged in public work. Subcontractors and contractors doing private work are also increasingly being asked to post a bond as assurance to prime contractors, project owners, and lenders that their work will be faithfully completed on time and all bills will be promptly paid.

Miscellaneous, license, and permit bonds are required by any firm that requires a license to operate or is subject to a wide range of financial responsibility or tax laws.

Court, probate, and fiduciary bonds are required to ensure the protection of litigants against nonjudicial loss of property, proper administration of estates, and faithful performance of fiduciary responsibilities to wards of the court and minors.

Insurance agents and brokers are the primary distribution system that insurance and surety companies use to meet the demand for surety bonds. A distinct minority of surety companies write bonds directly without the services of agents or brokers.

Direct-writing surety departments are usually part of insurance companies operating generally as direct writers. Most direct-writing insurance companies write property and liability insurance only and do not write bonds. In these companies producers are employees, not independent contractors.

Some direct-writing companies do not write surety bonds but serve as reinsurers for some classes of fidelity and surety bonds. Most direct-writing insurance companies also write automobile, homeowners, and life insurance but, to provide full services for all lines, make special contract arrangements to handle bond coverages for policyholders requiring them.

AGENTS, BROKERS, AND PRODUCERS

An *agent* represents the insurance or surety company under contract and has company authorization to distribute products according to established underwriting guidelines. A *broker*, on the other hand, represents clients to several different companies and is licensed to do business with any company. Legally, an agent usually represents an insurer, and a broker usually represents an insurance applicant or insured.

In practice, the terms "agent" and "broker" are nearly synonymous because most agents represent several companies, and brokers may represent insurance companies with regard to certain activities, such as premium collection. Both agents and brokers ethically and legally must work in the best interests of the insurance companies and the insurance purchasers. Chapters 6 and 7 of the CPCU 6 textbook, *The Legal Environment of Insurance*, discuss the legal aspects of agency relationships in greater detail.

A *producer* is the person in a brokerage or agency who is responsible for producing and servicing contract and other surety business. Because a producer can also be an agent or a broker, this chapter uses "producer" as an all-inclusive term to signify agents and brokers. The producer may be salaried by the agency or may earn only a commission on the business written. Producers must have enough education, training, and experience to provide contractors and sureties with a professional level of credit and financial prequalification services.

Although relatively rare, there are instances in which a very large contractor owns an insurance agency partially, or perhaps entirely, in order to save paying agents' commissions or to negotiate special terms directly with insurance or surety companies. In most cases the contractors want to gain control of insurance or surety costs and service. The disadvantage is that both the contractor and the surety lose the objective counsel and breadth of markets that an independent agent or broker can provide.

Forty to fifty years ago, some surety companies used *managing general agents* (MGAs) to serve as their field distribution forces and to accept business from subagents. MGAs had underwriting authority, within certain parameters, to bind the company on insurance as well as surety credit risks. Today, very few surety companies operate in this manner. Nearly all prefer to control underwriting in their own home offices and with their own field employees.

Most surety bonds require the advice of experts. Although many producers do not handle surety bonds every day, they should have a working knowledge of surety bonds in order to provide complete service to their contractor accounts.

PRODUCER'S ROLE IN CONTRACT BONDS

Opening the door to a sale is still a fundamental principle in any kind of selling. To do this in the "people" business of insurance and bonds, the producer must make as many contacts as possible in order to increase its own exposure in the field and to identify those contractors who perform work requiring bonds. This section discusses the means by which the producer can accomplish this essential task and provides several reasons bondable contractors may want to change surety companies or producers.

One way to enter the bonding arena is through other lines of insurance. Nearly every producer has small service or tradespeople insured who can serve as "centers of influence" by introducing the producer to contractors who perform work requiring bonds. If a producer has insurance companies for general liability or umbrella insurance, these centers of influence might be used as a means of acquiring an account. Sometimes, however, the reverse is true—obtaining the bond results in getting the other lines of insurance.

Attendance at bid openings and building trade shows or conventions help to display the producer's interest in the principal and may serve to open a few doors.

Getting to know suppliers who deal with contractors is another means of gaining exposure. Their recommendation of a producer is valuable and could result in a future sale. A method that has worked for some is a letter to known and well-established contractors, suggesting an interview.

There are many reasons why bondable contractors may want to change surety companies or producers. Some have relocated and do not like traveling long distances to secure bid bonds. Others may have been pressured politically into dealing with a producer who is not to their liking. Some get very poor service or may be dealing with a producer or insurance company that is not as competent as they desire.

Accountants are also influential and should not be overlooked as potential sources of referrals. Membership in business clubs can provide good business exposure by broadening the producer's contacts.

Surety credit is primarily a vehicle for providing prequalification services to project owners and prime contractors through the media of contract bonds. Once satisfied that the contractor will perform the contract faithfully, the surety guarantees the performance. The good faith and credit of the surety backs this guarantee. The surety is typically in only a partially secured credit position or is unsecured. Therefore, the surety underwriter must be careful to investigate fully the background, ability, business relationships, finances, and character of the contractors bonded. Sureties rely to a large extent on their producers to develop and evaluate this information as part of their prequalification responsibilities.

Prequalification Responsibilities

The professional surety producer plays an important role in the prequalification process. The producer is responsible for (1) compiling the necessary financial documents for the underwriter, (2) conducting a background investigation of the contractor's past contractual obligations, (3) assisting the contractor in selecting a surety company, (4) preparing a written credit analysis of the contractor's operations, (5) presenting the written analysis to the selected surety, and (6) helping to maintain open channels of communication between the contractor and the surety.

Financial Documents

The more knowledge the producer has about the contractor's financial status, the better its chances for developing an account that will be acceptable to the underwriter. The producer's role includes compiling the necessary documents for the underwriter. Many factors affect the desirability of an account, including the financial strength or weakness of the contractor's corporation or its personal assets. Sometimes a contractor's corporation is financially weak for some reasonable explanation. The contractor's willingness to give a personal guaranty through personal indemnity agreements can, in some cases, serve to strengthen the corporation sufficiently to make the bond writable. Some sureties will elect not to forgo premium if the contractor's personal proven wealth is used to shore up the contractual obligation. It must be verifiable wealth that is readily available and relatively liquid so that legal processes are not required for the surety to collect under its rights of subrogation should it become necessary to do so. Stocks of good quality, savings accounts, bonds, and other instruments of similar liquidity are generally acceptable.

A key element in bonding is liquidity. Assets vary in their significance, and those of particular interest to surety companies are the type immediately available for conversion to cash. A piece of land in an undeveloped area or a yard full of heavily encumbered earth-moving machinery will do little to meet payrolls or pay suppliers. Buildings, such as apartments or offices, may be fine long-term investments and look good on the balance sheet, but qualified buyers must be found before money is realized.

Objective assessment of a contractor's qualifications begins with a detailed analysis of financial performance and condition by the producer and surety underwriter. The analysis includes the relationship of work-in-progress and completed contracts to key balance sheet and income statement items, including costs and profits in excess of billings, billings in excess of costs, earned income, and gross profit or loss.

In assessing credit risk, the surety producer notes the contractor's percentage of completion profit estimates. A large part of a contractor's reported earned income and net worth may be based on the estimated cost to finish projects that are still in early stages of completion. This is a less desirable situation than that of a contractor whose reported earnings and net worth are a result of jobs that are completed or in advanced stages. Earnings in an advanced stage are not as subject to large future revisions resulting from estimating error, performance problems, or unforeseen contingencies as those in an early stage of completion.

If the contractor has a history of profitable operations and is in a sound financial condition relative to the work program and surety credit line desired, the professional surety producer will move on to the next stage of prequalification.

Background Investigation

In the next prequalification stage the surety producer interviews owners, suppliers, subcontractors, attorneys, CPAs, and bankers who have had business, credit, or professional relationships with the contractor in order to determine how well the contractor has lived up to its contractual obligations. Contractors who fail this stage of investigation do not receive further consideration, particularly if the investigation reveals a serious deficiency in character.

If any problems are related to factors beyond the contractor's reasonable control, or if the contractor has made simple mistakes that probably will not be repeated, further investigation and discussion with the contractor are warranted. If the contractor can overcome financial, organizational, or operational shortfalls, the professional surety producer will offer a candid appraisal of what steps the contractor can take to improve the chances of qualifying for surety credit. Following are a few of these shortfalls along with suggested remedies for each.

- *A contractor who cannot generate enough volume to cover overhead and fixed expenses:* Corrective measures might be to reduce overhead, sell assets, and reduce debt to bring fixed costs into line with available income opportunities. Alternatively, the contractor could develop market strategies to increase the volume of profitable work or employ some combination of fixed expense reduction and marketing strategies.

- *A contractor who has lost management control of project costs and performance:* Corrective measures could include evaluation of the type, complexity, and number of jobs undertaken to determine whether they relate to the contract management team's ability. A review of the contractor's cost accounting and internal controls (management information systems) is critical to determine if senior management is receiving a timely flow of information for monitoring and controlling work performance.
- *A contractor who has not developed and made funding provisions for continuity of the firm's ownership and management:* Corrective measures could include a buy/sell agreement with partners, key employees, or other contractors, funded by key employee life insurance and/or cash reserves, or Employee Stock Ownership Plans (ESOPs) or profit-sharing plans that allow key employees a sufficient equity in the business to continue operation following an owner's untimely death or disability.

Selection of a Surety Company

Selecting an appropriate surety company best suited to the contractor's needs requires evaluation of a number of factors:

- The surety's comfort with the type, range, and complexity of the projects it undertakes. Some sureties and underwriters have had bad experiences with certain types of contractors and will shy away from or lack confidence in them. Hazardous waste exposures, for example, might raise a red flag to many sureties.
- The financial capacity of the surety relative to the needs of the contractor.
- The surety's philosophy and operating plan relative to the size, type, complexity, geographic, or operational diversity of contractors in the surety's target market.
- The ability, creativity, and responsiveness of a surety's local and home office underwriters.
- The surety's pricing and risk philosophy relative to that of the subject contractor.
- Earnings and operational stability of a surety to provide the contractor with a stable long-term market.
- Quality of the working relationship between the surety producer and the surety company.
- Volume and quality of other business the surety handles for the surety producer.

Credit Analysis

Written analysis of the contractor's credit qualifications should be clear, concise, and comprehensive. A credit analysis should include all of the following items, with a discussion of the contractor's strengths and weaknesses:

- Company history
- Organization
- Management
- Type of work
- Performance track record
- Trade and bank credit relationships
- Outside professional members of the contractor's management team (accountant, attorney, banker)
- Financial performance and condition
- Five-year financial trend
- Bidding history
- Desired work program
- Future prospects

Recommendation of a "responsible" line of surety credit is a primary responsibility of a professional surety producer. Producers who encourage a contractor and surety to assume a larger credit line, or work program, than the contractor's organization, experience, finances, and market will safely allow do all parties a disservice. The contractor risks losing a business and personal assets, the surety risks losing a lot of money, and the producer risks losing a client and a surety market.

Some disreputable surety producers try to compete by offering contractors much larger credit lines without regard to the contractor's ability to manage a significantly expanded work program. Most surety underwriters do not allow themselves to be talked into such a situation, but it does happen occasionally. The professional surety producer must be certain that the credit facts will support the credit line recommendation. Responsible growth is to be encouraged, but reckless growth should be avoided at all costs.

Presentation

After a credit analysis is performed and the contractor's credit line is established, the contractor makes a formal presentation to the selected surety. In order to prepare for this presentation the contractor relies on the following assistance from the producer:

- Counsel as to the contractor's credit strengths and weaknesses, as viewed by the surety.

- Suggestions about how to capitalize on strengths, while overcoming weaknesses.
- Coaching on questions underwriters are likely to ask and indicating the relative weight given by underwriters to various aspects of the particular credit risk.
- Counsel as to the operations and business philosophy of the prospective surety company and individual underwriters.
- Review and discussion of the written analysis and presentation with the contractor before it is submitted to the surety. The contractor should be allowed to preview the written analysis for accuracy, completeness, and balance before it is given to the surety. The surety market is tight, and no opportunity should be wasted due to an incomplete or inaccurate credit submission.
- Assistance to the contractor and surety in overcoming any communication problems. This includes laying a good foundation in the early meetings between the contractor and the underwriters for open, timely communication, informing each party what can be expected from the other, and assisting both parties in meeting these expectations.
- Assistance to the contractor and surety in reaching a fair and reasonable compromise on issues where there is a legitimate difference of opinion.

Communications

Once a surety credit relationship has been formed, the professional surety producer has the responsibility of seeing that open channels of communication are maintained between the contractor and the field and home office surety underwriters. Normal communications include the following:

- *Quarterly or monthly reports on the status of work-in-progress.* This is derived from the contractor's cost-accounting records and is provided on a schedule that includes the following information: original contract price, current adjusted contract price, original estimated gross profit, costs to date, billings to date, current revised estimate of costs to complete.

  When jobs are completed, the contractor should provide the final contract price and gross profit. The contractor should fully explain any slippage in profit estimates and heavily under- or over-billed balances, as well as any necessary corrective action that is under way. The professional surety producer analyzes this information on a detailed spreadsheet that tracks individual job profit estimates and over- or under-billings, and provides underwriters with the spreadsheet and analysis.

This kind of complete communication gives the underwriter a good understanding and appreciation of the contractor's operations and capabilities. It builds confidence and rapport between the contractor and the underwriter, which is the basis of any unsecured credit relationship.

- *Quarterly or semiannual and annual financial statements.* Financial performance and condition, as reflected in the financial statements, should be received on a timely basis and submitted to the underwriter along with the professional surety producer's financial analysis. Interim financial statements may be prepared in-house or as a CPA compilation or review and should be available thirty to sixty days following the end of the quarter. A CPA who is knowledgeable of the construction business should audit the fiscal year-end financial statement in accordance with the American Institute of Certified Public Accountants (AICPA) Audit Guide for Contractors and should include the additional schedules recommended by the Audit Guide. Sureties expect to receive the annual audited financial statements no later than ninety days following the contractor's fiscal year-end. Failure to provide the audit by this time may jeopardize the contractor's surety credit.
- Sureties increasingly are requiring *annual business plans.* In the past, this information was conveyed through informal discussions with underwriters, usually following their analysis of the fiscal year-end audited financial statements. Today underwriters prefer to see formal written business plans. Even when not required by a surety, written business plans demonstrate professional management and enhance the surety credit relationship. The professional surety producer is an integral part of the contractor's management team and should be invited by the contractor to give objective input into the contractor's business plan. At a minimum, the business plan will include an evaluation of the contractor's strengths and weaknesses, market conditions, specific market threats and opportunities, and realistic financial goals over a reasonably foreseeable time period, usually three years, with continuous adjustments as changing conditions warrant.
- *Job site visits* by underwriters are a good way to cement the surety credit relationship and give the underwriters a direct feel for a contractor's capabilities. These visits should occur at least once or twice a year. The underwriter should also meet with estimators, field superintendents, and inside administra-

tors, all of whom share responsibility for successful projects. These parties can give the underwriter insight into the more critical aspects or interesting parts of the jobs in the field.

SURETY CREDIT LINES

The surety establishes annual surety credit lines after the field and home office underwriters have analyzed all of the credit facts and found them to be acceptable. The credit line is expressed as both a single job and an aggregate backlog limitation. For example, a $5 million/$15 million line means that the surety is willing to bond single projects up to a contract price of $5 million when the aggregate contract backlog of costs to complete does not exceed $15 million.

Credit Line Limits

The credit line is a facility that enables the professional surety producer to service the contractor's normal bond needs more effectively. The surety producer has authority to issue bid bonds within the terms and conditions of the credit line. The underwriter must approve any contract that falls outside of the credit line, limits, terms, or conditions before a bid bond is executed.

The credit line is normally conditioned on no material adverse change in the contractor's finances and management and is limited to jobs that are within the contractor's normal type of work and geography, subject to standard contract terms and conditions. The line normally stays in place for one year unless terminated earlier by the underwriter.

Bids

All bid bonds must be promptly reported to the underwriter and bid results furnished to the underwriter as soon as they are available. (Usually there are at least thirty days from bid opening to contract award.) Any irregularities in the contractor's low bid, or any spread greater than 10 percent between the contractor's low bid and the second bidder, must be communicated to the underwriter before the surety authorizes the final performance and payment bonds.

Increasing Credit Lines

Some producers compete by offering contractors larger credit lines. Some aggressive producers carry this too far and stretch the contractor's surety credit to a dangerous level. If the contractor becomes overextended in a work program, operational difficulties may develop and affect contract profit, administration, and cash flow.

In an overextended condition, one unforeseen contingency may result in the contractor's business failure. Examples of these contingencies are unreported, disputed change orders; slow receivables; and low bids. In a good credit relationship, the credit line is flexible and can expand. This allows the contractor to tackle a larger job or work program that offers a special profit opportunity and that makes sense within the contractor's overall risk profile, particularly with respect to the contractor's ability to finance the new proposal.

The credit line covers only the normal, anticipated bond needs. If a special situation develops that would cause a contractor to exceed the credit line, the contractor and surety producer should discuss the merits of the case with the underwriter. If the increase makes sound business sense, an exception will normally be granted.

The credit line provides a check on the producer and indicates the underwriter's general comfort level with the contractor's capacity and reliability.

Increasing Surety Capacity

The surety producer wants to place the contractor with a surety that has sufficient capacity to handle the business. Sometimes, however, a contractor may grow beyond the surety company's capacity. The constraint then becomes the surety's financial capacity, not the credit line. If a contractor appears to be outgrowing the existing surety, the surety producer should arrange a backup surety with adequate capacity. The producer should also ease the transition to the backup surety before the contractor reaches the original surety's limit and a crisis is reached.

RECENT HISTORY OF THE SURETY MARKET

For most of its history, surety was a specialized market. Several events in the twentieth century, however, fueled demand for construction and for surety backing.

- The building of twentieth-century America's infrastructure
- Post-World War II acceleration of construction activity to meet the demand following the Great Depression and the war
- The building of the interstate highway system and resultant real estate development
- The needs of a growing post-World War II "baby boom" population

Due to the large amount of capital needed to form and operate a surety company, multi-state licensing requirements, and the difficulty of generating market rates of return, only a limited number of major surety companies were able to meet this growing demand.

Because surety requires special credit expertise and a significant amount of time and special care to handle, many agents and brokers shy away from it. In fact, surety represents only a small part, approximately 1 percent, of the property-liability business. Thus, until the 1960s, surety producers tended to be small local agents. Usually one or two surety agents would share a local market, and all prospered nicely with little competition.

This situation was attractive to many surety underwriters, who found that they could significantly increase their income by moving into the agency business. They often took accounts they had handled as underwriters away from insurance agents who did not understand the surety business. The 1960s also saw the rapid development of national insurance brokers who grew by acquisition of local agencies. Many surety agents were attractive acquisition targets for national insurance brokers because of their relatively high levels of surety commission income and correspondingly high profits.

A Competitive Business

Because of the amount of time, effort, and handling required to service a surety account, surety commissions are substantially higher than insurance commissions. Insurance commissions generally range from 5 to 10 percent of premium, depending on the type of coverage. Surety commissions are based on a sliding scale, according to contract size, generally ranging from 25 or 30 percent on contracts below $2.5 million, to 5 percent on contracts above $7.5 million. Depending on the size and mix of their accounts, surety agents' commissions generally average between 20 and 25 percent.

Except for very large contractors, construction is a localized business. Competition forces contractors to stay close to the local subcontractor and material markets, and shipping costs discourage the movement of heavy equipment and materials over any long distance.

Because surety credit requires a close working relationship between the contractor, the surety producer, and the underwriter, surety services also tend to be provided at the local level. Presently, most local markets are generally served by at least three or four local or regional agents and a similar number of national brokers with local offices.

Technological Communications Changes

Technology may change the surety service situation as surety producers armed with laptop computers, fax machines, portable telephones, and access to good airline connections expand their territories without sacrificing service quality. Enhanced communications media and airline transportation enable producers to stay in close contact with their clients even when they are distant physically. The result will probably be more competition among a larger number of qualified surety producers in all local markets.

The high level of competition in the construction industry requires that contractors demand high-quality service from all members of their teams, including surety producers. Individual surety producers must therefore differentiate themselves from their competitors by offering high-quality value-added services. Producers must add value to the economic relationship or transaction. Producers who cannot adapt to the new market will lose business and eventually be forced to leave the field.

RISK MANAGEMENT SERVICES

The surety producer whose firm can provide professional risk management services can bring significant added value to the business relationship beyond surety services. The integration of surety brokerage and risk management services appears to be a natural development that can free the contractor to devote more time to acquiring and performing profitable construction work.

Insurance is only one of several ways to deal with loss exposures. Today the surety producer needs an organization that can provide valuable risk management support to the contractor, including the following:

- Analysis of the cost and benefit of self-insurance compared with available conventional insurance
- Evaluation of deductibles and self-insured retention levels within the contractor's ability to absorb and fund losses and in consideration of the statistical probability of loss within the deductible or self-insured retention
- Evaluation of job safety programs and loss control systems for effectiveness and efficiency
- Review of contracts for liability risk exposure, payment terms, and liquidated damages with attention to any unusual systems performance guarantee
- Exploration of alternative funding vehicles, including risk retention groups, purchasing groups, captive insurance companies, and other retention mechanisms, as well as loss-sensitive insurance pricing programs
- Monitoring of insurance companies' financial health and placement of risk only with financially sound companies

Although suretyship is a valuable service, many contractors view the surety bond as a "necessary evil"—a compliance requirement they must meet in order to obtain work. This attitude is both a problem and an opportunity to the professional surety producer.

A contractor's negative attitude towards surety would likely indicate some negative experience with surety from the past, either as a result of a credit prequalification problem or an encounter with an unprofessional surety producer, underwriter, or claims adjuster. The surety producer can turn this "problem" into an opportunity by explaining the benefits available to a contractor who works with a professional surety producer and underwriter:

- Objective counsel and feedback from an experienced independent professional who has the contractor's best interest at heart
- A confident relationship with a surety underwriter
- A reliable, stable, and adequate supply of surety credit
- Better planning and control of the business
- Help in avoiding costly management mistakes
- Improved overall credit standing

DEVELOPMENT OF TARGET MARKETS

The marketing effort will be more productive if it is focused on specific business segments. This is what is meant by "developing a target market." For example, by segmenting a general market group such as *subcontractors* into more specific trade groups, e.g., electrical, mechanical, or masonry subcontractors, the producer can tailor services, expertise, and promotional material to the particular needs of the specific group. The producer will also more readily develop a sphere of influence when efforts are focused on a narrow market segment. This will help generate referrals and word-of-mouth advertising within the targeted group. The marketing of any product or service involves four factors, or the "Four Ps": (1) product (service), (2) promotion, (3) position, and (4) price.

Product

The professional surety producer and the surety company must first have the education, training, knowledge, skill, and organization to provide the professional service (i.e., the product) that clients need.

Promotion

There are a number of ways a firm can promote its professional surety services, including (1) brochures, (2) targeted advertising, (3) seminars, (4) telemarketing and prospect calls, (5) involvement in construction industry associations, and (6) referrals by satisfied clients.

Brochures. Brochures and advertising should explain a firm's product and business philosophy without exaggeration or sales puffery. The message should be succinct and creative to stimulate interest, and all general claims should be supported by demonstrable evidence.

A firm's size and resources will generally dictate the extent of its advertising. Mass advertising, for example, is beyond the means of many small firms. All firms should take advantage of "free advertising," that is, writing articles for publication or getting quoted in the business or trade press. This cost-effective and subtle means of advertising also increases a firm's credibility.

Targeted Advertising. To maximize the impact of its advertising dollars, the surety agency should tailor and limit its advertising to targeted segments of its market. For instance, if an agency has special expertise in underground utility contractors, it should target its advertising to this specific group.

Seminars. Participating in professional seminars, either the firm's own or another organization's, is an excellent way to communicate to a target audience.

Telemarketing and Prospect Calls. In the past, some have viewed telemarketing in a negative light. Most people have experienced the nuisance sales phone call during dinner. Answering systems and secretaries insulate many from those callers during the work day. Most contractors need surety bonds, however, and many are not entirely satisfied or completely comfortable with their present surety relationship and therefore might be prompted or stimulated to consider a change of a surety relationship through a cold call or other informal contact.

Many contractors would welcome the opportunity to meet with a professional surety producer who would listen to their needs and offer constructive ideas or solutions. The objective of telemarketing or prospect calling is to introduce the professional surety producer to the contractor so that such a meeting can be arranged. By using effective telemarketing firms, or developing the in-house capability, a professional surety producer can save time in selling and providing professional surety services. Not every call will result in a sale, but market visibility and awareness will increase.

Construction Industry Associations. Active involvement in construction industry associations demonstrates the producer's commitment to its target markets and clients. An active role on association committees will also emphasize the member's experience and expertise.

Referrals by Satisfied Clients. Word of mouth is the most effective form of advertising because it carries the most credibility. Producers should not fear asking their clients to recommend them to their friends, subcontractors, and competitors. Satisfied clients will be glad to assist producers in finding additional business.

Success enables a producer or firm to continue providing excellent service. While some clients might not want to see their competitors benefit from their producer's or surety's service, most will realize that stable, effective surety prequalification improves the quality of competition in the industry. Unqualified competitors distort the bidding process by submitting bids they cannot fulfill. A producer or surety supporting unqualified contractors will develop a reputation among qualified contractors for not understanding the construction business well enough to recognize the requirements of a project.

There are two ways to grow in the surety production business:

1. By becoming visible and offering high quality services
2. By acquiring and retaining clients who succeed and grow

Position

The producer who has gained a favorable market position (perhaps 25 percent or more of a local market) and who has earned a reputation among local contractors and underwriters for professional quality service will be difficult to displace. The personal service nature of the business gives a decided edge to the well-established producer.

Some established producers, however, may become complacent and allow their service levels to slip, or they may fail to groom a successor to provide continuity to their business. These producers make inviting targets to young, aggressive producers seeking to establish themselves, or to other established producers who maintain high standards of service.

Price

Surety pricing is set by individual sureties who may either subscribe to rates established by the Surety Association of America (SAA) or file their own rates according to various state regulatory requirements. Rates must not be unfairly discriminatory; that is, principals with like risk characteristics should be charged the same rate. Most sureties now offer at least two or three rate levels to principals of a given class, based on financial strength criteria. For example, principals who are financially strong carry less credit risk and therefore pay a lower rate. Bond ratemaking and pricing will be discussed in greater detail in Chapters 9 and 10.

Sureties have relatively high fixed operating costs (principally underwriters' salaries and agency commissions) that total approximately 50 to 60 percent of premium income. The other 40 to 50 percent goes to cover claims, adjustment expenses, and profit.

To reach a reasonable rate of return for the risk undertaken, sureties should target at least a 20 percent underwriting profit. To reach their profit targets, sureties must keep claims to a minimum. To achieve this goal, competent underwriters and agents must be paid competitive salaries and commissions. Accordingly, sureties have little ability or incentive to compete on the basis of price.

Agents may quote a net premium rate to their clients and disclose their commissions. However, agents also have little incentive to compete by reducing commissions, since they must generate enough revenue to cover the cost of providing a high level of service.

MARKET LIFE CYCLES

Mature markets are characterized by slow market growth, a high level of competition among many firms, little differentiation between competing products or services, and resultant product standardization.

Markets, products, firms, and whole industries pass through a life cycle that consists of three phases: (1) innovation, (2) rapid growth, and (3) development into a mature market. Exhibit 3-1 illustrates this cycle.

- *Phase I—Innovation.* Phase I represents the early innovative and developmental stage in which research, development, marketing expenses, and investments exceed revenue.
- *Phase II—Rapid Growth.* Some unsuccessful products and firms never grow beyond Phase I. The successful ones normally advance to Phase II. At this point, profit accelerates rapidly and grows to a point where competition enters the market, product differentiation begins to draw some sales away from the initial innovator, and profit margins begin to erode.
- *Phase III—Mature Market.* Phase III represents the mature market stage, in which competition has greatly reduced differentiation between competing firms and products. All competi-

Exhibit 3-1
Market Life Cycle

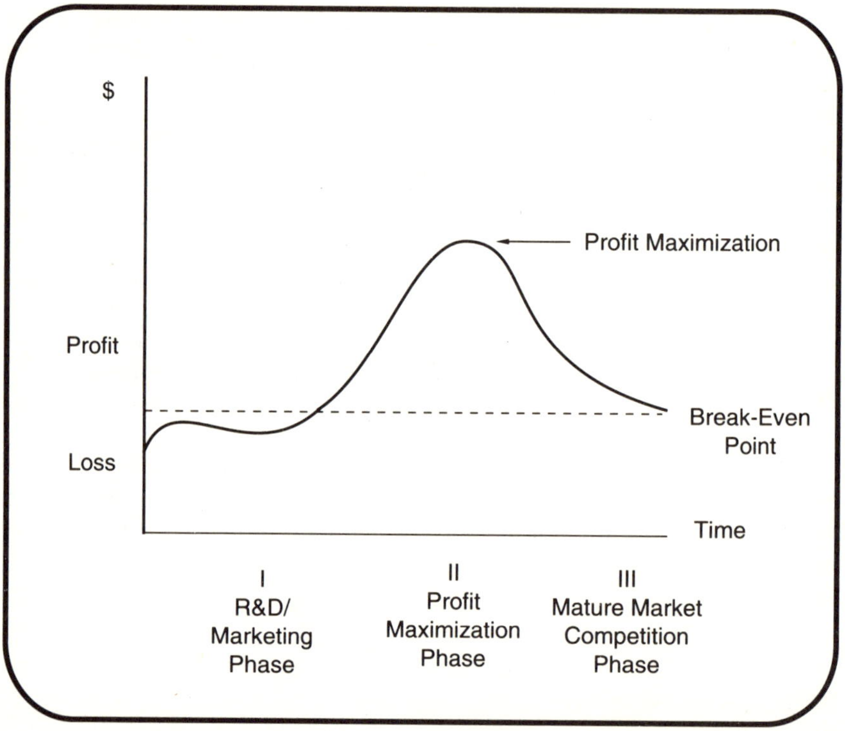

tors must therefore resort to severe price competition, bringing margins down to just above the break-even point. Those products and firms that fall below the break-even point eventually fail and leave the market.

A "mature market" is characterized by slow market growth and a high level of competition among many competitors with little differentiation between competing and standardized products or services. Examples of mature markets would include any commodities (food crops, lumber, metals, oil), basic materials (steel, cement, building supplies), and services (insurance, banking). In a mature market, price is the primary determining factor in the purchase decision.

The personal computer industry is a good example of the market life cycle. An innovator, Apple Computer, envisioned a need and a demand for a new product, which Apple developed and aggressively marketed with such success that the effort attracted many competitors. Fierce competition ensued. The price of personal computers dropped dramatically, along with competitors' profit margins, even while product quality greatly improved.

Growth Problems

Many firms in Phase II have difficulty meeting growth in demand. Capital, financing, cash flow, and management control problems may appear in this phase, causing companies to fail. The early stage of Phase II might be called the "shake-out" phase, when early entrants into the market experience growth problems and larger, better capitalized, or better managed firms enter the fray.

Most segments of the construction industry are well advanced into Phase III and wage stiff competition. The professional surety producer should look for well-managed and well-positioned clients that demonstrate an ability to grow profitably despite tough competition.

Market Segmentation

Market segmentation is the identification and development of market segments that are not presently being served or that could be better served. The professional surety producer should stay alert to new market segment opportunities and to new or changing areas of specialization in the market place.

The asbestos abatement market is an example of a relatively new field for contractors. Asbestos abatement services were not required until healthcare professionals determined the harm that friable asbestos causes to society; and individuals, organizations, and legislatures began to demand remedial efforts.

Laws and regulations mandated that asbestos of certain types and under certain conditions be removed from public buildings and the workplace. Initially, inadequate liability insurance and new technology kept nearly all sureties out of the market. This situation, in turn, restricted the supply of prequalified asbestos abatement contractors and led to excellent profit margins of 30 percent and more. Innovative professional surety producers developed liability insurance markets for asbestos abatement contractors, leading to the development of the surety market as aggressive new, and a few existing, sureties joined the business.

The asbestos abatement market today is probably approaching the profit maximization stage, as better availability of insurance and surety credit enables more contractors to enter the field. Many asbestos abatement contractors, who are experiencing the problems associated with rapid growth, working capital, cash flow, and management control difficulties, can benefit from the professional surety producer's objective counsel.

Managing the Market Cycle

Improved communication, information processing technology, and efficient capital markets are shortening the cycle time between Phase I (innovation) and Phase III (maturity). New markets should be located, and new or improved product and service capabilities should be developed, before the surety and client reach the apex of Phase II (rapid growth).

The professional surety producer should always try to stay ahead of the competition by developing new products and new markets, honing professional skills, and targeting market segments and contractors that offer above-average growth prospects. By developing a base of clients who are alert to new growth opportunities, who are well managed, and who can grow in their traditional markets, professional surety producers can leverage their growth and success.

DEVELOPING A BUSINESS PLAN

Any business in a competitive environment needs a well thought-out business plan. Both the surety producer and the contractor face competitors who want to take business away from them and who are actively planning a way to do so.

It would appear that only naive businesses would fail to plan, yet many businessowners confine their strategic thinking to a few quiet moments during their commute to work, never commit their thoughts to writing, and do not share them with their managers and employees. These people are easy prey for the entrepreneur who has carefully considered a plan and organized a team to carry it out effectively.

A good business plan requires time, discipline, and a willingness to include key people in the process. The following outlines the basic steps to developing a winning business strategy.

1. Form a planning group consisting of key managers from each functional area of the firm (marketing, operations, and administration) to be responsible for implementing the plan. People are more committed to a plan if they play an active role in its development.
2. State the business's philosophy and mission. These will serve as a standard against which plans and decisions can be measured. A sound business philosophy will take into account and balance the mutual needs of clients, employees, management, equity owners, and the community at large.
3. Identify the firm's strengths and weaknesses. Some items to consider include the following:

- Philosophy/culture (What is important to the firm?)
- Management quality and commitment
- Team motivation and dedication
- Resources (existing clients; qualified people; surety and insurance markets; professional, charitable, and social associations; equipment; time; and money)
- Continuity of ownership and management

Once identified, a firm should eliminate any critical weaknesses, building its plan on the foundation of its strengths. This is what will ultimately set the firm apart from its competitors.

4. Identify primary competitors' strengths and weaknesses based on the same factors as above. Once the competitors' strengths and weaknesses are identified, the firm can take advantage of the competitors' weaknesses and move to counter or, if possible, neutralize their strengths.
5. Identify market threats and opportunities:
   - Competitors' strengths and weaknesses
   - Competitors' business plans or lack of them
   - Competitors' continuity or lack of it
   - Potential changes in construction, insurance, and surety markets
   - Existing relationships of the firm and its competitors with insurance and surety markets
   - Potential new products, services, or substitutes, that is, bank letters of credit used as a "substitute" for surety bonds
6. Identify new business opportunities. Prioritize these opportunities and explain their priority in terms of the firm's and competitor's strengths and weaknesses or changes in market conditions or new products and services.
7. Develop preliminary new business objectives and action steps.
8. Determine what, if any, additional resources or development of resources are needed to achieve preliminary objectives.
9. Obtain and develop needed resources or modify objectives.
10. Develop concrete, measurable, attainable objectives and action steps.
11. Document all of the above.
12. State measurable objectives and action plans in writing. An action plan should incorporate the following elements:

- Specific action steps for each objective.
- Fixed responsibility to one individual for each action step and the related objective.
- A realistic time frame for reaching each objective.
- A firm due date for follow-up to see that each action step and objective is met. Due dates suggest a monitoring or control mechanism.
- Commitments from those responsible for each step and from the planning group.
- Action step monitoring before and after its due date.
- Assessment of progress at least quarterly to determine the reasons for success or failure.
- Action plan modifications as necessary.

13. Add or delete measurable objectives as objectives are reached or not reached and repeat the preceding process.
14. Review the entire business plan at least annually, changing goals and action steps as the firm's strengths and market conditions change.
15. Maintain competitive economic performance levels. If satisfactory performance is not reached within an agreed time period, a comprehensive reassessment may be necessary to determine whether such performance can be attained through adjustments in the plan or the staff. If not, these resources should be redirected to activities that will produce the highest long-term return on capital.

NONCONTRACT BOND PRODUCTION

Contract surety bonds represent roughly two-thirds of surety industry premiums. The remaining one-third of premiums relate to the noncontract lines of the surety business. This section discusses the production of some of the major categories of noncontract bonds: license, permit, and miscellaneous bonds, judicial bonds in civil proceedings, and financial guarantee bonds.

License, Permit, and Miscellaneous Bonds

The license, permit, and miscellaneous bonds business is normally considered an adjunct service to liability, property, and marine insurance accounts. These bonds normally have modest penalties of a few thousand dollars, usually $1,000 or $2,000, and seldom more than $10,000.

States and municipalities legislate statutory requirements for these bonds to ensure that principals comply with laws regulating their activities and that they meet minimum levels of financial responsibility. Most licensees comply with the law and, since these bonds carry only modest credit risks, sureties are fairly liberal in their underwriting standards. Sureties generally deny bonds only to principals who are in obvious financial difficulty or who are known to have poor character.

Surety companies compete for license, permit, and miscellaneous bonds on the basis of service to the agent and to the client. For very large Fortune 500 accounts, sureties offer substantial price discounts. Special service features include bulk reporting of premiums on a quarterly or annual basis and vesting underwriting authority in the agent or even in the client in some instances.

After checking with underwriters to ensure that the bonds are available, the producer should make an effort to promote sales of license and permit bonds by reaching out to present customers or their friends.

Premiums are usually quite low because bond amounts are not high. However, the surety service provided may work to the producer's advantage in obtaining or keeping other desirable lines. There are many producers who do not write license and permit bonds but somehow manage to write commercial and personal insurance. It would be a naive producer who provides the bond service while forgoing all of the rest of the business.

A producer who singles out or segments a market in which to sell license and permit bonds, like shoe stores, could try a pre-approach based on bond needs, that is, sales tax bonds or whatever other bond may be required of that class of business.

Leads from governmental departments requiring permits have brought significant business to some producers. A list of producers who handle license bonds is often maintained for the convenience of tradespeople.

Judicial Bonds in Civil Proceedings

Judicial bonds in civil proceedings are divided into court and fiduciary bonds. Court bonds are required by statutes or by the courts to protect the interests of litigants; fiduciary bonds, also required by statutes or the courts, protect the interests of minors, incompetents, heirs, and others.

Court Bonds. Court bonds are underwritten on the quality of legal counsel and the financial capacity of the principal. An example of a court bond is an appeal bond, which is a strict financial guarantee by a party who appeals a losing trial court decision to a higher court. The bond guarantees that all judgments will be satisfied and court costs paid in the event the appeal fails. Only the financially strongest principals qualify for unsecured appeal bonds. Most parties who appeal are required to post some form of cash or equivalent collateral with the surety.

Fiduciary Bonds. The attorneys for estates—and not the named fiduciaries—generally make the arrangements for obtaining fiduciary bonds. There are attorneys and law firms in every county, city, or community that specialize in fiduciary bond matters. These attorneys are proficient in probate matters and also understand sureties' requests and needs for underwriting information. Because fiduciary bonds are generally underwritten primarily on the basis of an attorney's character and reputation, agents and sureties try to identify and cultivate trustworthy attorneys for these bonds.

Fiduciary bonds are produced by agents who solicit this business from attorneys or serve the needs of their insurance clients. In most communities, there are only a few agents who specialize in writing these bonds. Because they are known to attorneys, these agents can sometimes capture a good share of the market.

Selling Judicial Bonds. Because premiums and rates for judicial bonds do not vary greatly from one surety company to another, business is not gained or lost on price. Business is lost because of neglect, incompetence, or an unwillingness to provide adequate service.

Perhaps the best way to generate business is to visit local attorneys to inquire if they are totally satisfied with their current bonding arrangements. Thorough advance preparation for these visits is the producer's best means of gaining new bond business.

Some surety companies and producers have developed a "mini bond kit," consisting of an expandable folder, or legal-size envelope, filled with commonly used bond forms, proper applications, powers-of-attorney, surety company seals, execution reports, and other things that may be useful.

A number of surety companies are agreeable to granting power-of-attorney to attorneys so that they may produce bonds more expeditiously. When this is accomplished, the producer is responsible only for billing the item. Because this arrangement saves them time, it is welcomed by many attorneys.

A "mini rate chart," as shown in Exhibit 3-2, helps attorneys determine the appropriate premium rate to charge for each of the various types of court, probate, and fiduciary bonds. It is suggested that the rate chart and mini bond kit be combined as a package and delivered personally to appropriate attorneys.

Some bond producers have increased business by advertising in local legal trade journals or bar association directories or by communicating with employees in the trust departments of banks, who can be

Exhibit 3-2

Sample "Mini Rate Chart"

Obverse

Crowley Fire and Marine Insurance Co.

Bond Rate Chart

The following are "quick reference" rates intended to help you rate the majority of bonds that you execute. If you have any doubt as to rate, you may leave that portion of the Execution Report blank, and we will fill in the rate and return the agent's copy to you by return mail.

Judicial

Fiduciary:

Your state, U.S.A.

Up to $2,000—$10 per M (thousand) per year

$2,000–$50,000—$20 plus $5 per M per year on portion over $2,000

Minimum Premium $20 per year

Plaintiff:

Generally $20 per M on the penalty of the bond. Check first—these vary.

Minimum Premium $20 per year

Bonds of Administrators, Executors, Guardians and Trustees Under Will

Where the bond is double the value of the personal property, reduce final premium 20%.

Where bank is Co-Fiduciary, discount final premium 33⅓%.

License

Range from $5 to $20 per M per year, depending on class and location

Minimum Premium $20 per year

Reverse

Public Official

Generally $3.50 per M per year for officials who do not handle tax money.

Peace officers and subordinates, $5 per M per year.

For officials handling money, see your State page in Public Official section of manual.

Minimum Premium $20 per year.

Fidelity

A. Individual and Schedule
   Usually $5 per M per year for Commercial and Professional.
   Use application #625

B. Blanket
   Refer to company office for rating. Premiums vary depending on class of business.
   Use application F-660

   Special discount when attached to a package policy—20%

Contract

Must be prequalified.

Class B—General Contractors. Work on buildings and underground work.

First $500,000 — $12 per M
Next $2,000,000 — 7.25 per M
Next $2,500,000 — 5.75 per M

Please call if in doubt on rates.

If you are not certain which application is needed, see summary sheet in your bond kit.

Reprinted from Richard D. Turner, Stephen Horn II, Peter R. Kensicki, *Multiple-Lines Insurance Production* (Malvern, PA: Insurance Institute of America), vol. 2, p. 52.

good contacts for probate bonds.

Often overlooked is the opportunity to work out a bonding arrangement with other producers who do not have bonding facility or inclination. There are others who may not have time to properly service bonds but will pass the referral or request on to a friendly competitor.

Political associations, direct and indirect, can be good referral sources. Reviewing occupations of customers and their children can also be of considerable benefit. Some present clients, for example, may have jobs somehow connected with courts, banks, or as subordinates to elected officials. These clients can serve as a means of introduction or may even be in a position to direct bonds to a producer who asks for the business. It pays to watch new business auto applications or to review long-standing files for hints of bond potential.

It is important to appoint a backup attorney-in-fact should the producer not be available to execute the bonds.

Qualifying as a Bond Representative. To qualify as a bond representative, one needs the approval of a licensed agent by the insurance or surety companies that will be writing the bonds.

The first step in obtaining a power of attorney is completion of a request for power of attorney. This usually consists of a one-page form calling for the name of the producer as it is to appear on the power; a three-year history of bond premiums written by the agency; names of other surety companies that may have granted a power, including the date and amount and a question about any revocation by other sureties; and the amount of power being requested.

It is recommended that the applicant for a power of attorney personally visit the bond department of the surety company in order to see how the bonds are underwritten and processed.

Upon approval, a formal contract, or *letter of authority*, is drawn, outlining the producer's discretionary authority to execute various classes of bonds up to certain limits and calling for indemnity to the surety company in the event of loss resulting from any violation. It is a serious obligation and must be signed by both the surety company and the producer. The standard letter of authority usually grants power to execute administrator and executor, guardian, certain bankruptcy, public official, and license bonds. Bid, contract, supply, fidelity, forgery, defendant, and miscellaneous bonds are in the "refer" category and will be authorized by specific letter when necessary. A surety company may grant more liberal authority to those possessing greater qualifications or experience.

Once appointed, the producer becomes an attorney-in-fact and is supplied with an adequate number of powers of attorney. Exhibit 3-3 is a specimen copy of a Standard Form Power of Attorney. These powers may be placed in the government offices where signed bonds are ultimately filed, including city offices and with specific court

Exhibit 3-3
Specimen Form—Power of Attorney

CROWLEY FIRE & MARINE INSURANCE COMPANY
Malvern, PA

Power of Attorney

KNOW ALL PERSONS BY THESE PRESENTS: That THE CROWLEY FIRE & MARINE INSURANCE COMPANY, a corporation organized under the laws of the state of Pennsylvania, and having its principal office in the City of Malvern, does hereby constitute and appoint
____________of____________its true and lawful Attorney(s)-in-Fact to sign, execute, seal, and deliver on its behalf as Surety, and as its act and deed, any and all bonds, policies, undertakings, or other like instruments as follows:

Any such obligation in the United States, up to $____________.

This appointment is made under and by authority of the following resolution passed by the Board of Directors of said Company at a meeting held in the principal office of the Company, a quorum being present and voting, on the____________ day of____________, 19___, which resolution is still in effect:

"RESOLVED, that the President or any Vice-President be hereby authorized, and empowered to appoint Attorneys-in-Fact to affix the corporate seal; and with or without writings so executed by such Attorneys-in-Fact shall be binding upon the Company as if they had been duly executed and acknowledged by the regularly elected officers of the Company."

IN WITNESS WHEREOF, THE CROWLEY FIRE & MARINE INSURANCE COMPANY has caused these presents to be sealed with its corporate seal, duly attested by its Vice-President this __________ day of ____________, 19___.

THE CROWLEY FIRE & MARINE INSURANCE COMPANY

____

(seal) Vice-President
STATE OF PA) ss:

Reprinted from Richard D. Turner, Stephen Horn II, Peter R. Kensicki, *Multiple-Lines Insurance Production* (Malvern, PA: Insurance Institute of America), vol. 2, p. 55.

clerks. Such placement reduces the need for attaching a power to each bond issued. However, a reasonable supply of powers should be retained in the producer's office for attachment to bonds when required.

Acceptance of the power of attorney carries with it the responsibility to perform in a manner displaying professionalism and good judgment. Bonds, once issued, cannot be easily recalled or canceled, and mistakes can be very costly.

Financial Guarantee Bonds

The vast majority of financial guarantee bonds are written by sureties who specialize in this business, and most guarantee principal and interest payments on municipal bond issues. In effect, the surety's guarantee allows the municipal bond buyer, or investor, to rely on the surety's credit rating and not just that of the borrowing municipality.

All financial guarantee sureties who guarantee municipal bonds have the highest investment grade, Standard & Poor's or Moody's credit ratings of AA or AAA, so that they can upgrade the credit of municipal bond issues. To meet the credit rating agencies' (Standard and Poor's and Moody's) very high credit standards, financial guarantee sureties must maintain very strong, liquid balance sheets with net worths greater than $150 million. The sureties must also maintain stringent risk-based capital requirements with higher risk guarantees backed by a larger percentage of capital. Investors enjoy the added security of a surety's guarantee that all principal and interest will be paid. This is especially helpful to small investors or individuals who may not have the time and expertise to analyze the municipalities' credit or who may be uncomfortable with a less than investment grade debt security.

The borrowing municipality benefits by broadening the market acceptance of its guaranteed municipal bond securities. The AA or AAA rating that the surety provides reduces the interest rate the borrower must pay. Since the surety premium is less than the borrower's interest savings, this is a good deal for the borrower.

Financial guarantee sureties, specializing in municipal bond guarantees, follow very stringent underwriting policies. Their track record is so good that they have experienced only one loss incident: Washington Public Power Service, popularly known as the "WHOOPS" bond default in the early 1980s.

Most of the financial guarantee bond business is produced by investment bankers and placed directly with the financial guarantee insurance market. Some of these markets will pay a small commission (5 to 10 percent) to insurance agents or brokers if value is added. Alternatively, the agent or broker may negotiate a fee for service with the investment banker and municipality. Most agents and brokers lack the expertise and client relationship to add any significant value to these transactions and thus have difficulty competing with investment bankers in this market.

Standard sureties write miscellaneous financial guarantees only for principals of very high financial integrity and usually for terms that do not exceed two or three years. Miscellaneous financial guarantees are produced by insurance agents and brokers, usually on behalf of existing property and casualty insurance clients.

SUMMARY

This chapter discussed the surety bond distribution system and the distinctions between agents, brokers, managing general agents, and producers. Surety bonds offer the producer high commission business opportunities, a chance to specialize, and an opportunity to round out insurance coverages for commercial clients.

The role of a surety producer as a primary prequalifier and the surety prequalification process were discussed, including the proper use of surety credit lines. Bond producers were warned against encouraging credit lines that exceed a contractor's capacity to perform.

Marketing an intangible service such as suretyship, which is not generally well understood by contractors and project owners, offers the surety producer an interesting challenge. The chapter reviewed the historical development of the market for surety services, the producer's role in marketing these services, and the key marketing concepts (the four Ps): product (service), promotion, position, and price.

Markets, products, firms, and whole industries experience life cycles. This chapter examined the cycle's three phases—innovation, rapid growth, and development into a mature market—as well as market growth problems, market segmentation, and market cycle management.

Any business in a competitive environment requires a well-devised business plan. A step-by-step process of business planning has great value in achieving business goals and objectives.

The chapter concluded with a discussion of three general categories of noncontract surety bonds: license, permit, and miscellaneous bonds; judicial bonds in civil proceedings (court and fiduciary); and financial guarantee bonds.

CHAPTER 4

Bond Underwriting

The major goal of underwriting is the development and maintenance of a profitable, growing book of business. The achievement of this goal depends on providing appropriate coverage; establishing effective producer relationships; and maintaining selection standards, pricing standards, and a high level of professional competence.

Normal underwriting activities include hazard identification and evaluation, pricing, the determination of policy terms and conditions, the selection decision, and the monitoring and servicing of accounts that are accepted. Underwriting activities also can include risk management services, marketing, product design, creation of rating programs, preparation of underwriting manuals, participation in bureaus and associations, and formulation of broad underwriting policy. Exhibit 4-1 summarizes these activities.

Bond underwriting is one of the most challenging of all underwriting fields. Bond underwriters perform extensive financial analysis and often address complex legal matters. This chapter examines the general techniques used in underwriting the following major kinds of bonds:

1. Noncontract bonds
    a. Public official bonds
    b. Judicial bonds in civil proceedings
        (1) Fiduciary bonds
        (2) Court bonds
    c. License and permit bonds
2. Fidelity bonds
3. Contract bonds

Exhibit 4-1
Underwriting Activities

Activities Performed by All Underwriters

- Hazard Identification and Evaluation
- Pricing
- Determination of Policy Terms and Conditions
- Risk Selection Decisions
- Monitoring and Servicing Accounts

Activities Performed by Some Underwriters

- Risk Management Services
- Marketing
- Product Design
- Creation of Rating Programs
- Preparation of Underwriting Manuals
- Participation in Bureaus and Associations
- Formulation and Monitoring of Broad Underwriting Policy

Adapted from *Principles of Property and Liability Underwriting,* Chapter 1, J.J. Launie, J. Finley Lee, Norman A. Baglini, Third Edition 1986, Insurance Institute of America, Malvern, PA 19355.

There are significant differences between these bonds because the obligations under each vary greatly. As a result the underwriting of each kind of bond also varies.

BOND UNDERWRITING IN GENERAL

In examining the underwriting of bonds in general, expense factors, subjective factors, and financial reports should be considered.

Expense Factors

In order to get a better perspective of surety and fidelity underwriting expenses, it is helpful to compare them with similar expenses in the property-liability business as a whole. As indicated in Chapter 1 in Exhibit 1-5, underwriting expenses incurred as a percent of premiums written for fidelity and surety were somewhat higher than for the total property-liability industry for 1981 to 1990.

Exhibit 4-2 shows that these total underwriting expenses incurred have two components: (1) commissions and brokerage incurred and (2) other underwriting expenses incurred. These expenses in the surety field are much higher in both categories during the period (21.2 and 26.8 percent of premiums written, respectively) than those in the total property-liability business (12.0 and 14.3 percent). The expenses in

Exhibit 4-2
Underwriting Expenses Incurred
From 1981 to 1990
Ratios to Premiums Written

Category	Commissions and Brokerage Incurred		Other Underwriting Expenses Incurred		Total Underwriting Expenses Incurred
Fidelity	14.2	+	18.8	=	32.9
Surety	21.2	+	26.8	=	48.0
Total Property-Liability Industry	12.0	+	14.3	=	26.3

Adapted from *Best's Aggregates and Averages*, Property-Casualty, 1991 Edition, pp. 136, 137. © A.M. Best Company—used with permission.

the fidelity field are also somewhat higher in both categories (14.2 and 18.7 percent). The main reason for high costs in surety is that underwriters do a significant amount of work assisting their producers or agents in prequalifying their clients. This includes assisting in the preparation of a complete credit presentation, including all documentation required for proper analysis of the principal.

Exhibit 4-3 shows underwriting expenses incurred from 1981 to 1990. Commissions and brokerage incurred as a percent of premiums written have decreased in recent years for fidelity, surety, and the total property-liability business. The average for the decade is higher in all three categories than for the year 1990. Some of this decrease may be attributed to competition in the industry and to the surge in "new financial guarantee" writings, which until 1986 were included as part of the surety line.

For other underwriting expenses incurred, those incurred in surety for 1988, 1989, and 1990 (31.4, 31.1, and 30.7 percent respectively) were higher than the 26.8 percent for the period. Some of this increase may be a result of the stricter and more complex underwriting controls and the switch over of the "new financial guarantee" business to its own line for reporting purposes. This was mandated by the National Association of Insurance Commissioners (NAIC).

A surety underwriter must weigh a variety of factors in the process of underwriting any given bond. The underwriter must also consider how several major factors can counteract each other. Nevertheless, an analysis of the facts alone cannot produce the desired underwriting results. The underwriter must incorporate additional considerations into the assessment of the risk.

Exhibit 4-3
Underwriting Expenses Incurred—Ratios to Premiums Written

Category	Year	Commissions and Brokerage Incurred	Other Underwriting Expenses Incurred	Total Underwriting Expenses Incurred
FIDELITY	1981	17.2	21.7	38.9
	1982	16.0	24.5	40.6
	1983	16.0	24.8	40.8
	1984	15.6	22.8	38.4
	1985	13.8	18.6	32.4
	1986	14.8	15.5	30.2
	1987	13.3	14.0	27.3
	1988	13.1	17.6	30.7
	1989	12.8	18.6	31.5
	1990	14.1	20.0	34.0
	1981 to 1990	14.2	18.7	32.9
SURETY*	1981	26.3	25.7	52.0
	1982	25.8	26.3	52.1
	1983	22.8	25.2	48.1
	1984	22.8	23.2	46.0
	1985	16.4	18.5	34.9
	1986	21.0	24.9	46.0
	1987	22.2	28.1	50.4
	1988	20.2	31.4	51.6
	1989	20.3	31.1	51.3
	1990	20.7	30.7	51.4
	1981 to 1990	21.2	26.8	48.0
TOTAL PROPERTY-LIABILITY INDUSTRY	1981	12.6	14.7	27.4
	1982	12.6	15.3	27.9
	1983	12.7	15.7	28.4
	1984	12.7	12.7	27.9
	1985	12.0	13.9	25.9
	1986	11.9	13.2	25.1
	1987	11.9	13.4	25.3
	1988	11.8	13.9	25.7
	1989	11.5	14.4	26.0
	1990	11.3	14.7	26.0
	1981 to 1990	12.0	14.3	26.3

*Includes Financial Guaranty since 1986.

Adapted from *Best's Aggregates & Averages*, Property-Casualty, 1991 Edition, pp. 136,137.

Subjective Factors

Subjective factors is a catch-all category for an underwriter's personal assessment about the character of a principal. For instance, most underwriters would concur that a principal's "moral character" is a significant factor in underwriting. Characteristics may include the person's honesty, sincerity, motivation, methods of business operation, and treatment of employees and other business associates. These characteristics are difficult, if not impossible, to quantify. Since the underwriter is, in effect, evaluating the bond applicant's integrity, the underwriter must develop a personal (subjective) method for judging whether the applicant shows satisfactory evidence of good character.

Financial Reports

Financial reports are important not only because they present factual information concerning the firm's financial condition, but also because they reflect the quality of the firm's overall management. The care with which the reports are prepared, the management attitudes they reveal, and the details they provide about the use of assets, debt management, and capital formation tell a great deal about the firm and its owners.

Owners of most small firms provide to the surety the same data they give to their banks. Larger firms submit reports prepared by outside accountants, either public accountants or Certified Public Accountants (CPAs). Their reports are either fully audited (and unqualified), audited (but qualified or limited in some way by the auditor), or unaudited. Since financial analysis plays a crucial role in underwriting unsecured surety credit obligations, most underwriters require professionally prepared financial statements.

If credit reports reflect financial strength and favorable payment records, some underwriters at times provide a small first bond without fully audited financial statements. Essential in these cases is a favorable relationship between the bank and the principal, acknowledged in writing by the principal's bank.

UNDERWRITING NONCONTRACT BONDS

Noncontract bonds include all bonds except contract and fidelity bonds. They cover a variety of situations, each requiring different treatment from an underwriting standpoint. This section examines underwriting factors for the following categories of bonds:

1. Public official bonds
2. Judicial bonds in civil proceedings
3. License and permit bonds

Within each category there are many subcategories of bonds, and statutes and regulations often prescribe requirements associated with them. (AFSB 153 treats in greater detail the underwriting factors for noncontract bonds.)

Public Official Bonds

Most elected and appointed officials who handle public funds must give public official bonds to qualify for office. The bond functions as an instrument to protect public assets from certain acts by the public official.

The most outstanding characteristic of public official bonds is that they generally are for faithful performance of duty, not just for honesty. *Malfeasance* (wrongdoing), *misfeasance* (improper execution of a lawful act), and *nonfeasance* (failure to perform duty) of official duties are included under a bond if there is a potential for monetary damages. Generally, dishonest individuals cause most losses. Sometimes the dishonest individual is not the one bonded, but a subordinate for whom the bonded individual is responsible. Therefore, a bond for the faithful performance of duty makes the bonded (and generally honest) individual accountable for the actions of subordinates.

Underwriting Variability. The extent of risk associated with different bonded officials varies considerably. A notary public has no opportunity to embezzle public funds. The city treasurer, however, controls a substantial amount of funds. The hunting and fishing license agent has a seasonal responsibility, but the sheriff's responsibility is year-round. Tax collectors need insurance to protect them in case of robbery and burglary, but other municipal officers might not have the same need.

Public official bonds do not protect the individual who is bonded, but the governmental body that requires the bond. In some cases, there is no statutory provision dictating when and how the official can be relieved of responsibility. Officials cannot limit their liability without leaving office, and yet they cannot leave office without fulfilling their duties. Meanwhile, the bond continues to guarantee faithful performance.

The governmental body that requires the bond is generally the only one that can present a claim, and it can do so only as prescribed by law. The surety cannot protect itself in any way from the legal requirements. Regardless of the limitations the surety prints in its form, the law dictates what the bond should cover.

The bond amount and the term of office usually are prescribed by law. Despite all the potential legal and political entanglements, most surety companies are eager to write public official bonds because they have proven to be profitable.

Background Checking. An application is usually the primary source of underwriting information for public official bonds. It contains personal references and banking facilities audit procedures used by the public office, as well as financial information. The reputation of the official is a paramount consideration of the surety underwriter. The surety sometimes briefly reviews the training and work experience of the applicant and often requires a clearance of accounts of the prior official to screen carryover problems. It is impossible to be sure that there are no hidden problems within the ranks of subordinates, but checking the records and clearing the predecessor helps reveal major problems in most cases.

Sureties do a great deal of class underwriting on public official bonds. But they also have insisted on evidence of sound accounting practices and regular, proper audits. This has helped to reduce losses.

Loss Control. There are many ways to limit losses caused by misdeeds of public officials. One way is for the governmental body to whom the public official reports to designate the official depository of funds and securities. A bonded public official who does not select the depository cannot be held responsible for the funds if the bank fails. Another way to control losses on public official bonds is to require insurance against robbery and burglary or broad-form crime insurance so that moneys in the custody of public officials will be insured in case of such loss. The need here may extend to the bonding of all employees for whose conduct the official is responsible. Probably the most conventional method to reduce the amount of losses is to require that the governmental body make annual audits to help discover losses while they are still small.

Public Employees Blanket Bonds. These are special bonds for governmental employees who do not have to file individual bonds. The governmental body must determine whether it wants an *honesty form* or a *faithful performance form*. The honesty form is less expensive than the faithful performance form, which provides broader coverage. Public employees blanket bonds may be written for (1) a department, a division, an office, or an institution of any state, county, or local subdivision, (2) public utilities, and (3) public schools.

The public employees blanket bond is presently written as a part of the simplified crime program as either coverage form O or P. Coverage form O protects against loss caused by employee dishonesty on a per loss basis, whereas coverage form P covers loss on a per-employee basis. The rating is based on the number of ratable employees, the amount of the bond, and whether the bond is an honesty form or a faithful performance form.

Judicial Bonds in Civil Proceedings

Judicial bonds in civil proceedings are a second type of noncontract bond. There are two major categories of judicial bonds in civil proceedings, fiduciary and court bonds. These bonds are very different in nature and are associated with different underwriting considerations.

Fiduciary Bonds. A *fiduciary* is a person who manages the affairs or funds of another or who is otherwise in a position of trust. The principal (fiduciary) should have experience in those official duties and must generally have qualified legal counsel in order for a surety company to underwrite the bond. This is required because a fiduciary's duty is to handle the affairs of an estate in a legally prescribed manner, which means, among other things, that the fiduciary must not engage in any risky, unprofitable operations or investments. Some states have a list of the kinds of investments that can legally be made. Advice of counsel on matters such as these is essential. Some form of reporting is required of most fiduciaries either annually or at the end of their term of service.

Term. The term of the bond does not expire until the fiduciary performs the obligations under the bond. The term of the fiduciary often extends over a number of years, in which case it may be advisable to call for a periodic accounting by the attorney. Such accountings are common in connection with guardian bonds. By frequently delivering to the court an accounting of all activities to date or since the last accounting, the fiduciary can obtain the court's approval for those actions (while the records are still available) and be exonerated for those activities before the term of service expires.

Forms. The court often requires the bond to be on the court's form, although many courts accept the surety company's form. The court usually sets the bond in a fixed amount based on the value of the personal property the fiduciary expects to receive. Real property cannot be sold validly without court order. If it is found that the bond amount is not large enough, an additional bond may be required. The bond is for the fiduciary's term; a short-term obligation is easier than a long-term obligation to underwrite and accept. There is no cancellation provision in the bond form, so the bond remains in force until the court has relieved the fiduciary of all responsibilities. The estate pays the bond premium as an expense of the fiduciary.

Data. Sureties underwrite most fiduciary bonds not only on the basis of data on the application, which includes a brief financial statement, but also to a great extent on the basis of the competence of the principal's counsel. Some underwriters state that they underwrite law firms more than they underwrite principals.

Types of Fiduciary Bonds. The most commonly issued fiduciary bond is written for administrators. An *administrator* is a fiduciary the court appoints to conduct the affairs of the estate of someone who has died without a will. (If there is a will, the will names an *executor* to perform these duties.) There are several special types of administrators, but their duties are basically the same. They assume control of the decedent's personal property, collect debts due the estate, and preserve assets so they can be properly distributed when dictated by the court. The administrator, like the executor, is legally required to give notice by publication calling for timely claims against the estate. In some cases, the estate assets must be appraised and an inventory filed showing the appraised values.

Administrators or executors also take care of the decedent's expenses associated with death, including funeral costs. They must pay the federal, state, and local taxes that have accrued. Administrators or executors draw up the inheritance tax forms although they may not be the ones required to pay the tax. When they have performed their duties, administrators must file an accounting with the court showing receipts, disbursements, and balances on hand. They must also ask for relief of liability based on evidence that assets have been properly distributed and ask for discharge of the surety. If administrators fail in any of these activities, they are responsible for the debts incurred and for any charges against the estate because of incorrect handling. Administrator bonds are generally short-term obligations because they can be handled within several months or, at most, within a year or two.

A common long-term fiduciary bond is the *guardian bond.* There are different types of guardians. Generally, a guardian administers the estate of a minor or preserves rights and assets of a minor who is involved in litigation. This means collecting the funds as well as investing, reinvesting, and maintaining records of the use of funds and paying costs for the minor's education, support, and maintenance under court order. The court typically requires an annual accounting, and the surety often requires a copy of this accounting.

In many jurisdictions the fiduciary who takes charge of an incompetent's estate also is called a guardian. In others, this person (or persons) is called a "committee," a "conservator," a "curator," or a "custodian." The obligation under the bond remains the same, regardless of the title.

Many kinds of fiduciaries perform special duties. Some of them are "masters," "referees," or "trustees." They may be required to sell real estate or to close some legal proceeding when there is more than one party involved and some neutral third party must act. An example of this condition is a "master in partition," who helps conduct the final closing of the sale of real estate in divorce proceedings.

Another group of fiduciaries, called "receivers," helps to manage or liquidate a business in financial difficulty. They muster the assets of a failing business and dispose of those assets only as the court directs. In a federal bankruptcy situation, the receiver does not dispose of, but holds, assets until the creditors in bankruptcy elect a trustee.

Trustees in reorganization proceedings to rehabilitate a business are appointed on the basis of competency by the judge of the bankruptcy court. The surety underwriter must carefully evaluate the qualifications of these people in view of the loss exposures involved. In some jurisdictions, individuals, usually attorneys, specialize in business reorganization and are familiar with all appropriate laws.

Court Bonds—Plaintiffs' and Defendants' Bonds. In numerous kinds of litigation, one of the parties bringing suit must post a bond to protect the other party. This type of surety bond is called a *court bond* and is required by statute or court decree.

There are many types of court bonds, but this discussion will be limited to *litigation bonds*, or plaintiffs' and defendants' bonds, which include appeal, replevin, injunction, mechanic's lien, and bail bonds.

Plaintiffs' bonds are required of people bringing suit at law against others. Most sureties review the financial status of plaintiffs for whom they are writing bonds.

Defendants' bonds protect plaintiffs while their suit is being tried by the court. This protection is needed because defendants may want to regain possession of assets attached by the plaintiff, or to have protection while continuing in lawful activities. Defendants' bonds usually allow the defendant to (1) retain or regain possession of property (that has been attached by the plaintiff) pending the outcome of the suit or (2) suspend the execution of a judgment, order, or decree of the court while the defendant seeks reversal of an unfavorable judgment in a higher court. The latter adds to the underwriter's concern because the defendant has already lost the case once. Consequently, many surety underwriters consider writing defendants' bonds only with full collateral. This raises the question, why would a defendant want a court bond when full collateral is required? The reason is that, in most cases, there is no other alternative for the defendant but to obtain a surety bond.

Considering the low premiums for court bonds, the litigation bond system is probably advantageous to all concerned. Courts are not designed to accept collateral. They cannot determine whether collateral is adequate and cannot maintain premises for the safe storage of collateral. These activities require the surety's expertise.

Underwriting Plaintiffs' and Defendants' Bonds. The results of court cases are extremely useful sources of underwriting information. Sureties are more cautious when underwriting defendants' bonds than plaintiffs' bonds. They may require only an application from a plaintiff that includes a brief form financial statement. For a defendant, a surety may require some form of collateral. No underwriter should assume that the court's decision will favor the principal.

In every case, the bond must be underwritten to account for the possibility that the principal will lose and will have to pay the face amount of the bond. The court generally prescribes the face amount of the bond such that the value of the property in question, plus an amount for costs, interest and damages, is included in the total amount.

Appeal Bonds. Among the more common types of plaintiffs' and defendants' bonds are appeal bonds. They must be filed by principals who wish to contest a judgment by appealing to a higher court. The bonds may be limited either to costs of the appeal (*costs* on *appeal bonds*) or to stay of execution on the judgment, order, or decree (*stay of execution* or *judgment value bonds*). Whether the bond is for the *appellant* (appealing party who lost in lower court) or the *appellee* (party who won in lower court and against whom appeal is taken), it is understood that the principal will prosecute the appeal and perform as ordered if the appellate court (higher court) affirms the lower court's judgment.

Attachment Bonds. The purpose of many plaintiffs' and defendants' bonds is to prevent or to allow continued use of property. (These bonds are described in detail in Chapter 2.) An *attachment bond* responds to this need before a court renders a judgment. An *attachment* is a legal device requiring the property to be held in custody (often by the sheriff) so it cannot be sold, transferred, or removed from the court's jurisdiction. It is often used if a defendant is a nonresident. The attachment bond, which the plaintiff furnishes, documents an agreement to indemnify the defendant for loss or damage arising out of the attachment if the court decides that a statutory ground for attachment did not exist or if the plaintiff fails to recover a judgment against the defendant.

A defendant uses a *release of attachment bond* to dissolve the attachment. This frees the property for sale or other disposition, and the plaintiff then looks to the bond for satisfaction of any judgment in the plaintiff's favor. It is possible that the same surety may write bonds for the plaintiff and the defendant, which is one reason why the underwriter should not evaluate the merits of any case. The underwriter must be an impartial judge of the financial capacity of the plaintiff and the defendant. The surety may require collateral from one or both parties.

Replevin Bonds. A *replevin bond* is similar in some ways to an attachment bond. Replevin means to take back. A replevin is an action by a person who claims ownership of personal property, wishes to recover possession of specific articles of personal property, and alleges that another person has unlawfully taken or withheld that property. Unlike an attachment bond, a replevin bond does not prevent someone from taking property, but it guarantees that the property will remain in the same condition and will not be sold or otherwise disposed of. Both of these bonds are underwritten about the same way, except normally the replevin bond is for a smaller amount and is needed quickly.

As with attachment bonds, there are two primary types of replevin bonds. The plaintiff must furnish a replevin bond in order to secure property. This bond documents the plaintiff's agreement to return the property if the court so orders, and that the bond will pay all costs and damages adjudged to the defendant. The defendant may in turn furnish a *counter-replevin bond* to recover replevined property, thereby regaining possession of the property until the court makes a final decision. This bond is conditioned for redelivery of the property to the plaintiff, if the defendant is so ordered, or to otherwise comply with the order of the court. Since this is a type of defendant's bond, a surety may require collateral.

Injunction Bonds. Another kind of plaintiffs' and defendants' bond is the *injunction bond*. An injunction is a court order that requires a defendant to do, or to refrain from doing, a particular thing. Property is not necessarily part of an injunction. An order granting an injunction may be conditioned upon the plaintiff's furnishing a bond documenting agreement to indemnify the defendant against loss if it is decided that the court should not have granted the injunction. The defendant may furnish a *dissolve injunction bond,* which nullifies the injunction and allows the defendant to proceed as if the injunction were never issued. This bond guarantees payment of any damages the plaintiff may sustain because of the defendant's performance of acts prohibited by, or nonperformance of acts required by, the original injunction. Underwriting an injunction bond or a dissolve-injunction bond depends on whether there is a strong likelihood of the other party's liability or serious doubt about the bonded party's responsibility that would require the posting of collateral. Financial responsibility of the bonded party is also a criterion.

Mechanics' Lien Bonds. A *mechanic's lien bond* (or *bond to discharge a mechanic's lien*) is designed to discharge a lien against real estate filed by one who has done work or furnished materials for the construction of a building or other improvements on property. The owner who wishes to sell property but has not paid all workers may not be able to close a sale without a surety bond to discharge mechanics' liens. A general contractor must often bond away liens that subcontractors and material suppliers place on the property. The surety may require the contractor to furnish collateral if an unpaid bill from a subcontractor or supplier is in dispute.

Bail Bonds. A *bail bond* secures the release of a person involved in a criminal action. The bond is conditioned on the principal's appearance in the court where the charge is pending and submission to trial and orders of the court. Failure to appear means the entire penalty of the bond becomes due and payable as a forfeiture. Specialty surety companies write virtually all bail bonds.

License and Permit Bonds

License and permit bonds are required by the federal government, or any state, county, municipality, or other political subdivison as a condition to issuing a license to engage in a certain business or activity, or to granting a permit to exercise a particular privilege.

Licensing laws often require firms to provide surety in support of the promise to lawfully conduct business. The scope of the bond varies according to the law, the locality, the nature of the guarantee, and the parties who have a right of action under the bond.

In order to understand the obligation of the bond, the underwriter must understand the law requiring the bond, the bond form, and any regulatory requirements. Most of these bonds fit within one or more of the following groups.

Compliance or Privilege Bonds. Construction related businesses may be required to give *compliance or privilege bonds* to public bodies to guarantee that the business will be conducted, or privileges exercised, in conformance with building and trade codes. The bond penalties are usually nominal, and sureties write them freely for applicants who are well known, well regarded, and whom the producer recommends. Typical businesses for which these bonds are written are drain layers, electricians, oil burner installers, and plumbers. While most license bonds are compliance or privilege bonds, a surety must exercise additional care where there is direct third-party liability.

Liquor license bonds are a type of compliance bond that carry penalties for noncompliance. However, in many locales where the government restricts the number of outstanding licenses, noncompliance seldom extends to such a degree that it must require penalties. Local governments often can control minor infringements by operators by mere threat of license revocation.

Good Faith Bonds. *Good faith bonds* include bonds that protect the general public against fraud, misrepresentation, and unfair practices of licensee-principals. Enterprises to which such bonds are issued include car dealers, collection agencies, employment agencies, and pawnbrokers. Good faith bonds must be underwritten cautiously, but businesses of good reputation and sufficient financial worth present low risk.

Buyers' Bonds. Sureties issue *buyers' bonds* required by public bodies to guarantee that buyers will pay farmers for goods. These buyers cannot usually pay farmers until they re-sell the goods, and the bonds guarantee that the farmers will get paid. Examples of buyers who must obtain these bonds are dealers in agricultural products, livestock auctioneers, livestock dealers, and milk dealers. Underwriting considerations include favorable references and sound financial conditions.

Tax Bonds. *Tax bonds* guarantee the payment of taxes levied under the laws or ordinances requiring these bonds. For example, in a retail business, the public pays sales tax to the retailer, but the tax money is commingled generally with other business funds and loses its identity. In this case, the surety is liable for the payment of the tax funds if the business fails to remit the taxes due to the government. These bonds, outright financial guarantees, apply to cigarette tax, gasoline or fuel tax, liquor tax, and sales tax.

Underwriters must understand both the laws mandating these bonds and the principal's moral, legal, financial, and ethical reputation, which must be beyond reproach. The financial information must be current and verified by the underwriter. Available assets should be liquid enough to pay the bond penalty easily if this becomes necessary. The principal must have strong net worth because the full bond penalty is often involved when a loss does occur on a financial guarantee bond of this type.

Underwriting License and Permit Bonds. As in most surety lines of business, the best way to understand how any given license and permit bond is underwritten is an example. Consider the following different bonds and the particular qualities of each required of one firm. As the discussion of the various bonds progresses, it becomes clear that the scope of the underwriting tests changes according to the bond.

A gasoline distributor must obtain several types of bonds. One is a license bond allowing the distributor to do business. The limit of liability is small, and the bond is written freely if the applicant is well known and respected by the producer.

The same distributor may wish to hang a sign above the sidewalk outside the company office, for which a permit bond is required by law. The law also may allow a third-party action if the sign falls on the third party. The underwriter requires adequate liability insurance on the premises.

The gasoline distributor may need a permit bond to dig up a

sidewalk while installing a tank below ground. This bond may require financial underwriting to ensure that the firm has enough liquidity and net worth to perform the intended construction project.

A gasoline distributor collects taxes and must prove financial responsibility commensurate with the amount of taxes to be collected, determined by the amount of sales anticipated for a given period of time. For this tax bond, which is a financial guarantee, the distributor must either have liquid assets in excess of the bond amount or post collateral with the surety.

UNDERWRITING FIDELITY BONDS

Fidelity insurance, a form of crime insurance, covers theft by employees. It has the following special characteristics that make it unique among crime insurances:

- *Property exposed to loss is accessible.* The nature of the employment relationship provides the employee an opportunity to learn the firm's routines; schedules; habits; fellow employees; and the existence, absence, or relative effectiveness of management controls.
- *Losses can be hidden.* Unlike burglary and robbery, which by definition are "visible" crimes, employee theft of money and information can be made "invisible." The theft can be obscured or covered for varying lengths of time, given the employee's knowledge of routines, schedules, and other information about the firm.
- *The probability of severe loss greatly exceeds that in other kinds of crime.* The thief's access to property continues until the crime is discovered. The length of the time of access, in turn, contributes to the size of loss. Even the robberies that get the most notoriety are more often than not the result of "insiders."
- *Management control systems are the primary loss control devices.* Safes, vaults, alarm systems, and other security systems are secondary defenses against fidelity losses. Management's monitoring of the revenue, merchandise, and raw material that flow into and out of its possession is the first line of defense.
- *Management may be reluctant to accept that thieves may be among its employees.* Employers are frequently unwilling to believe that their employees might steal from them. The reluctance to accept this reality leads to practices that contribute to opportunities for theft or at least that exacerbate exposures to loss.

- *Management may be reluctant to prosecute employee thefts.* Many employers will not sign complaints or testify freely at criminal proceedings against their employees. The reasons for this appear to be a wish to avoid damaging publicity; an acceptance of the culprit's "hard luck" story; and a desire to have the whole affair quickly resolved, especially when there is a promise of restitution.

The following characteristics of fidelity crimes pose additional problems for underwriters:

1. Losses, when reported, are already fairly large, and the final determination of the amount of loss greatly exceeds the initial report.
2. The widespread reluctance of employers to accept the reality of dishonest employees creates a problem of adverse selection against the insurance company.

Underwriting Considerations

A fidelity bond usually covers an indefinite term. There is, however, an annual rating period. Because the relationship between the insurer and insured is a long-term one, it must begin on a sound basis. The underwriter must be satisfied that certain conditions exist prior to bonding:

1. The management of the insured firm should be of the highest moral character so that the moral hazard is nonexistent.
2. The insured should be profitable. Profits indicate competence within a given market, management planning and control systems, financial ability to respond to recommended loss control expenditures, and the understanding by employees that good performance should be rewarded.

   A new firm may not be profitable because it has heavy capitalization expenses and because it is still developing markets for its products or services. At the very least, the underwriter must be assured that the firm's founders have meaningful, sufficient experience in related work.
3. Burglary and robbery loss control systems are in place and maintained. Appropriate defenses against external crime also are a deterrence to employees.
4. Amounts of insurance are within the limits prescribed by the company.
5. Management controls exist and are maintained. These controls are evidence of management concern. With few exceptions, the absence of these controls is sufficient reason to decline the account.

Fidelity Loss Control

Fidelity loss control is synonymous with management controls. The controls described below apply to all kinds of firms and are minimal standards for acceptability. As limits of liability increase, so should the stringency of these controls.

Selection Practices. For a small sole proprietorship or a large multinational corporation, an underwriter will look to see that the following selection practices are in place:

- New hires are screened, and their references are checked. Applicants with gaps in employment history must have satisfactory explanations. Employers must ensure that those with convictions for crimes of dishonesty are placed in positions where employee theft is essentially impossible.
- Seasoned employees up for promotion should be reviewed, especially when the promotion or transfer is into a sensitive position.
- Management must remain sensitive to employee behavior in order to detect unreasonable or unexplained behavioral changes.

Periodic Audits. Underwriters pay attention to the frequency of audits. Audits generally test accounts receivable, cash accounts, inventories, and disbursements such as accounts payable and travel and entertainment expense accounts. The tests are samplings of these accounts, the results of which are measured against industry- or company-wide norms. They allow the early detection of malfeasance and are a highly visible way of communication to employees that management is monitoring performance.

The frequency of audits is usually a management decision, but the underwriter should feel free to require an increase in frequency if the amount of insurance exposed to loss or the nature of the risk so warrants. Generally, an audit should occur at least annually. Insurers often establish limit of liability thresholds at which audits must be conducted by Certified Public Accountants rather than by internal auditors.

Small businesses may not have internal auditors, and the expense of outside auditors may be too high. An underwriter may forgo audits in these cases if (1) bookkeeping records are sound and up-to-date, and (2) there are reasonable grounds to believe that owners are exercising personal supervision on a daily basis.

Monthly Bank Account Reconciliations. Few things are more tempting to employees with personal cash flow difficulties than to be given authority over a checking account where they know the superiors fail to reconcile the bank statements. Underwriters check to see that accounts are reconciled by a person in authority who does not prepare or make deposits or prepare or sign checks or drafts.

Divided Responsibilities. Employees who regularly handle merchandise should not have responsibility for handling cash. Similarly, those regularly handling cash should not handle merchandise. For a small business, this may not be practical; and the owner should make frequent spot checks.

Physical Inventories. Physical inventories by persons other than those directly responsible for merchandise, parts, materials, or control records should occur at least annually.

Annual Vacations. All nonowner employees should take annual leaves of not less than five consecutive days. This allows different people to be assigned to different positions, thus revealing irregular behavior on the part of, or unusual procedures engaged in by, the vacationing employee. The employee who never takes vacations often has the best opportunity for theft.

UNDERWRITING CONTRACT BONDS

Many underwriters believe that underwriting contract bonds is the only "real underwriting" in surety although many other bonds, particularly the financial guarantee bonds, also require skill in financial analysis. Nevertheless, it is true that, in contract underwriting, the intricacies of accounting become intertwined with those of business, presenting perhaps the greatest challenge to the underwriter.

Underwriting the Contractor: Three Factors

A contract bond client is underwritten every time a bid is contemplated. The total surety credit line is reviewed when each fiscal period is completed. As a party to this account, the surety lends its financial capacity to the principal to guarantee the principal's obligation to the obligee.

In doing so, the surety runs the risk of having to assume the principal's (contractor's) obligation to the obligee. The surety underwriter's job is to see that this risk is within an acceptable range. This means making certain that the contractor can fulfill its obligations and is therefore worthy of receiving unsecured credit from the surety. Surety underwriters evaluate the credit worthiness of their clients in light of the *three Cs of credit:* character, capacity, and capital. These considerations are discussed below.

Character. *Character* is the moral and ethical nature of an individual or business entity. In evaluating the character of a principal, a surety underwriter looks for honesty, integrity, fair dealing, and a sense of commitment to one's work.

The surety underwriter looks for evidence of good character in the personal and employment history of bond applicants. The underwriter focuses on the following:

- Success in school, employment, or business
- Evidence of increasing responsibility
- Career focus—numerous occupations may reveal the attempt to bury an unfavorable history or may show a lack of commitment
- Reverses or bankruptcies—some contractors learn from their mistakes, but the test is the frequency or pattern of such mistakes
- Trade payment record—reflects management ability and a sense of fairness and understanding in financial dealings with others

The underwriter will require a completed application or background information sheet accompanied by financial statements. This information is updated as new bonds are requested. Many underwriters expect to see *at least* the three most recent year-end statements, though statements for the past five years are preferred by most. If the year ended more than six months prior, they will expect an interim statement. A contractor's public accountant or CPA may not be required to audit this interim statement, but the underwriter will spot check, or verify, assets. If the financial statements are not audited, the underwriter must do extensive research to verify the statement before writing any bonds. The amount of research required is, at least to some extent, based on the financial strength of the contractor and the size of the bonds to be written.

Capacity. *Capacity* is a contractor's ability to perform a project successfully. The surety underwriter considers the following factors in measuring (or evaluating) a contractor's capacity:

- Business organization
- Performance record
- Plant and equipment
- Financial resources
- Credit reports
- Management control
- Bank credit line

Organization of the Contractor. Information furnished by the applicant in the application or supporting documents indicates how long the contractor has been in business and the "age" of the firm. The ownership of the organization should be documented. If it is a sole proprietorship or partnership, the contractor should provide information about life insurance and continuity planning.

The underwriter should also review the experience of other members of the firm if substantial work programs are anticipated. (*Work program* refers to the outstanding contracts, either as bids or as work in progress at a given point in time.) This is important because, as the contractor's workload grows, it is likely that the contractor will delegate jobs to other firm members, about whose expertise the underwriter must be convinced. The underwriter measures the experience of the contractor and its managers and other key personnel in terms of education and years of experience and the size, complexity, and location of projects successfully completed. Prior employment history, length of service, and experience with contractors known for their organizational strength and success are also important factors.

Performance Record and Future Plans. The underwriter reviews a history of the contractor's work program and the growth pattern of the contractor's current work program in order to be certain that a contractor is not expanding too rapidly. Performance records are checked by contacting the owners of completed work or architects and engineers on previous projects. An underwriter should not be overly impressed by letters delivered by the contractor from satisfied customers.

The underwriter typically requests a list of the most important jobs the contractor has completed in the last five years. Each job on this list should include the name and address of the owner and architect, the kind of work and location, the contract price, profitability, and the year completed.

If an underwriter is evaluating a contractor who is bidding on a job that is consistent with successfully completed work in terms of size, number, type, complexity, location, labor markets, and owner, then it is not difficult to project whether the contractor has the capacity to handle the pending work, provided there is no adverse change in the contractor's organization and finances. However, when the contract work involves new markets or is of a number, type, size, or complexity that is different from the contractor's experience, it is more difficult to evaluate capacity. The underwriter must therefore make a more careful underwriting decision because many surety losses are attributed to contractors who, because of competitive pressures, sought to expand into new types of work or geographical areas.

An underwriter should approach any such strategic move cautiously, with extensive evaluation of the risks involved. The underwriter must be certain that the principal has the financial capacity to assume the additional risk of the planned venture. Surety underwriters usually advise their clients to seek the sureties' counsel and advice well in advance. The underwriter's counsel is valuable because it is based on broad experience in many different markets and situations.

Plant and Equipment. Depending on the size and type of contract, either or both of these items can be a crucial measure of capacity. Road building, for example, requires special heavy equipment, while a large heating, ventilating, and air conditioning job requires a sheet metal shop. Nevertheless, both are examined for the same reason—the underwriter must make certain that the contractor has or can obtain the physical capacity or production resources needed to complete the contract work. An appropriate mix of well-maintained equipment is essential to the high level of productivity demanded by today's competitive market.

Most underwriters also are concerned about the method used to obtain these resources. Equipment may be owned or leased, or leased with a purchase option. Tax considerations play a role in the contractor's decision to lease or buy. A contractor who elects to own equipment or hold it under a long-term lease should consider carefully the availability of work in the future. Idle equipment, especially if encumbered, is a financial burden because it eats away at profit and reduces the return on a capital investment. Some underwriters prefer to see equipment purchased outright because the effect of the purchase on the contractor's financial condition will be visible immediately.

If debt is used to finance equipment, the contractor needs to consider the effect that debt leverage has on the firm's financial health. Debt must be serviced whether or not the contractor has work. Without job cash flow, fixed debt service payments come directly out of working capital, which reduces liquidity. This, in turn, can limit or reduce the contractor's surety credit line, thereby adding to the difficulty of getting work to generate the cash flow to service the debt.

It is important that the contractor have the amount of equipment needed but not be overburdened with debt. A contractor who has higher debts than competitors is at a disadvantage in bidding work, since debt service expenses will be higher. Inability to get work leads to problems in servicing debt and maintaining surety credit.

Work in Progress. Although the historical cost value of plant and equipment are included on the balance sheet of a firm, they are assets that the contractor often overrates and that the surety cannot evaluate precisely from information in the financial statements. Another item that is difficult to evaluate is the *status of work in progress*, which gives the financial status of the work on hand. Such items are traditionally valued by standard accrual methods of accounting and do not reflect the estimated profit or lack of profit without some analysis.

For example, accounts receivable indicate that the contractor has an asset, but it may be only a paper asset which should have a corresponding payable as a liability. Accounting records do not always reflect the liability, but once the contractor has billed the owner, these are considered an asset. In fact, the contractor may have overbilled the customer either by front-end loading or by billing for an amount in excess of the costs incurred. The underwriter uses a status report similar to that in Exhibit 4-4 to analyze billings and costs and to compare the contract price with estimated costs to complete. This information, which is used to adjust assets and liabilities shown on the financial statements, is probably the single most significant item for the underwriter to consider when dealing with large contractors.

Work-in-progress charts reveal the trend of the contractor's business over time. For long-term construction projects, it is essential to know what percentage of the project has actually been completed at any given time and how rapidly the work progresses. This information provides additional insight into the contractor's capacity.

Credit Reports. Credit reports are another way to measure capacity. The surety checks subcontractor, supplier, and lender references to determine if and how the contractor has satisfied obligations to these parties. Their responses have a direct bearing on the evaluation of the character as well as the capacity of the contractor. Successful performance requires the support and commitment of subcontractors, suppliers, and lenders. Any weakness in relationships with these parties can impair the contractor's ability to perform, i.e., capacity.

Since the underwriter might expect references furnished by the contractor to make favorable comments, the underwriter also looks at trade credit reports from companies such as Dun & Bradstreet and the National Association of Credit Managers. A long record of slow payments or any lien foreclosures will prompt the underwriter to either reject the contractor or dig deeper into its investigation of the contractor's trade credit.

There are numerous sources of credit information, but the Dun & Bradstreet Report is probably the one source used most by surety contract bond underwriters. These reports give a sketch of the history of the firm, its organization, and its owners. They also provide a summary of payment records from suppliers. A brief form of financial statement should also be included. This statement is incomplete from the underwriter's viewpoint but serves as a point for comparison with the more thorough statement the accountant supplies.

Credit reports do not provide all the details an underwriter needs, but they offer clues for further appraisal. Chapters 7 and 8 more thoroughly explore credit terminology and laws, as well as credit

Exhibit 4-4
Status of Contracts

STATUS OF CONTRACTS

Name and Address of Contractor

Uncompleted Contracts as of 19

Contract Description and Location	I Contract Price Including Approved Change Orders	II Contractor's Estimated Cost At Time of Bid (1)	III Total Amount Billed to Date Including Retainage (2)	IV Total Costs to Date	V Revised Estimated Remaining Costs To Complete (3)	VI Estimated Completion Date
1						
2						
3						
4						
5						
6						

Contracts Completed During Last Fiscal Year or Since Last Status of Contracts Report

Contract Description and Location	Final Contract Price	Total Cost	Gross Profit of Loss

1 Include contractor's original estimated total cost plus cost of all change orders and extra work orders approved to date.
2 Do not include "claims" or "disputed items." If desired, attach an explanation.
3 See instructions on reverse side.

This information prepared

By ____________________

Date ________________ ,19 ______

investigations and reports. Reading a few reports will not give many clues to a novice underwriter, but comparing the style and content of thirty or forty reports helps a new underwriter determine the vital concerns in a report. The novice must learn how to spot such concerns in order to concentrate on them in subsequent analysis.

Related to a credit report is a bank letter or bank report. Many sureties question bankers, and some bankers question sureties. The exchange is mutually helpful, but it should not be haphazard. The underwriter usually asks questions related to three major areas:

1. What are the account balances (current or at any given statement date)?
2. Can the amount of loans be confirmed? Are the loan commitments being met as agreed?
3. Has a written authorization for future loans been arranged? May the surety be furnished with a copy? (This item is usually obtained through the contractor rather than directly from the bank.)
4. Are there any restrictive covenants? (Examples of restrictive covenants might include maintaining required financial ratios, restricting dividends, or prohibiting the incurrence of any additional debt.)

On new accounts that were previously bonded by another surety, underwriters will be concerned that the contractor may have some problems that are not readily apparent. For example, the prior underwriter may have restricted or denied the issue of some new bonds, and the contractor will likely want to move from this "uncooperative" surety to one that "wants the business." Since such an account may represent a potentially large loss, the underwriter will make every effort to determine the real reasons the contractor wants to switch sureties.

Management Control. The basic elements of construction contracting are a matter of bidding and building. A contractor's demonstrated ability to control the processes of project estimating, bidding, job supervision, and cost control is, therefore, vital to the success of the contractor and vital to accurate determination of capacity.

Estimating. Estimating is the first step in the construction process. A contractor must exercise great care in taking-off and pricing materials, in accurately estimating labor hours and costs, and in scheduling each segment of the job. Competition has reduced available gross profit margins for many contractors to about 5 percent or less. Accordingly, there is little room for error in the contractor's price estimate.

Bidding. Bidding is the second step in the construction process. The contractor must carefully organize, control, and double-check subcontract and material prices as they are submitted by telephone only hours and sometimes even minutes before the bid opening deadline. In the contractor's bid room, numerous elements of a contract are bid by suppliers and subcontractors to the contractor by telephone in a short period of time. Procedures for taking bids and listing them in order of price and qualification of the bidders must be well established. Any gaps or failures in communication or judgment at this point can be costly. Good teamwork is essential.

If awarded the contract, the contractor must have the ability to manage the job profitably in order to succeed. This requires realistic, yet aggressive scheduling, expert supervision of labor and subcontractors, and close attention to the documentation and pricing of contract change orders.

Cost Controlling. Good cost records and a reliable cost control system are primary tools in managing a contractor's work program—in part because current work records are needed to estimate new work. Job cost information should be accurate and timely. Cost accounts should be organized for easy comparison to the cost estimate for each work phase and cost category of the job. The cost estimate is the baseline for measuring actual costs. Each phase should include the costs of materials, labor, subcontracts, and other direct costs. Planned overhead and profit should also be included.

Project superintendents should carefully measure costs and submit them to the head office, preferably on a daily basis (certainly no less often than weekly). Management should review all costs on every job weekly and should know if costs for each phase are below or above budget and why. When costs begin to exceed budget, they are eating into profit. Corrective action should be taken immediately to maintain control of the job in order to realize the estimated profit.

Continuity Planning. Many construction firms succeed under the strong management and leadership of one or two key individuals. A continuity plan is a formal plan that establishes who will own and manage the firm in the future once these individuals are either no longer involved, or involved to a lesser degree, in the firm's operations. Without a continuity plan, the firm and its surety credit will suffer if these individuals are no longer involved as a result of death, disability, or retirement.

In evaluating capacity in terms of continuity planning, the underwriter considers two factors: (1) continuity of management and (2) continuity of ownership. If the key person is not an owner, but an employee, then a successor should be identified. Larger firms generally have an internal succession plan. Smaller firms may have to look outside the firm for a successor. In the latter case, funds should be set aside because it will probably require a financial incentive (in the form of cash or ownership) to attract a talented successor. Key person life insurance is a common way to ensure that needed funds are available in the event of death. In addition, it is advisable to build cash reserves for disability or retirement.

Most often the key person is the sole or principal owner. In this case the problem of continuity is one of ownership as well as management unless the business is to be discontinued upon completion of the then existing jobs. Since an ongoing construction firm has real economic value, the heirs ordinarily would like to receive its full value, not just the net proceeds of an orderly liquidation. This may be accomplished through a formal buy-sell agreement between the owner and key employees, or between the owner and outside interests.

To limit the financial impact of a key person's death, the buy-sell agreement should be funded by cash reserves accumulated for this purpose or by life insurance. If debt is used to fund the sale, then the firm must carry the debt service burden. Since the amount of debt required is usually substantial, this will have a detrimental effect on the firm's credit capacity. The buyout is frequently accomplished with a combination of cash, life insurance, and debt.

If the firm is expanding, it probably needs to employ all of its cash for working capital. Moreover, a growing company does not usually have much excess credit capacity. Consequently, any use of cash or debt to fund a sale will reduce liquidity, working capital, and available credit capacity. Shrinkage, rather than continued growth, would be the likely result. A shrinking firm may find it hard to meet a fixed debt obligation. Expanding firms generally find life insurance to be the most economical way to fund a buy-sell agreement.

The risk of serious injury or physical disability is, except for older people, statistically greater than the risk of death. Accordingly, the purchase of disability insurance on owners and key employees should be considered in any continuity plan. The fact that construction sites expose owners and key employees to a greater-than-average safety risk should heighten interest in key person life insurance, disability insurance, and safety programs. Therefore, surety underwriters have a great interest in contractors' continuity plans.

Capital. *Capital* is the surety's third consideration in underwriting a contractor. It is a measure of the contractor's financial ability to assume the risks of business activity. It is also an indication of past success and commitment to the growth of the business as measured by the level of retained earnings. Moreover, the composition of capital—debt versus equity and liquid versus fixed assets—also says something about the contractor's judgment about the importance of financial stability and the independence of the firm.

Equity Versus Debt Capital. As an unsecured creditor, a surety examines a contractor's *equity capital*. This is the portion of assets the contractor owns and is viewed by the surety as a cushion to absorb any operating losses. The larger this cushion, the lesser the likelihood that the surety will have to step in and provide financial assistance or assume the obligations of the contractor.

If the majority of a contractor's assets are purchased with debt, the lenders have a greater interest than the contractor in the assets that support the business. This is not a healthy situation. If the contractor runs into problems and is unable to make timely debt payments, the lenders may foreclose their claims to the firm's assets. Short of foreclosure, lenders may demand restrictive covenants that can circumscribe a contractor's ability to manage the business. In the event of bankruptcy, the creditors will liquidate the business or place it under the control of a receiver, who will then operate the business for the equitable benefit of the creditors.

Unless a surety manages to get itself into a favored position as a creditor, its claim for indemnity by a principal likely will be subordinate to many other claims by secured creditors, mechanics' liens, etc. A surety must consider this eventuality in choosing whether to underwrite a contractor.

A prudent contractor makes certain that the potential claims of lenders do not amount to more than a minority interest in the business. The contractor wants to have enough equity capital to absorb any operating loss or unforeseen contingency, and still make timely payments to lenders, subcontractors, and trade creditors. This means having enough liquid assets to meet current obligations even in the event of an unforeseen financial setback. Most underwriters do not like total debt to exceed half of the contractor's capital base.

Working Capital. *Working capital* is the conventional measure of a business firm's liquidity. By accounting standards, working capital consists of current assets less current liabilities. *Current assets* are cash and other assets that can reasonably be expected to be converted to cash within a year or within the firm's normal business cycle. *Current liabilities* are obligations coming due within the next year or within the firm's business cycle. Sureties typically like current assets to be more than 1.3 times current liabilities.

Contract Backlog. Sureties define *backlog* as the estimated cost to complete all open work. (Some contractors define it as the amount left to bill.) The backlog represents the surety's obligation or exposure at any given point in time. The surety's exposure, however, also may be greater than the amount left to bill. Underwriters therefore examine the backlog carefully. They are interested in the backlog of bonded as well as unbonded work. Problems related to the unbonded work can affect the contractor's performance on bonded obligations.

The surety requires the contractor to maintain prudent levels of net worth and working capital relative to the work backlog. This makes the underwriter more comfortable because, if problems arise, the contractor has enough money to solve them without cash from the surety.

Thirty or forty years ago, demand for construction was high, the number of contractors was relatively small, and gross profit margins of 15 to 20 percent were common. In that favorable economic environment, sureties believed that a contractor should have enough working capital to carry the 10 percent retention that owners customarily withheld under their contracts pending final completion of the work. The surety convention, or "rule of thumb," required a contractor's working capital to be equal to at least 10 percent of the backlog (estimated cost to complete the work outstanding). Thus, if profit margins deteriorated to zero or delays forced the contractor to wait for final payment, at least the contractor could finance the investment in the project (the 10 percent retention) out of working capital. This conventional *10 percent rule*, called "ten times net quick," is still followed by many underwriters today. At the least, it is a benchmark to which many of them relate. Underwriters may comment, for example, that an applicant is a "10 percent case" or a "5 percent case."

Over the years, increasing competition has squeezed profit margins to the point where 5 or 6 percent gross profit or less is all that some construction markets will allow a contractor to earn. Also, many owners now withhold less than a 10 percent retention. It is not uncommon for owners to retain 10 percent until a project reaches, say, the 50 percent stage of completion, resulting in an overall retention of 5 percent. This seems only equitable since a contractor should not be expected to finance any part of the project for the owner. If the owner retains more than the contractor's profit margin, the contractor's funds are, in effect, being invested in the project. (This tends to keep the contractor focused on the job and creates some protection for the surety.)

Today, sureties tend to vary the benchmark ratio of working capital to backlog, depending on the size of the contractor and type of work performed. Because competition among contractors has generally reduced profit margins and increased the degree of credit risk, underwriters have become more conservative in defining an adequate amount of working capital. They tend to be more liberal, however, toward those general contractors who can pass on some of the contract retention by holding back retention from their subcontractors.

For a small general contractor, sureties generally expect to see working capital in an amount ranging from 8 to 12 percent of backlog. For a large general contractor, they might expect 5 to 8 percent. For a small, heavy equipment contractor whose equipment and labor costs are high, and less of the project is subcontracted, the surety might want 7 to 11 percent. For a large, heavy equipment contractor, 4 to 7 percent might be the norm.

Sureties require subcontractors to have a higher percentage of working capital to backlog. Subcontractors are not usually paid until the contractor is paid. A small subcontractor might be expected to maintain 10 to 14 percent, while large subcontractors might be held to 6 to 9 percent. Exhibit 4-5 shows typical ranges for working capital requirements.

Balance Sheet. The major divisions of a contractor's balance sheet reflect the capital considerations discussed to this point. The *balance sheet* is a snapshot of a firm's assets, liabilities, and equity or net worth. It measures financial condition, or ability to meet both expected and unexpected obligations that arise in the course of business.

Statement of Operations and Retained Earnings. The *statement of operations and retained earnings* is a "report card" of financial performance over a fiscal period. A surety first looks for profits to determine that the contractor is a viable concern and worthy of credit. Surety underwriters note the degree of variability in contract volume, gross profit, overhead, and net profit over time, seeking ways to enhance their knowledge of the particular business and risks in the contractor's marketplace.

If the contractor is expanding and requires a growing line of surety credit, the underwriter looks critically at any failure to retain profits in the business. The contractor is expected to keep profits in the business to increase the "equity cushion," thus avoiding a substantially increasing credit risk to the surety. Underwriters are not against growth, but they want it to be balanced with sufficient working capital and net worth so as not to raise their credit risk to an uncomfortable level.

To identify financial trends and to gauge a contractor's performance, underwriters need at least three years, and preferably five years, of financial data. Since they are unsecured creditors, most sureties insist on audited financial statements so they can be reasonably certain that the financial information on which they base their decisions is accurate.

Schedule of Work on Hand. The surety carefully analyzes the contractor's schedule of completed and uncompleted work such as the one shown in Exhibit 4-6 to get a better picture of the contractor's financial status, as well as some information concerning the contractor's ability to make accurate estimates on jobs. This schedule includes the following five items for each open job:

- Adjusted contract price (including change orders)
- Original estimated gross profit

Exhibit 4-5
Working Capital Guidelines

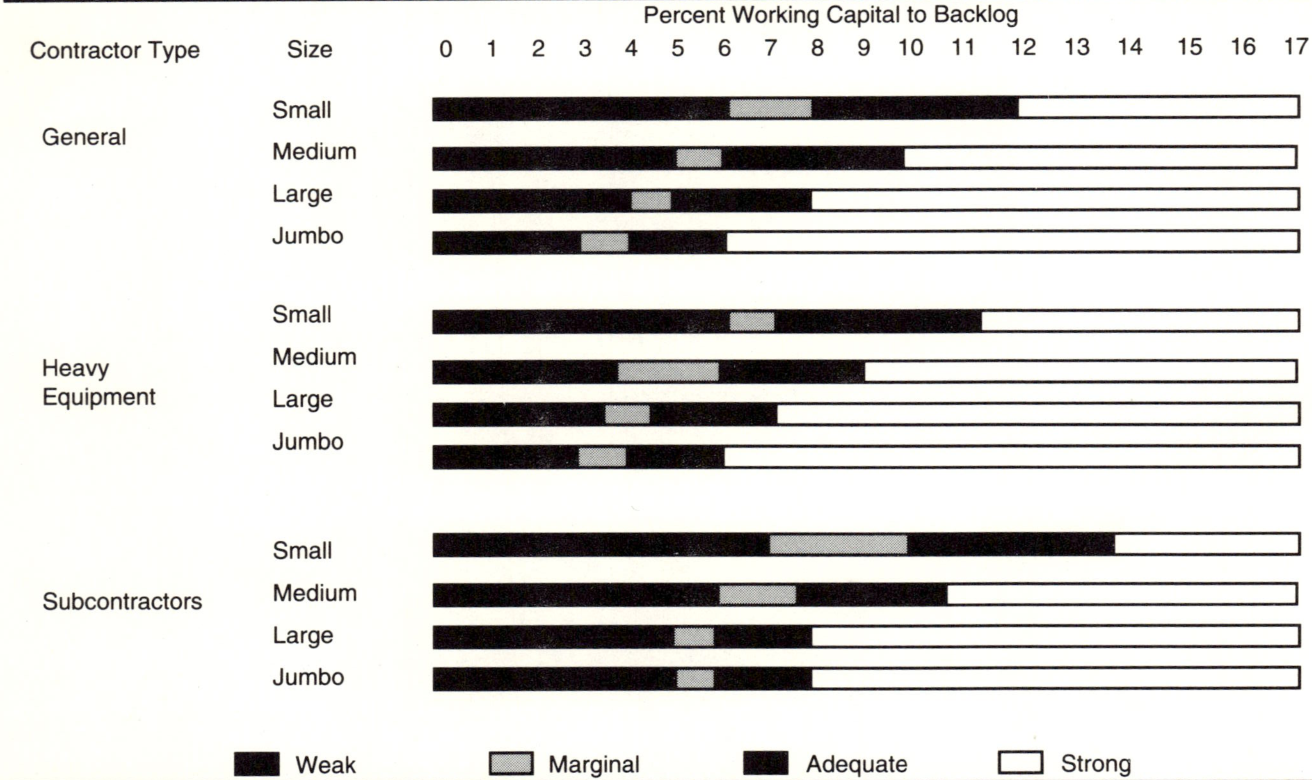

Reprinted with permission of CIGNA Bond Services.

Exhibit 4-6
Schedule of Position

CONTRACTOR ________

SCHEDULE OF POSITION ON COMPLETED AND UNCOMPLETED PROJECTS
(To include all costs, bonded and unbonded, over ________)
(Projects ________ and under may be assembled as one project)

REPORT AS OF ________

LAST REPORT AS OF ________

JOB NUMBER/NAME	A CONTRACT PRICE (Including Change Orders)	B BILLED TO DATE (Including Percentages)	C COSTS TO DATE (Including Sub-Percentages)	D REVISED ESTIMATED COST TO COMPLETE	E REVISED TOTAL ESTIMATED COST OF PROJECT (C + D)	F % COMPLETE (C + B)	G TOTAL ESTIMATED GROSS PROFIT (LOSS) REVISED (A – E)	H ESTIMATED GROSS PROFIT EARNED TO DATE (F + G)	I EXCESS OF BILLINGS OVER (UNDER) COSTS (B - C)	J OVERBILLED (UNDERBILLED) (I – H)	K ORIGINAL ESTIMATED GROSS PROFIT	EST COMPL DATE

PROJECTS COMPLETED SINCE PRIOR REPORT

JOB NUMBER/NAME	FINAL CONTRACT PRICE	TOTAL COST	FINAL GROSS PROFIT (LOSS)	ORIGINAL GROSS PROFIT	DATE JOB ACCEPTED BY OWNER

COMMENTS/REMARKS

REPORT PREPARED BY: ________

TITLE: ________

- Amount billed to date
- Costs to date
- Revised estimated costs to complete

The underwriter first looks to see how much profit the contractor earned on jobs that are not yet complete, since that figure depends heavily on the contractor's estimate of the final outcome. Profit on jobs that are closer to completion is a more accurate figure than those in early stages. Reported profit earned on completed or nearly completed jobs is a much more reliable indication of cash assets than expected or estimated profit derived principally from substantially unfinished work. This is why most underwriters insist on receiving audited financial statements prepared by professional CPAs who specialize in auditing contractors. A CPA's audit confirms that a contractor's estimates are reasonable.

Underwriters look at past profit margins on jobs that are similar in size, type, and duration to the current work. If they find that profit margins on prior jobs were quite a bit lower than what the contractor estimates for the current work in progress, the contractor and CPA will be requested to explain and justify the apparently optimistic forecast.

Overbillings. A contractor who bills an owner for more than the costs incurred to date on a job is in an *overbilled position*. It is a common and accepted practice to *front load* or submit an "unbalanced bid," that is, to bill an owner more on items that appear early in the project schedule, and then bill correspondingly less on items that appear later in the performance of a contract.

For example, an early item, such as clearing/grubbing and site preparation, might represent 2 percent of the total cost of a project. The contractor might front load a bid by charging 4 percent. Then, on a later item, say finishing carpentry with an actual cost of 4 percent, the contractor would bill the owner for only 2 percent, thereby balancing the "unbalanced" bid. The contractor has not overcharged the owner, but has recovered more costs in the early phases to offset the initial costs of preparing the estimates and bid. These costs are not included in the itemized contract estimate.

This practice of overbilling is not inappropriate. Owners are aware of it and are generally willing to accept it, up to a point, as an equitable practice. If a contractor becomes aggressive in overbilling to the point where the owner believes that the overbilling is excessive, then the owner is likely to object and perhaps refuse to pay the overbilled amount.

Experience has taught surety underwriters that a contractor who has some losing jobs that were overbilled in their early stages may bid low on new work in order to create new overbilling to cover the cash flow deficit in the later stages of the losing jobs. This may be the cause of aggressive overbilling.

Sureties accept an overbilled condition so long as the contractor keeps the funds liquid and does not withdraw the overbilled funds from the business. If the contractor withdraws the overbilled amount, invests it in fixed assets, or uses it to cover cash flow deficits of losing jobs, the surety would become alarmed at the strong possibility that the overbilled funds will not be available to put back into the job when needed and that it will have to pay some of the contractor's bills.

Underbillings. *Underbilling* exists when a contractor incurs more costs on a job than have been billed to the owner. Underbilling may be intended to offset earlier overbilling amounts, or it might reflect some difficulty on the job. If the job is a loser and the contractor has not yet recognized that fact in revised profit estimates, the losses may appear first as underbillings. If there is a dispute with the owner or some items of work have not been done properly, the contractor might have incurred costs that cannot be billed, which would show up as underbillings. Unbilled change orders can also be a source of underbilling and may reflect poor administration on the job.

Certainly the small profit margins available today in most sectors of the construction market will not support contractors financing owners' projects. A contractor who is underbilled on a project has made a financial investment in the job and is carrying part of the financing by investing money in the job. Further, unless a provision for cost of funds has been included in the project estimate, the contractor is making an interest-free, unsecured loan to the owner. This is an unwise business practice.

Underbillings are a cause for surety underwriters' concern. Most contractors are not sufficiently capitalized to finance any portion of a project beyond the initial startup. Net underbillings at the middle or later stages of a project are a harbinger of loss and may suggest significant problems. As a result, sureties and the American Institute of Certified Public Accountants Guidelines require work-in-progress schedules to be included in contractors' audited financial statements. In addition, underwriters may ask for quarterly schedules of work on hand so that they can keep abreast of changes in the profit and billing status of the contractor's work program and the current backlog level.

Underwriting the Contract Document

The contract required of the contractor by the owner, obligee, or by statute is first presented in the form of the bid specifications and general terms and conditions. The underwriter should determine if the contractor is familiar with the type of work at hand, but many other portions of the contract also interest the underwriter as indicated by the following questions:

- Are there clauses included that are as yet untried in the law—new requirements inserted for the exclusive benefit of the owner?
- Has the contractor considered these clauses in the bid?
- Are new legal requirements of the locale where the contract will be performed contrary to standard practice? Some of the current federal grant programs require that a portion of the work using grant funds be assigned to a minority contractor or supplier. The underwriter would want to ask the following related question: Is a minority contractor available for the work, or must one be brought in from beyond the immediate vicinity at a higher cost than anticipated?
- How soon must the contract be completed?
- Is a shutdown allowed for winter snow or other unfavorable weather conditions?

The underwriter also must address the contract provisions for completing the work on time. If the work is not finished, the standard solutions are *liquidated damages* (a reasonable sum that the parties stipulated in advance) or a *penalty clause* (generally an amount per day for each day the work is not done). Nebulous, uncommon damage clauses leave the contractor uncertain as to the amount of money due in the event of failure to complete the project on time. With a penalty clause, the contractor can at least build in costs for time beyond that which is allowed if it is known at the beginning that more time will likely be needed.

In most contracts the owner requires a *maintenance clause* or guarantee from the contractor as to the fitness of the contractor's work. The most common guarantee provides that the work will be free from poor workmanship and defective material for at least one year from the acceptance date of the contract. This guarantee is so standard that it is included in the performance bond rate. The exact wording of the clause is important. Contractors should read it carefully, and underwriters should be aware of every maintenance clause in order to be certain that the standard acceptable level of maintenance, and not a higher standard, is contemplated.

Although not common, *efficiency guarantees* present a much greater risk. These guarantees state that the completed project will function up to specific standards as required. If it does not, the contractor will redo the work until it is acceptable. As a result, the contractor may become responsible for the design of the project and errors of the engineer, architect, or inventor. The contract becomes virtually impossible to price under these conditions and is a very high surety risk. Exceptions to this rule exist in roofing contracts, where the manufacturer of the roofing product may guarantee the material. In this case, the obligation of the contractor is to install the product properly. This arrangement is fair to all concerned since the manufacturer is in the business of manufacturing roofing materials designed to last many years, and the contractor is in the business of properly installing roofs on buildings.

Maintenance periods of other than one year can be written successfully when the contractor is financially strong and willing to pay the additional charges typically associated with the extended period of maintenance. Reduced rates apply when the owner withholds *retainages* until the maintenance period is finished.

Owners commonly withhold retainages of 10 percent from payments of estimates due contractors on bonded jobs. The billing presented by the contractor is limited to the work actually completed. Payment is generally made, less the 10 percent retention, within the month. Each month a new bill is presented. The owner frequently, but not always, reduces the amount of retained percentages to 5 percent or less when the original work is 50 percent completed.

Retained percentages in excess of 15 percent create a hardship on most contractors, since any retainage in effect requires the contractor to partially finance the construction project. From the underwriter's viewpoint, reasonable retainage ensures that the surety has some money available if the contractor cannot complete the project.

Owners make progress payments on some construction projects as contractors reach different stages of construction when each stage is easily ascertainable and when monthly billing would be difficult to estimate accurately. This *milestone* arrangement is typical for projects too small for cost accounting or when similar units are being built one after the other.

Monitoring Underwriting Information

The underwriter receives many different types of information relating to the contract. This information must be organized and kept for future reference. A contractor's status, as well as conditions for a project, can change from day to day. The underwriter must, therefore, monitor all data closely and continuously. One surety company uses the contract summary form in Exhibit 4-7 for this purpose. Some of the information is summary data from items previously discussed, and some information is not available until the bid results are obtained. Contractor and subcontractor bidding results also have places on this form. Bids that reflect differences in excess of 10 percent generally need an explanation. The surety may require bids differing by more than 15 percent to be re-estimated, and other bonding can be restricted until the contractor is proven capable of making a profit on this job.

Exhibit 4-7
Underwriter's Contract Summary Form

APPLICANT	NAME AND ADDRESS	( ) INDIVIDUAL ( ) PARTNERSHIP ( ) CORPORATION ( ) JOINT VENTURE	SUBMITTED BY DATE UNIFORM COMMERCIAL CODE FILING? ☐ YES ☐ NO ☐ BLANKET ☐ SPECIFIC
OBLIGEE	NAME AND ADDRESS		APPROVED DECLINED
PROJECT			REMARKS

BOND DATA		OTHER BIDDERS	BIDS
	BID DATE		$
	BID BOND		$
	PERF BOND		$
	PAYT BOND		$
	MAINT (NO YRS)	ENGINEER'S ESTIMATE	$

	WORK SUBLET DESCRIPTION	BONDED?	AMOUNT
CONTRACT PRICE $			
COMPLETION TIME			
PENALTY $			
PAYMENTS (How Made? Cash?)		TOTAL	$

WORK ON HAND (INCLUDE OUT-STANDING BIDS AND THOSE TO BE BID)	DESCRIPTION AND LOCATION OF WORK	COST PLUS OR LUMP SUM	BIDS IN LINE?	CONTRACT PRICE	% COMP	AMT UNCOMPLETED
				$		$
				$		$
				$		$
				$		$
	SPECIAL EQUIPMENT—SPECIAL HAZARDS? (For Either new Job or Work on Hand			PLUS NEW CONTRACT		$
				TOTAL UNCOMPLETED WORK		$

Experience				
	LARGEST PREVIOUS CONTRACT	CONTRACT PRICE $	KIND OF WORK	DATE COMPLETED
	LARGEST PREVIOUS WORK PROGRAM	AMOUNT $	KIND OF WORK	DATE PERFORMED

Financial Information (STATEMENT ON REVERSE SIDE)					
	BANK CREDIT (Amt., Name of Bank, How Secured)		D & B RATING		STATEMENT DATE
		CURRENT ASSETS	$	TOTAL ASSETS	$
	INDEMNITY	CURRENT LIAB	$	TOTAL LIAB	$
		NET QUICK ASSETS	$	NET WORTH OR STKHDRS EQUITY	$

It is also possible that the surety will forfeit the bid bond if the contractor cannot expect to complete the job for the bid price and the amount of the difference between bid prices is more than the amount of the bid bond. However, forfeiture does not often happen. The contractor must still pay the penalty since the surety would have an indemnity agreement with the contractor.

Exhibit 4-7 also includes a section on work-on-hand. This section is not a complete analysis of work-on-hand, but a brief list of the incomplete work, including work under bid but not yet awarded.

A review of this list gives some indication of the size of the work program, including the current bid which would show if the work program and the job size are stretching the contractor's financial ability. If the contractor is overextended, underwriters may restrict future bidding to smaller jobs until the work program is reduced or the contractor demonstrates that larger jobs and programs can be profitably undertaken.

Although underwriters have rules about acceptable sizes of jobs or programs, they must use them with caution today in light of the inflationary economy. For example, one underwriter might base decisions on the rule that a single job size or uncompleted program not exceed ten times available working capital. Others, however, have been cautioned against using this rule. The choice depends on company philosophy, the underwriter, and the situation.

A careful analysis of net quick assets balanced with the review of net worth, and a comparison of those figures in a prior accounting period indicates trends are more valuable than rules of thumb. Chapters 5 and 6 describe in greater depth accounting and financial statements as well as ratio analysis. Some underwriters prefer the use of ratios while others prefer to stay with dollar amounts. National financial averages such as those Dun & Bradstreet publishes provide the underwriter with information for comparison of the contractor under consideration with other contractors. Locality differences, labor negotiations pending, and individual contractor characteristics are additional considerations in evaluating the contractor's financial status.

Indemnity Agreements

Another underwriting consideration is the strength of indemnitors. An *indemnitor* is someone who agrees to stand behind the contractor and lend financial support to the surety on the contractor's behalf. Indemnitors are typically the majority owners (and spouses) of the firm, but they also can be third parties. Personal assets outside the firm may help make a strong case better, but they never make a weak case sound. If owners are not willing to stand behind their own firms, it is unlikely that the surety will wish to continue the relationship.

The purpose of requiring a written indemnity agreement is to ease and increase the ways for the surety to obtain relief and to maintain the indemnitor's interest in seeing that the bonded contracts are performed. In most cases the surety has a right at law to be reimbursed for the loss it pays, but some owners of construction companies may attempt to use the corporate structure to avoid personal losses. If they will not indemnify a surety willingly, they may not find a surety willing to bond their firm.

Extending a Line of Credit

A contractor sometimes may want an indication of the size of work program the surety believes the contractor can handle and how big a job the surety is willing to bond both currently and in the future. Most underwriters can indicate ranges of job sizes and work programs that are acceptable to the surety, and some sureties will extend a line of credit to bond a contractor's future projects.

Distinct from discussions about what projects a surety will approve are the negotiations between underwriters and producers concerning limitations of a contractor's capacity. These negotiations give the producer or local underwriter reference points from which to decide whether a given job is pushing the higher limits of the contractor's capabilities. Generally, the contractor is aware of these limitations long before the surety company must express its views. A contractor's lack of awareness of capacity limitations is an underwriting consideration.

When the surety extends a line of credit for future jobs, periodic analysis of work in progress by the surety is necessary to monitor the credit line. The extra work associated with document preparation when a surety extends a credit line makes credit line availability more attractive to large contractors who bid frequently and who regularly provide comprehensive work-in-progress information.

Sufficient Underwriting Time

Because the financial risks of underwriting contract bonds can be great, the underwriter should take all the time needed to give each application the most complete consideration. The underwriter must weigh the pressure to complete the application review against the need for information and the cooperation needed from the contractor and should follow standard guidelines in reviewing the application.

Information Need Versus Time Pressures. Probably no single mistake has hurt contractors more than hurrying underwriters and giving them less than the necessary information when considering a bid. This is particularly true with new firms or with firms getting their first bonds. Since producers usually do not have the authority to write contract bonds without the consent of the underwriter, and since some producers handle so few bond accounts, delay may result. Neither the producer nor the contractor may expect this delay.

Communicating the need for appropriate and sufficient information to contractors has been a goal of all the major surety company underwriters. Even with all required papers in hand, the surety still may need a week or more to consider a new account. The underwriter must follow guidelines when reviewing an account and may have to seek additional information for review and acceptance.

Cooperation Needed. In most cases, the longer a surety works with a principal, particularly a contractor, the better able the surety is to provide service on a timely and informed basis. The close relationship between a surety and a contractor requires a high degree of mutual cooperation. Work increases as a construction firm prospers, and the complexity of information required for the surety grows with the contractor's increasing management skills. Switching sureties causes the evaluation process to go back to ground zero. Yet many firms change sureties because they believe that a new surety will look at the situation differently and be inclined to extend more bonding credit.

Rule-of-Thumb Guidelines. The importance of rule-of-thumb underwriting guidelines is best illustrated by an example. One underwriter in a surety branch office some years ago compared his decisions with another underwriter over a period of weeks. The decisions all related to first bond submissions for new accounts. Both underwriters had the same information and had worked for the company for about the same length of time. Neither ever agreed on what the most significant reason for a declination was; yet, each always declined the same accounts. On accounts they decided to accept, they generally agreed on approximate line of credit limitations. The use of similar underwriting guidelines in establishing limitations therefore guards against making underwriting decisions for purely subjective reasons and establishes a standard for accepting accounts.

SBA Surety Bond Guarantee Program

The federal government is involved in surety bonding through the *Small Business Administration (SBA) Surety Bond Guarantee Program*. The purpose of the program is to make surety bonds available to small business applicants through a government guarantee program.

A 1970 amendment to the Small Business Act of 1958 (15 U.S.C. 694a-c) established SBA's program to provide financial help for small businesses in the federal procurement market for construction and nonfederal markets requiring bonding. The SBA can guarantee up to 90 percent of a surety's losses on bonds issued to small businesses that otherwise could not obtain bonding without the SBA guarantee. SBA regulations allow a 90 percent bond guarantee for all contracts (1) of $100,000 or less or (2) awarded to small, disadvantaged firms. Contracts between $100,000 and $1.25 million awarded to nonminority contractors are guaranteed at not more than 80 percent.[1]

The government initially intended that the SBA program would encourage emerging minority contractors. The program now assists construction firms that are deemed capable of building the type of work they wish to bid, but for whom the financial qualifications are a bit riskier than a surety underwriter would accept. In effect, the federal government becomes a financial risk bearer similar to a reinsurer. In order to qualify, the contractor must meet all qualifications set by the surety and the SBA. The process of submission and review involves additional time for approval and a great deal of paperwork. However, the requirements help the contractor learn about the financial responsibilities involved in the work desired.

Contractors who take advantage of this program must show a potential for graduation from the program. In theory, if a firm cannot increase its management capability and grow without continuing assistance, it cannot continue to participate in the program. In practice, contractors are seldom dropped from the program so long as they continue to qualify as a "small" business.

The SBA charges 20 percent of the premium and assumes the agreed upon 80 or 90 percent of the losses. This program is not an assigned risk program, but a shared effort between industry and government to solve a problem neither can effectively solve alone.

Role of Insurance in Credit Prequalification

In response to the litigiousness of American society, the insurance industry has raised premiums, restricted some coverages, and limited the availability of liability insurance. This situation has created a tendency for design firm professionals and owners to pass liability on to contractors by writing strict hold-harmless agreements into their contracts. These clauses hold the contractor financially responsible for any harm to third parties arising out of the design or construction of the project—without regard to negligence. Some prime contractors, in turn, try to pass this risk on to their subcontractors.

A single uninsured claim could financially devastate a contractor. The mere cost of defending a liability suit, even if the contractor is not found at fault, can be financially debilitating. Accordingly, underwriters must screen contracts carefully for contractual liability and hold-harmless clauses. When these clauses exist, underwriters may insist that they be removed or require evidence of the contractor's liability insurance protection. If neither requirement is met, they may refuse to write the bond.

Accommodation Underwriting

There is a significant credit risk associated with bonding construction contractors. Owners rely on the surety to prequalify contractors and to eliminate contractors who lack the qualifications for performance of the contract. For these reasons, it would be economically unsound and morally wrong for a surety to provide its guarantee in the absence of prequalification, or as an accommodation to other business considerations on behalf of the contractor or the surety producer.

For other than contract bonds, where the bond penalty is relatively small and the underlying obligation is routine, sureties will in some cases write bonds as an accommodation to a customer or agent who brings them a substantial volume of other insurance or surety business. This is called *accommodation underwriting*. The underwriter's consideration here is whether the surety can sustain a loss on the bond as an accommodation and still profit from the overall business relationship with the contractor or surety producer.

CHARLES SQUARE EXCAVATING—A CASE STUDY

The following hypothetical case study is based on the application for bid bond (Exhibit 4-8) and financial statements (Exhibit 4-9) of Charles Square.

Charles Square is thirty years old and relatively inexperienced. The following review of the supporting documents (Exhibits 4-8 and 4-9) of the case identify the points in favor of and against writing the bond. The reader should then compare the pluses and minuses and decide whether the surety should guarantee Charles' work.

Positive Features

The first item on the application is that the applicant's business and the bonding agency are located in the same city. This means that a local producer is working with Square and is probably very well aware of his personal background. There is also a relatively small bid bond of $5,000 and a contract bond of $50,000. The bond is to the local city Department of Public Works. Since it is a bid bond, Square does not yet have the job, so there is time to use this fact as a point for evaluation. These are all points in favor of the account.

In line eight of the application, notice that the contract calls for hauling cinders already purchased, so no credit guarantee on the purchase price is involved. The contract involves only hauling. In line nine, notice that the estimate of cost by the city engineer and the contractor are the same. The next item in favor of this contract is that the work is to be completed in the relatively near future, i.e., by the last snowfall. The contractor does not have to worry about a long delay in time before payments are made because payments are to be made as billed. In line seventeen, notice that the retainage is 5 percent, not an unusual amount. In line twenty-four, the information about contract work underway indicates that a substantial amount of the work this contractor normally does must occur during good-weather months. The new job can be done during his off season.

Under the section entitled, "Experience," notice that the contractor has several years of experience and has done several jobs for the same people. This means his customers must have thought enough of him to call him back for a second job. Nevertheless, it is customary for the surety to request reference letters from previous customers. In line thirty-two, it is clear that the principal's age is not a problem because he has been working in the construction field for six years and has worked with his father, who has been in the business for many years.

In the general section, line thirty-five shows that the contractor thinks his bank has a great deal of faith in him. This is an advantage since it means he has confidence in his bank, and his bank has confidence in him. Notice in line forty-three that several of the types of references given are appropriate for a contractor. He did not put down, for instance, his pastor and his doctor, but professional people in the building trade.

Turning now to the financial statement (Exhibit 4-9), notice that the good points here appear to be a relatively substantial amount of cash in the bank and a relatively small amount of current accounts payable. Notice also that, while there is a substantial note payable to the bank, it is due on equipment notes, and the equipment book value is considerably higher than the amount of the note. The same condition is true for the real estate; although there is an encumbrance, it is not nearly as high as the value listed on the real estate. In the final pages of the financial statement, notice that the contractor carries some life and fire insurance.

Negative Features

This is the first time this individual has been bonded. It appears to be the first time he has undertaken this type of work. It also may be the first time he has given an estimate. Therefore, the underwriter may be relying exclusively on the engineer's estimate, and the contractor may not be capable of accurately bidding the job. Although the application indicates that payments will be made when billed, customers may delay payment. As a result, there may be cash flow problems. The contractor's cash position must be excellent in order to withstand delays, and his financial statement indicates that this may not be so.

The general quality of the information in the application and the fact that this person was never previously bonded should warn the underwriter that there are certain things that need careful review with a good insurance producer. For instance, the limit of liability in line twenty-eight for general liability insurance is far too low for today's environment. The same is true for the property damage liability limit. The auto liability limit, although more realistic, is still probably not high enough, and it could realistically be two or three times higher.

A hold-harmless agreement is in effect for which there is no insurance, and this is indeed a weak point. The individual probably presumes that since he has completed the question on this application, the firm with which he has his insurance would automatically make an endorsement. This probably will not happen unless the producer is very close to the account and has carefully reviewed the application.

A disadvantage offsets the previously noted advantage with regard to banking facilities. The principal may be disappointed when he finds that First City State Bank and Trust Company will not give him whatever amount he needs. Although they have expressed a confidence in his financial standing, they have not made any written disclosure that would indicate the amount of credit line established.

The financial statement itself has significant disadvantages. Although it appears to be carefully thought out, the statement is not fully audited. Therefore, it is not clear that the person completing the information was indeed qualified to do so. As a result, numerous items will have to be verified. There is no indication that the book value of equipment or real estate is realistic. In addition, the accounts receivable are not thoroughly aged, although it appears that some of the accounts are quite old.

Finally, the end of the financial statement in the section on life insurance shows that Charles does not have nearly enough life insurance for family use, let alone for business use. The fire insurance limit on his house is not as high as the amount of value listed on the financial statement. With replacement cost insurance being available, full replacement cost insurance should be considered, if possible, for $80,000 rather than $64,000 as listed. If Charles has chosen inappropriate risk retention amounts on his personal insurance, this may reflect inappropriate judgment, generally, on his part.

Given the preceding information, the reader should decide whether a bond should be issued for this contractor. A solution for this case is not presented because, under certain conditions and in certain territories, a bond could be written. Under other conditions in other territories, this submission would be unacceptable.

Exhibit 4-8
Application for Contract or Bid Bond

hereon listed, it will be necessary to return this blank for completion.

APPLICATION FOR CONTRACT OR BID BOND **Bond No.**..................

Agent ....Bonding Agency of First City.................... Location ....49 Church St.................

NOTE—Copy of Contract, Specifications, Plans, Bond Form required (in case Bid Bond, Advertisement and Instructions to bidders), and Applicant's Financial Statement must accompany this Application and all questions be fully answered.

1. Full name of Applicant....Charles Square Excavating.................... Age ....30....
   (If corporation, give exact corporate title)
2. Business address (street, city and state)....R. D. # 4, First City....................
3. If Applicant is a firm, name all partners of firm; if a corporation, name principal officers and directors.

NAME	AGE	ADDRESS
Charles Square	30	

4. Bonds required; Bid **Proposal Bond, $**....5,000. (10%)....; **Contract Bond, $**....estimated $50,000.
   Labor and Material Bond, $....estimated $50,000....; **Maintenance Bond, $**....5,000.....
5. To whom is bond to be given?....First City Department of Public Works....
   (Give full name and address. If a corporation, give exact title)
   Address ....4 Court House Square, First City....................

NOTE—If the required information is not given in response to the questions

6. If bond applied for is Proposal Bond, will it operate as a final bond? no Date of Bid one week from today

Date Bids to be Opened bid day Approximate amount of bid $ 50,000.

If bond applied for is Performance Bond, how was Bid secured? will be by this bid bond

7. **Amount of Contract: $** .... **Date awarded** to be 30 days after bid date **Date of Contract** ....
(If contract price is per unit of measure, give also probable total of contract)

8. Nature of Contract (Give concise description of proposed work and locality) hauling cinders already purchased by First City from County Utility Power plant

9. Name and address of Architect or Engineer in charge City Engineer

What is his estimate of cost of work? $ 50,000. Your estimate? $ 50,000.

10. **Other Bidders** on above contract including highest and lowest:

NAME	ADDRESS	BID
1.		
2.		
3.		
4.		
5.		

If more than five bids, tabulate them on separate paper and attach to above

Continued on next page

TERMS OF CONTRACT

11. Date work is to be commenced........first snow........Date work is to be completed........last snow of season or pile runs out.

12. Penalty for non-completion on time........Premium for advance completion........

13. Is there a strike clause in the contract?........no........An arbitration provision?........no........

14. Payments, when to be made on contract?........when billed........

15. Amount of advance payment, if any $........none........

16. Are payments to be made wholly in cash?........yes........ If not, in what?........

If payments are in stocks, bonds, warrants or other securities, advise fully what arrangements made for disposing of same ....

17. Percentage reserved from payments until completion........5%........

18. How long must work be kept in **Repair** after completion? ....none........

Is this **Repair or Maintenance** guarantee limited to defects in workmanship or materials? ....

If not, describe guarantee fully........

19. Will construction bond remain in force for the maintenance, repair or guarantee period?........N/A........

If not, will separate bond be required?........ and in what amount? $........

20. What portion of work is guaranteed after completion and value of same? ....N/A........

....

Percentage of payments retained until expiration of maintenance period? ....

21. State approximate amount of this contract which will be **Sublet $** none, and describe below the principal **Sub-Contracts:**

AMOUNT	CHARACTER OF WORK	NAME OF SUB-CONTRACTOR	ADDRESS	BONDED?

If more than five sub-contracts tabulate them on separate sheet and attach to above

22. Have you purchased or made binding contracts for the materials needed for this contract, and within your estimates? N/A

23. How are deliveries assured to you? N/A City owned cinders

24. Give information below about all your **Contract Work Under Way,** or for which you are committed.

	CONTRACT PRICE	KIND OF CONSTRUCTION	LOCATION OF WORK	SURETY	% COMPLETED	Expected Completion Date	NAME AND ADDRESS ENGINEER OR ARCHITECT
a.	1,500.each	five home	sewer systems per	month, next	four	months	Modern Homes
b.	1,200.	farm pond	south of town 6 miles	none	just	started	Walter Hinds
c.							
d.							
e.							

Continued on next page

questions hereon listed, it will be necessary to return this blank for completion.

25. Have you applied to any other company for this bond? no State name of company and reasons why declined none

26. Give names of surety companies with which you have previously dealt never previously bonded

27. Do you carry Fidelity Bonds on your employees who handle funds? no

28. State amount and character of Insurance you will carry on this contract and name of company issuing each policy. Fire, $ none (Amount); (Company); Compensation, $ statutory (Amount); Yours (Company); Windstorm or Extended Coverage $ (Amount); General Liability $ 25/50,000 (Amount); General Property Damage $ 5,000 (Amount); Automobile Liability $ 50/100,000 (Limits); Automobile Property Damage $ 10,000 (Limits); Owners Protective Liability $ none (Limits); Owners Protective Property Damage $ none (Limits);

Does contract contain a "hold harmless" agreement under which you agree to indemnify and hold harmless the Owner for any claims for personal injury or property damage? yes If so, have you had your Liability and Property Damage policy specially endorsed to protect you? no, please do.

Will any explosives be used in performing the contract? no If so, have you arranged to have your General Liability and Property Damage Policies endorsed to provide coverage? no, please do.

NOTE— If the required information is not given in response to the

EXPERIENCE

29. How many years have you been in business under your present name? two, three before as partner

30. What projects have you completed in your own name? regular sewer jobs for homes gravel hauling

CONTRACT AMOUNT	CLASS OF WORK	WHEN COMPLETED	NAME AND ADDRESS OF OWNER
3,500	excavation for G. Hand	last year	G. Hand, First City
5,000	gravel hauling, G.Hand	this spring	G. Hand, First City
10,000	septic sewers	last year and this	Modern Homes

31. Have you or any of your associates ever failed to complete any work awarded to you or to any organization with which you or they have been connected? If so, where and why? no

32. What is the construction experience of the principal individuals of your organization?

INDIVIDUAL'S NAME	PRESENT POSITION OR OFFICE	YEARS OF CONSTRUCTION EXPERIENCE	MAGNITUDE AND TYPE OF WORK	IN WHAT CAPACITY
Charles Square	owner	6	all levels	various
Adam Square	father of owner	35 years	foreman, Gen. Const. Co.	

GENERAL

33. Is your present plant sufficient for this contract? yes Estimated cost to put it in good shape for this work, $........ State what new plant will be purchased, advising cost and how you will pay for same (Use separate sheet if necessary) ....

Continued on next page

34. With what bank have you arranged a loan for the purpose of handling this contract? First City State Bank & Trust

35. What is the amount of such loan? $ whatever we'll need

36. What security, if any, has the bank required for the loan? signature

37. When and how must you repay the loan? as we get paid

38. Have you assigned or will you assign to other than your surety your payments on this or any other contract or any part thereof? no

39. Are you having **any** controversy with **anyone** over **any** contract or payment of labor or material bills on **any** contract? no

40. Are there **any** mechanics' liens filed on **any** of your work anywhere? no

41. Are there any judgments, suits or claims pending against you? no

42. Are you interested in more than one line of business? yes If so, give particulars we'll consider each job on its own basis

43. References: Give only Engineers or Architects, or Owners, for whom you have done work:

NAME	ADDRESS	BUSINESS
Edward Short, President	First City State Bank & Trust	
Matthew Modern	Locust Street, First City	Owner, Modern Homes
Philip Price	City Hall	City Engineer
Mark Everhart	Lincoln Ave., First City	Architect

The undersigned does or do hereby represent that the statements made . . .

. . . and shall be liberally construed as against the undersigned.

Signed, sealed and dated this Dec. 6 this year **day of** ...., **19**........

If Individual sign here:

Witness: Linda Taylor .... Charles Square ....(Seal)

If Co-Partnership sign here:

Witness: ....(Seal)

........................(Seal)
(Individually and as a co-partner)

........................(Seal)
(Individually and as a co-partner)

........................(Seal)
(Individually and as a co-partner)

If Corporation sign here:

....
(Name of corporation)

Attest: .... *Secretary* By .... *President*

Continued on next page

ADDITIONAL INDEMNITY

In consideration of THE IIA CASUALTY INSURANCE COMPANY executing or procuring the execution of the bond or bonds herein applied for, the undersigned, jointly and severally, does or do join in the foregoing agreement; and the undersigned, if a corporation, warrants that it is financially interested in the performance of the obligation which said bond or bonds applied for are given to secure, and asserts that it is fully empowered to obligate itself thereby; and the undersigned, warrant(s) that the undersigned has or have a substantial, material and beneficial interest in the obtaining of said bond or bonds, and join(s) in the foregoing agreement as an inducement to THE IIA CASUALTY INSURANCE COMPANY to execute said bond or bonds.

The provisions of Section 204.075, Wisconsin Statutes, are hereby specifically waived, if applicable.

.... **(Seal)** Charles Square, First City .... **(Seal)**
(Indemnitors Signature and Address) **(Indemnitors Signature and Address)**

.... **(Seal)** .... **(Seal)**
(Indemnitors Signature and Address) **(Indemnitors Signature and Address)**

.... **(Seal)** .... **(Seal)**
(Indemnitors Signature and Address) **(Indemnitors Signature and Address)**

INDEMNITOR(S) ACKNOWLEDGEMENT MUST BE NOTARIZED

STATE OF Incorporation } ss:
COUNTY OF Harmony }

On this Dec. 6 this year day of ...., 19........, before me personally appeared

Charles Square

to me known to be the person(s) or member(s) of the partnership or officer(s) of the corporation that signed the foregoing instrument and acknowledged the execution of the same to me.

Betty May Smith

If Indemnitor is a corporation, a certified copy of resolution of Board of Directors authorizing officers to execute agreement must accompany this application.

Exhibit 4-9
Financial Statement of Charles Square

FINANCIAL STATEMENT

Name: Charles Square

Business Address: R. D. # 4 (Street) First City (City) (State)

Statement of Assets and Liabilities as of Dec. 31 **19** last year
Insert date, otherwise statement will be returned.

This statement must be made up by Applicant, his or its Bookkeeper. Agents not allowed to do this.

Assets	$	¢	Liabilities	$	¢
Cash in Bank (as per Schedule "A")	7,384	00	**Notes Payable** (as per Schedule "I"):		
Cash on Hand	300	00	(a) To Banks Regular	157,395	00
Certified Checks deposited with bids			(b) To Banks for Certified Checks		
Stocks, Bonds, etc. (as per Schedule "B")			(c) To Material Furnishers		
Accounts Receivable from completed contracts, including retainage and excluding claims not approved for payment (as per Schedule "C")	9,845	00	(d) To Others (exclusive of equipment)		
Earned Estimates and Retainage on uncompleted contracts shown by Engineers' or Architects' estimates (as per Schedule "D")			**Equipment Notes Due Within One Year** (as per Schedule "G")		
Work Performed and Unbilled (as per Schedule "D")	1,000	00	**Owing Sub-Contractors,** Account of Retained Percentage, Earned Estimates and Work Performed and Unbilled (as per Schedule "J")		
Other Accounts Receivable (as per Schedule "E")			**Accounts Payable** (as per Schedule "K")	3,363	00
Materials in Stock not included in any items above (present value)			(a) Not Past Due $3,363.		
			(b) Past Due $		

Continued on next page

Assets			Liabilities		
(a) Available for Contracts Under Way $			**Income Taxes:**		
(b) Other Materials ..$			(a) Unpaid balance under Filed Returns		
Total Current Assets			(b) Reserve or Estimated Amount Payable on Profit for Period Immediately Preceding		
FIXED ASSETS					
Notes Receivable (as per Schedule "F")			**Miscellaneous Taxes** and other Accruals		
Equipment at Book Value (as per Schedule "G")	253,129	00	**Total Current Liabilities**		
Real Estate (as per Schedule "H")			**Equipment Notes Due After One Year** (as per Schedule "G")		
Used for Business ..Value $					
Homestead ....Value $ 80,000	80,000	00			
Held as Investment. Value $			**Encumbrance on Real Estate** (as per Schedule "H")	15,000	00
All Other Assets (explain fully if credit expected)			**All Other Liabilities**		
Car and furniture	5,000	00	**Capital Stock** (paid up) if a corporation		
			Surplus and Undivided Profits		
Total Assets			**Total Liabilities**		

CONTINGENT LIABILITIES

Are there any judgments, suits or claims pending against you? no

Have any of your notes or accounts receivable, or retained percentages been assigned, pledged, sold or discounted? no If so, explain fully

Are you acting as surety or bondsman for others, or as indorser on their notes or accounts? no

....

Are there any liens for labor or materials filed on any of your work anywhere? ......no......

....

Are you having any controversy with any one over any contract or payment of labor or materials on any contract?

....

..........no..........

Have you any other contingent liabilities? ....no..........

STATEMENT OF EARNINGS

For period beginning ......1-1...... 19..last year.., and ending ......12/31 last year...... 19.......

Gross Revenue		$ 153,946.
Direct Costs	$....................	
General and Administrative Expenses (including all depreciation)	$....................	$ 107,420.
Profit before Income Taxes		$ 46,526
Federal and State Income Taxes **Reserved and/or Paid** on Above Profit		$ 23,096
Net Profit		$ 23,430

Dividends Paid $.................... **List Net Profits by years for the four preceding years:**

19......., $ 11,500. ; 19......., $....................; 19......., $....................; 19......., $....................

Continued on next page

SCHEDULE "A"

NAME OF BANK	LOCATION	AMOUNT ON DEPOSIT
First City State Bank & Trust	Church Street	$ 5,280 savings
		2,104 checking

SCHEDULE "B"—STOCKS, BONDS, ETC.

NAME OF SECURITY	No. Shares	Par Value	Market Value	Dividends Paid Past Two Years	If Any Pledged, State To Whom And For What Purpose
				none	

SCHEDULE "C"—ACCOUNTS RECEIVABLE FROM COMPLETED CONTRACTS

AMOUNT	WHEN DUE	IS IT GOOD?	FROM WHOM DUE (Name and Address)	NATURE OF CONTRACT	Amount of Contract
4,000	9/30 last	year yes	Modern Homes	septic sewers	
3,500	10/25 last	year yes	G. Hand	on account	
2,345	various small jobs -- all real current & good				

SCHEDULE "D"—ACCOUNTS RECEIVABLE ON UNCOMPLETED CONTRACTS

Current Earned Estimates	Retainage Earned And Withheld	Work Performed And Unbilled	Designation of Contract and Name and Address From Whom Due	Amount Of Contract	Estimates Paid To Date
1,000	various accounts				

SCHEDULE "E"—OTHER ACCOUNTS RECEIVABLE

AMOUNT	WHEN DUE	FOR WHAT IS IT DUE?	IS IT GOOD?	Name and Address of Party From Whom Due

SCHEDULE "F"—NOTES RECEIVABLE

AMOUNT DUE	WHEN DUE	FOR WHAT DUE	HOW SECURED	Name and Address of Party From Whom Due

Continued on next page

SCHEDULE "G"—EQUIPMENT

Quantity	Description and Capacity of Items	Age Of Items	Purchase Price	Depreciation Charged Off	Book Value	Encumbrance How Payable
	See attached list					

SCHEDULE "H"—REAL ESTATE

LOCATION AND DESCRIPTION OF PROPERTY	In Whose Name Is Title?	What Rents Per Month	Present Forced Sale Value	Amount of Mortgage
Home	Charles & Susan		40,000.	15,000.

SCHEDULE "I"—NOTES PAYABLE

AMOUNT	NAME AND ADDRESS OF PARTY TO WHOM PAYABLE	For What Purpose	What Security	When Due
157,395	First City State Bank & Trust		Equipment	various

SCHEDULE "J"—AMOUNTS DUE SUB-CONTRACTORS

Current Earned Estimates	Retainage Earned And Withheld	Work Performed And Unbilled	Designation of Contract and Name and Address To Whom Due	Amount of Contract	Estimates Paid To Date
			none		

SCHEDULE "K"—ACCOUNTS PAYABLE

AMOUNT	NAME AND ADDRESS OF PARTY TO WHOM PAYABLE	FOR WHAT?	Date of Purchase	Date Expect To Pay
1,363.	Jake's Service Station	Gas & oil	12/15	when billed
2,000.	various small bills		within past mo.	within 30 days

Continued on next page

IF A CORPORATION ANSWER THESE QUESTIONS

When Incorporated .... In what State incorporated..
Authorized Capital $......................Subscribed Capital $......................Capital Paid in Cash $....................
Capital Paid in Equipment or Otherwise $................................ Total Paid-up Capital $................................

NAMES OF OFFICERS AND DIRECTORS	Number Of Shares Owned	Financial Worth Aside From Interest In The Corporation
President	....	....
Vice-President	....	....
Secretary	....	....
Treasurer	....	....
Directors	....	....
....	....	....

Has the corporation or any of its officers ever failed in business? .... If so, give particulars.
....
....

Are any of the above officers engaged in any other line of business? .... If so, give particulars.
....
....

IF A CO-PARTNERSHIP ANSWER THESE QUESTIONS

Name And Address Of All Individuals Comprising Co-Partnership	Age	Mention Individual Property Holdings (Real and Personal) Of The Firm Members Not Included In Above Statement. Also State Encumbrance Upon Same, If Any*
....	....	....
....	....	....
....	....	....

***Separate statements shall be filled out and signed by each member of the firm showing his individual assets and liabilities exclusive of his interest in the firm's business.**

CO-PARTNERSHIP QUESTIONS (continued)

Has the firm or any member of the firm ever failed in business? .... If so, give particulars ....

Are there any judgments, suits or claims against the firm or any of its members? .... If so, give particulars ....

Is partnership general or limited? .... If limited, explain fully ....

Are any of the firm members engaged in any other line of business? .... If so, give particulars ....

....

INDIVIDUALS, CO-PARTNERSHIPS OR CORPORATIONS MUST COMPLETE FOLLOWING

Are you engaged in any other lines of business? .... no ....

Have you ever failed in business or compromised with creditors? .... no ....

Has any surety company ever paid a loss on you as an **individual,** or if a **firm** on any of the firm members, or if a **corporation** on any of the officers? .... no .... If so, state name of surety company and give full particulars ....

Continued on next page

Have you ever defaulted on a contract? no

If you have furnished bonds before give names of your sureties N/A

Have you any established credit lines at banks? yes If so, state amount, $ no restrictions

Name and address of banks First City State Bank and Trust, First City

and advise what security banks require signature

State whether you are at this time **Discounting** your bills, paying in 30 to 60 days, or more Discount & 30 days

Are you paying any bills by **Notes?** no

Do you have your books periodically audited by a licensed or certified public accountant? no

If so, give name of accountant and date of last audit

ADVISE FULLY REGARDING INSURANCE CARRIED

Life Insurance 30,000 (Amount) Charles (On whom carried) Susan, wife (To whom payable) Ohio Life (Company issuing) $ 1,500 (Cash surrender value)

Fire Insurance 64,000 (Amount) home (On what carried) Milltown Mutual (Company issuing)

Workman's Compensation and/or Liability Insurance yours (Limits) (In what company)

Other Insurance—State amount, character of insurance and companies issuing Auto -- yours

GIVE NAMES OF CONCERNS FROM WHICH YOU BUY	ADDRESS	CITY	STATE
Holleran Dodge & Plymouth	Jessup Street, First City		
Jake's Service Station	Cherry Street, First City		
Mack Truck	Allentown, Pennsylvania		
John Deere	Franklin Drive, First City		

For the purpose of inducing the IIA Casualty Insurance Company to issue or procure . . .

. . . to other companies for the purpose of securing reinsurance or co-insurance.

IF INDIVIDUAL Sign Here:

Witness: Susan Squire .... Charles Squire ....

IF CO-PARTNERSHIP Sign here:

Witness: ....

(NAME OF FIRM)

....................Member of Firm

....................Member of Firm

....................Member of Firm

(INDIVIDUALLY AND AS CO-PARTNERS)

IF CORPORATION Sign Here:

Attest: ....

(NAME OF CORPORATION)

.... By ....

SECRETARY PRESIDENT

Subscribed and sworn to before me this..........day of.........., A.D. 19.......

....

NOTARY PUBLIC

December 31, last year
Charles Square

EQUIPMENT OWNED	AMOUNT VALUE
No.1 Snow Plow	650
No.2 Snow Plow	300
Snow Plow frame and lift accessories for trk	525
Rogers Lo-Boy Trailer	3,300
Stone Rake	250
1989 Dodge Pick-up, 4 wd	8,100
Snow Plow and Accessories for Pick-up	1,000
1990 Dozer	38,000
1977 580 Case Backhoe	4,700
1988 Cat 951 Loader	39,000
1985 Mack Tri-Axle Dump Truck	32,000
1987 Mack Tri-Axle Dump Truck	38,000
1991 Miller AC-DC Portable Welder/Accessories	3,000
Shop Equipment	3,904
1977 International Lo-Boy Tractor	8,000
1984 International Single Axle Dump Truck	18,000
Extra Dump Body	500
1990 Dodge Pick-up	9,000
1984 International Dump Truck	9,000
Safety Equipment	300
Car Trailer	700
1975 Mack Dump Truck	7,000
Cinder Spreader	1,000
1989 Dodge Pick-up	7,600
Plow for Above	1,300
Total Value	$235,129

SUMMARY

The major types of surety bonds are noncontract bonds, fidelity bonds, and contract bonds. Generally the most intensive underwriting is applied to construction contractors. Contract bonds account for about two-thirds of the surety industry premium volume.

The three factors considered in underwriting contract bonds for construction are character, capacity, and capital. The major sources of underwriting information are the application for the bond, documents showing financial data, and the contract document itself.

Since the total amount of the surety's bond liability generally far exceeds the net worth of the bonded contractor, the surety may be risking more than the contractor. Yet, the premium the surety charges for prequalification service and for assuming the credit risk is, in effect, a service fee. It is generally somewhat lower than what a bank would charge for a letter of credit.

As a result of the high risk and low premium, surety underwriters must be conservative in their underwriting policies or credit standards. No amount of capital can compensate for a lack of character or weak capacity. In the final analysis, the use of unsecured credit depends on one person's faith and trust in another.

Chapter Note

1. 15 U.S.C. 694a-c.

CHAPTER 5

Financial Statements

When a surety agrees to stand behind a principal, it creates a business opportunity for that principal in much the same way as a bank creates a business opportunity for a person or company to whom it lends money. In some sense, both are extending credit, and both will only do so if the applicant is found to be worthy of receiving credit. Banks and sureties evaluate creditworthiness by reviewing an applicant's financial status as reflected in its accounting and financial statements. This chapter explains who prepares accounting and financial statements and how they are prepared, the components of financial statements, and how the procedures for and analysis of construction accounting differ from those used for most businesses.

FINANCIAL STATEMENT PREPARERS

The quality of a financial statement depends on the technical competence of the preparer and the procedures used to determine and present financial information. To be certain that a statement is of sufficient quality and thus reliable enough to use in making a decision about extending surety credit, an underwriter should know about the qualifications and biases of, as well as the procedures used by, the statement preparer. This section discusses the various statement preparers and the reliability of statements prepared by each.

Internal Personnel

Internal, or in-house, personnel who prepare statements from the principal's books and records can be officers or employees of the principal. The reliability of these statements depends on who compiled the information. For instance, in the mind of a surety, the reliability of a statement prepared by a part-time bookkeeper for a small firm might differ from the reliability of a statement prepared by the chief financial officer of a large corporation. In addition, the reliability of a statement prepared manually, using few or no accounting controls might differ from the reliability of a statement prepared mechanically, using advanced accounting and computer systems.

With certain exceptions, an underwriter would probably be unwilling to rely solely upon a statement prepared by internal personnel primarily because of the preparer's bias. For instance, the chief financial officer for a large corporation may be just as reliable as an outside certified public accountant (CPA), but because of ties to the company, that officer may not be objective. The officer's bias in favor of the company might "color" the presentation of the company's financial condition. As a result, regardless of the confidence a surety may have in the quality and accuracy of internally generated figures, a surety would want corroboration from an independent accounting firm.

Registered Public Accountants

The Department of Accountancy in each state licenses registered public accountants. There are no uniform educational standards established for eligibility, and applicants are not usually required to pass a written examination. Because they do not need to meet the standards established for a CPA, registered public accountants may not render an opinion about the financial statements they prepare. Accordingly, their accounting functions are usually limited to those of a bookkeeping service; and, as a general rule, they are not accepted as independent accountants by sureties.

Certified Public Accountants

Surety underwriters typically form their impression of an account on the basis of the account's financial statements. It is often easy to tell at a glance whether a statement was professionally or carelessly prepared. Eligible contractors have failed to interest sureties in their business because of inadequately prepared financial statements.

Most sureties require not only that their clients engage CPAs, but also that CPAs are highly qualified specialists in particular accounting fields. As no one doctor could treat all health problems, neither can one CPA address all aspects of accounting for all different types of businesses. Depending on the accounting complexities of a given business organization, different degrees of expertise are required.

To become certified, the accountant not only must pass the Uniform CPA Examination administered by the Board of Accountancy of each licensing state, but also must have a minimum of several years of accounting experience. The CPA must adhere to a strict code of ethics as established by the American Institute of Certified Public Accountants (AICPA), the standard leader in the accounting profession. The AICPA, the Financial Accounting Standards Board (FASB), the U.S. Securities and Exchange Commission (SEC), and the American Accounting Association (AAA) serve as the four independent authoritative bodies in establishing national accounting standards. Because of these educational and professional requirements, a surety typically considers a financial statement prepared by a CPA a reliable basis on which to make a credit decision. The CPA's role in preparing financial statements and the different kinds of opinions offered by the CPA are discussed in Chapter 6.

A CPA's services extend well beyond the preparation of financial statements. CPAs recommend changes in internal controls and accounting methods and counsel a company on the most advantageous financial and tax reporting systems. The CPA may also make recommendations for automating payroll and other bookkeeping functions and regularly visits a company's office to monitor the implementation of new procedures. Tax planning is one of the CPA's most critical roles, and CPAs should be available to discuss financial trends and developments with the users of financial statements.

In construction accounting, a highly accurate cost recording and job allocation system is essential in tracking line item costs versus the job budget, and costs should be recorded and allocated at least on a weekly basis. As mentioned, one of the most important services the CPA can perform for a client is assisting in the selection and programming of a computer system that is most adaptable to the contractor's particular needs. This establishes an early warning system and enables the contractor to identify and address unanticipated cost escalations promptly and to periodically produce a reasonably reliable balance sheet and income statement for internal use by company management.

ACCOUNTING PREPARATION METHODS

CPAs prepare financial statements and tax returns on a cash basis or on an accrual basis. In selecting a method, the CPA considers the fact that although cash basis accounting is acceptable, and possibly advantageous, for tax purposes, it creates a less accurate picture of the organization's financial position. For construction firms, the cash and accrual methods are not acceptable under *generally accepted accounting principles* (GAAP) for financial reporting purposes, but they are acceptable for tax accounting.

For the construction industry, two variations of the accrual method can also be used for financial and tax reporting. The percentage-of-completion and completed contract methods evolved in response to uncertainty about the final cost of a contractor's project. These accounting methods are discussed below.

Because the percentage of completion and completed contract accounting methods are complex and specialized, they are discussed briefly below and in greater depth under "Construction Accounting." The XYZ Construction Company will be examined using the four accounting preparation methods.

Cash Basis

The *cash basis method* eliminates all accounts receivable, accounts payable, and accruals from the balance sheet. The income statement reflects only cash receipts as revenues, from which cash paid for direct construction costs are deducted to arrive at a gross profit or loss. The general and administration (G & A) expenses incurred are subtracted from this amount, other income received is added, and other expenses paid are subtracted. The result is *net profit before taxes*.

It may be helpful in understanding the cash method to think of individual federal income tax returns. Individuals must report income from salaries, bonuses, commissions, dividends, interest, and any other sources. They then reduce the total income by itemized deductible expenses or by the standard deduction. This is strictly a cash-in/cash-out declaration. If someone else owes the filer money, this money is not reported on the tax return as part of adjusted gross income. Nor is the money the filer owes a deductible expense.

The same accounting principles apply to a business organization when it reports income on the cash basis. Open accounts receivable and payable are neither recognized as income or expenses nor added to or deducted from the balance sheet.

The *modified cash basis* allows for depreciation and accrued taxes. Exhibit 5-1 shows the balance sheet of the XYZ Construction Company, and Exhibit 5-2 shows the income statement for the XYZ Construction Company. Both are based on the modified cash method.

Exhibit 5-1 shows the working capital (current assets – current liabilities) is slightly less than the net worth (capital stock + retained earnings – treasury stock).

Exhibit 5-2 shows that the 1991 net profit after taxes of $569,338 plus the retained earnings of $5,565,320 from December 31,1990,

Exhibit 5-1
Balance Sheet (Modified Cash Method)

XYZ CONSTRUCTION CO., INC.
BALANCE SHEET
12/31/91
(MODIFIED CASH METHOD)*

CURRENT ASSETS		CURRENT LIABILITIES	
Cash	$2,404,900	Current portion of long-term debt	$ 15,116
Marketable securities	3,616,040	Accrued and withheld payroll taxes	21,184
Inventory	216,024	Accrued expenses	37,889
Prepaid expenses	106,922	Income taxes payable	6,514
Total current assets	$6,343,886	Total current liabilities	$ 80,703
		Long-term notes payable	6,688
		Capital stock	175,000
Fixed assets	18,194	Treasury stock	(16,000)
Other assets	18,969	Retained earnings	6,134,658
Total assets	$6,381,049	Total liabilities and capital	$6,381,049

* Unlike the Cash Method, the *Modified* Cash Method allows accrued expenses, depreciation, and bad debts on the income statement.

WORKING CAPITAL	
Current assets	$6,343,886
Current liabilities	– 80,703
	$6,263,183

NET WORTH	
Stock	$ 175,000
Treasury stock	(16,000)
Retained earnings	6,134,658
	$6,293,658

equals the retained earnings of $6,134,658 of December 31, 1991. This amount is carried to the retained earnings in the balance sheet in Exhibit 5-1.

The advantage and primary purpose of using the cash method is to mitigate or defer tax liability into future accounting periods. It is, therefore, a good method for tax reporting. The disadvantage is that it serves little or no purpose in obtaining credit because it does not disclose vital financial information such as accounts receivable and

Exhibit 5-2
Income Statement (Modified Cash Method)

XYZ CONSTRUCTION CO., INC.
INCOME STATEMENT
FOR THE YEAR ENDED 12/31/91

Cash receipts	$72,640,919
Cash disbursements	68,969,781
Gross profit	3,671,138
General administrative expense	2,928,238
	742,900
Other income	149,698
	892,598
Other expenses	3,008
Net profit before taxes	889,590
Provision for income taxes	320,252
Net profit after taxes	$ 569,338
Retained earnings 12/31/90	$ 5,565,320
Retained earnings 12/31/91	$ 6,134,658

NOTE 1— In addition to the elimination of accounts receivable and payable on the balance sheet, all entries relating to timing differences in recognition of income were also omitted; i.e., C&E/Billings, Billings/C&E, and deferred taxes.

NOTE 2— Income statement revenues are given for example purposes only to illustrate how the Cash Method would be stated. It cannot be used where annual revenues exceed an average of $5,000,000.

payable on the balance sheet and the income statement.

However, the cash basis method can be used for tax purposes only by companies with average annual receipts of $5,000,000 or less. Within this limitation, a firm may use the accrual method for financial reporting and the cash method for tax purposes.

Accrual Basis

The *accrual basis method* states receivables, payables, and prepaid and accrued expenses on the balance sheet. Revenues, which are stated on the income statement, consist of all amounts billed during the year. All direct job costs, including accounts payable and accrued job expenses, are then deducted from completed contracts and contracts in progress to arrive at the gross profit or loss. Exhibits 5-3 and 5-4 show the

Exhibit 5-3
Balance Sheet (Straight Accrual Method)

XYZ CONSTRUCTION CO., INC.
Balance Sheet
12/31/91
(Straight Accrual)

CURRENT ASSETS		
Cash		$ 2,404,900
Marketable securities		3,616,040
Accounts receivable		10,520,993
Inventory, at cost		216,024
Prepaid expenses		106,922
Total current assets		$16,864,879
FIXED ASSETS		
Property and equipment		
Auto	$21,604	
Trucks	18,519	
Tools	4,088	
	$44,211	
Less: Accumulated depreciation	26,017	18,194
OTHER ASSETS		
Cash value of life insurance	13,915	
Intangible assets	5,054	18,969
TOTAL ASSETS		$16,902,042

CURRENT LIABILITIES		
Current portion of long-term debt		$ 15,116
Accounts payable		6,023,258
Accrued and withheld payroll taxes		21,184
Accrued expenses		37,889
Income taxes payable		1,967,490
Total current liabilities		$8,064,937
Notes payable	$21,804	
Less: Current maturities	15,116	6,688
STOCKHOLDERS' EQUITY		
Authorized 50,000 shares Common stock $5.00 Par value: issued and outstanding 35,000 shares		175,000
Treasury stock, at cost		(16,000)
Retained earnings		8,671,417
Total stockholders equity		8,830,417
TOTAL LIABILITIES/ EQUITY		$16,902,042

balance sheet and income statement of XYZ Company using the straight accrual method of accounting.

The net profit after taxes for the year 1991 of $3,497,762 shown in Exhibit 5-4 plus the retained earnings of $5,173,655 from December 31, 1990, equals $8,671,417. This amount also appears in Exhibit 5-3 in the retained earnings portion of stockholder's equity. The $8,671,417 of retained earnings for the straight accrual method in Exhibit 5-3 is somewhat higher than the $6,134,658 calculated under the modified cash method shown in Exhibit 5-1.

Exhibit 5-4
Income Statement (Straight Accrual Method)

XYZ CONSTRUCTION CO., INC.
Income Statement
For the Twelve Months Ending
12/31/91
(Straight Accrual)

REVENUE			PERCENT
Completed contracts and contracts in progress		$85,687,776	100.0
Less cost of revenues		77,440,976	
Gross profit		$ 8,246,800	9.6
General and administrative expenses			
Officers' salaries	$682,460		
Other salaries	924,587		
Rent	300,000		
Utilities	36,818		
Telephones	18,609		
Legal-accounting	23,407		
Entertainment	15,689		
Travel	27,065		
Depreciation	14,603		
Bad debts	35,000		
Bonuses	850,000	2,928,238	3.4
		$ 5,318,562	
Other Income			
Interest earned	$133,608		
Gain on sale of fixed assets	16,090	149,698	
		$ 5,468,260	
Other Expenses			
Interest expense		3,008	
Net profit before taxes		$ 5,465,252	6.4
Provision for income taxes		1,967,490	
Net profit after taxes		$ 3,497,762	4.0
Retained earnings 12/31/90		$ 5,173,655	
Retained earnings 12/31/91		$ 8,671,417	

Most businesses use the accrual basis. Like the cash basis method, the accrual basis can control taxable income by withholding billings at the end of a fiscal year.

Exhibit 5-5 shows significant factors the underwriter should consider using the straight accrual method. The advantage of the accrual

Exhibit 5-5
Factors for Underwriter (Straight Accrual Method)

XYZ CONSTRUCTION CO., INC.
SIGNIFICANT FACTORS FOR THE UNDERWRITER
(Straight Accrual)

Working Capital

$16,864,879	(Current assets)
−8,064,937	(Current liabilities)
$ 8,799,942	

Net Worth

$ 175,000	(Capital stock)		Total assets	$16,902,042
(16,000)	(Treasury stock)	OR	Less:	
8,671,417	(Retained earnings)		Total liabilities	8,071,625
$ 8,830,417				$ 8,830,417

Working capital stated above is on an "as declared" basis by the CPA; i.e., before the underwriter adjusts certain current assets and liabilities for analytical purposes.

method is that it portrays a more accurate and usually stronger financial condition. It is therefore more useful than the cash basis method in obtaining credit. On the other hand, it is less conducive to controlling taxable income.

Percentage-of-Completion Method

The *percentage-of-completion method* recognizes income or losses from incomplete contracts, but it does so only as this income is earned. This method works by applying a formula used to determine actual costs incurred to the total estimated costs upon completion. Balance sheet treatment is also given to the cost/billing relationship. It is similar to that used with the completed-contract method, except that earned income is added to the costs incurred and is used in arriving at earned revenues. Exhibits 5-6 and 5-7 show how the XYZ Construction Company balance sheet and income statement for the year ending December 31, 1991, would be prepared using the percentage-of-completion method.

Notice in Exhibit 5-7 that the retained earnings amount of $8,458,717 for December 31, 1991, appears in the balance sheet in Exhibit 5-6 under stockholders' equity.

Exhibit 5-8 shows jobs in progress and accounts for the jobs on a percentage-of-completion basis. Notice that the revenues earned as

Exhibit 5-6
Balance Sheet (Percentage-of-Completion Method)

XYZ CONSTRUCTION CO., INC.
BALANCE SHEET
12/31/91
(Percentage-of-Completion)

CURRENT ASSETS		
Cash		$ 2,404,900
Marketable securities		3,616,040
Accounts receivable		4,604,902
Earned estimates and retainage		5,916,091
Cost and estimated earnings in excess of billing		309,604
Inventory, at cost		216,024
Prepaid expenses		106,922
Total current assets		$17,174,483
FIXED ASSETS		
Property and equipment		
Auto	$21,604	
Trucks	18,519	
Tools	4,088	
	$44,211	
Less: Accumulated depreciation	26,017	18,194
OTHER ASSETS		
Cash value of life insurance	$13,915	
Intangible assets	5,054	18,969
TOTAL ASSETS		$17,211,646

CURRENT LIABILITIES		
Current portion of long-term debt		$ 15,116
Accounts payable		2,604,198
Due subcontractors		3,419,060
Accrued and withheld payroll taxes		21,184
Accrued expenses		37,889
Billings in excess of costs and estimated earnings		1,714,213
Income taxes payable		6,514
Deferred taxes		769,067
Total current liabilities		$8,587,241
Notes payable	$21,804	
Less: Current maturities	15,116	6,688
STOCKHOLDERS' EQUITY		
Authorized 50,000 shares common stock $5.00 par value; issued and outstanding 35,000 shares		$ 175,000
Treasury stock, at cost		(16,000)
Retained earnings		8,458,717
Total stockholders' equity		8,617,717
TOTAL LIABILITIES/ EQUITY		$17,211,646

Exhibit 5-7
Income Statement (Percentage-of-Completion Method)

XYZ CONSTRUCTION CO., INC.
STATEMENT OF EARNINGS
FOR THE TWELVE MONTHS ENDING
12/31/91
(Percentage-of-Completion)

REVENUE			PERCENT
Completed contracts	$50,081,975		
Contracts in progress	33,581,984	83,663,959	100.0
Less cost of revenues			
Completed contracts	46,205,537		
Contracts in progress	31,235,439	77,440,976	
Gross profit		$ 6,222,983	7.4
General and administrative expenses			
Officers' salaries	$ 682,460		
Other salaries	924,587		
Rent	300,000		
Utilities	36,818		
Telephones	18,609		
Legal-accounting	23,407		
Entertainment	15,689		
Travel	27,065		
Depreciation	14,603		
Bad debts	35,000		
Bonuses	850,000	2,928,238	3.5
		$ 3,294,745	
Other income			
Interest earned	$ 133,608		
Gained on sale of fixed assets	16,090	149,698	
		$ 3,444,443	
Other expenses			
Interest expense		3,008	
Net profit before taxes		$ 3,441,435	4.1
Provision for income taxes			
Current	$ 394,160		
Deferred	844,756	1,238,916	
Net profit after taxes		$ 2,202,519	2.6
Retained earnings 12/31/90		$ 6,256,198	
Retained earnings 12/31/91		$ 8,458,717	

Exhibit 5-8

XYZ Construction Co., Inc.—Uncompleted Jobs in Progress 12/31/91 (Percentage-of-Completion)

Job No.	Description	Contract Price	Total Estimated Costs	Costs to Date	Estimated Costs to Complete	Billings to Date	Percent Complete	Total Estimated Gross Profit	Gross Profit Earned	Revenues Earned	Costs and Earnings in Excess of Billings	Billings in Excess of Costs & Earnings
76	Smith Building	26,409,817	24,561,129	11,717,509	12,843,620	12,664,902	47.7%	1,848,688	881,824	12,599,333	309,604	65,569
79	Jones Library	15,664,003	14,724,162	6,819,617	7,904,545	7,564,367	46.3%	939,841	435,146	7,254,763		
80	Johnson Hotel	29,778,013	27,544,662	12,698,313	14,846,349	15,376,532	46.1%	2,223,351	1,029,575	13,727,888		1,648,644
Totals		71,851,833	66,829,953	31,235,439	35,594,514	35,605,801		5,021,880	2,346,545	33,581,984	309,604	1,714,213

It is to be assumed that all three of these jobs were started subsequent to 1/1/91, and all revenues were earned during this accounting period. If any had been earned in 1990, they would have been deducted from 1991 revenues on the income statement.

Restating Revenues Earned:

Total Billings	35,605,801			
Less: Billings in excess of costs	4,370,362	(35,605,801 – 31,235,439)	OR Costs to Date	$31,235,439
	31,235,439		Plus Gross Profit	$ 2,346,545
Plus	2,346,545	Gross Profit or Income Earned		$33,581,984
	33,581,984	Revenues Earned (carried to income statement)		

Exhibit 5-9
Completed Contracts (Percentage-of-Completion)

XYZ CONSTRUCTION CO., INC.
COMPLETED CONTRACTS
12/31/91
(Percentage-of-Completion)

	CONTRACT PRICE	COSTS	GROSS PROFIT	%
Kelly Office Tower	$17,690,843	$16,806,300	$ 884, 543	5.0
Miles Convention Center	23,876,460	22,324,490	1,551,970	6.5
Cross Department Store	31,006,890	27,906,201	3,100,689	10.0
Miscellaneous	11,414,646	10,444,401	970,245	8.5
	$83,988,839	$77,481,392	$6,507,447	7.7
Less: Gross profit in prior periods			$2,631,009	
Gross profit this period			$3,876,438	

listed in this exhibit are the same as the revenue from contracts in progress on line two of Exhibit 5-7.

The gross profit of $2,346,545 on uncompleted jobs is shown in Exhibit 5-8. If this amount is added to the gross profit earned during 1991 on completed contracts of $3,876,438 shown in Exhibit 5-9, the gross profit is $6,222,983, shown in Exhibit 5-7 on line six.

Exhibit 5-10 shows significant factors for the underwriter to consider when using the percentage-of-completion method. Working capital and net worth are both calculated.

Exhibit 5-11 shows federal and state tax calculation for the XYZ Construction Company using the percentage-of-completion method. An assumption of 36 percent was used for federal and state taxes combined.

Completed-Contract Method

Like the percentage-of-completion method, the *completed-contract method* addresses cost variations that occur as a contract is being completed. The completed-contract method does not recognize earnings or losses generated from uncompleted contracts on a company's income statement. These costs are treated in a special way in the balance sheet through the completed-contract method. Exhibits 5-12 and 5-13 show costs in excess of billings, and billings in excess of costs, on each uncompleted contract.

Exhibit 5-10

Factors for Underwriter (Percentage-of-Completion)

XYZ CONSTRUCTION CO., INC.
SIGNIFICANT FACTORS FOR THE UNDERWRITER
(Percentage-of-Completion)

Working capital

$17,174,483	(Current assets)			
−8,587,241	(Current liabilities)			
$ 8,587,242				

Net worth

$ 175,000	(Capital stock)		Total assets	$17,211,646
(16,000)	(Treasury stock)	OR		
8,458,717	(Retained earnings)		Total liabilities	8,593,929
$ 8,617,717				$ 8,617,717

Working capital stated above is on an "as declared" basis by the CPA; i.e., before the underwriter adjusts certain current assets and liabilities for analytical purposes.

Exhibit 5-14 shows a comparison of the four accounting methods for the XYZ Construction Company. Although profits, retained earnings, total assets, working capital, and net worth may vary according to the method used, notice that net worth minus working capital is always $30,475. (This formula is a good way to check if the accountant has made any mistakes.) Net worth minus working capital should always be the same, regardless of accounting method used.

COMPONENTS OF THE FINANCIAL STATEMENT

The components of the *financial statement* include (1) the report of independent CPAs, (2) the balance sheet, (3) the income statement, (4) statement of retained earnings, (5) statement of cash flows, (6) notes to the financial statement, and (7) supplemental information. The components usually appear in this order. Each component is discussed below.

Report of Independent Certified Public Accountants

This report indicates which of the three methods (audit, review, compilation) the CPA has used to attest to the financial status of the company. Of the three methods of attestation, the audit is the most detailed, thorough, and reliable. The next most rigorous method is the review, although there may not be any direct confirmation of assets

Exhibit 5-11
Tax Calculations (Percentage-of-Completion)

XYZ CONSTRUCTION CO., INC.
FEDERAL AND STATE TAX CALCULATIONS
(Percentage-of-Completion)

Tax calculations using a 36 percent factor for federal and state taxes

Completed contract basis net profit from tax return	$1,094,890	Percentage net profit before taxes	$3,441,435
	x 36%		x 36%
Current taxes due	$ 394,160		$1,238,916
		Less current due	394,160
		Deferred taxes	$ 844,756

Arriving at balance sheet deferred tax liability using the income statement approach

Deferred taxes 12/31/90	$920,445
Deferred taxes 12/31/91	844,756
Difference	$ 75,689
Deferred taxes 12/31/91	$844,756
Less difference	75,689
	$769,067

and liabilities. Compilations are the least reliable of the three forms of attestation, since they may be taken directly from the principal's financial statements with perhaps no accounting tests or verifications made. If an audit was performed, the report will also express an opinion about the company. If a review or compilation was used, a disclaimer would be included. These three forms of attestation will be discussed in greater detail in Chapter 6.

Balance Sheet

The *balance sheet* shows total assets, liabilities, and net worth (or equity). Net worth as shown on the balance sheet should approximate the company's liquidated value, that is, all assets converted to cash and all liabilities paid as of the statement date.

The financial condition represented on the balance sheet is only true for a given point in time. It is continually fluctuating and can change significantly within short periods of time because of calculated, miscalculated, or totally unanticipated events. The analyst must therefore assess any given balance sheet along with balance sheets prepared for the previous three to five years.

Exhibit 5-12
Balance Sheet (Completed-Contract Method)

XYZ CONSTRUCTION CO., INC.
BALANCE SHEET
12/31/91
(COMPLETED-CONTRACT METHOD)

CURRENT ASSETS		CURRENT LIABILITIES	
Cash	$ 2,404,900	Current portion of long-term debt	$ 15,116
Marketable securities	3,616,040	Accrued and withheld payroll taxes	21,184
Accounts receivable	4,604,902	Accrued expenses	37,889
Earned estimates and retainage	5,916,091	Accounts payable	2,604,198
Costs in excess of billings		Due subcontractors	3,419,060
Inventory	216,024	Billings in excess of costs	4,370,362
Prepaid expenses	106,922	Income taxes payable	394,160
Total current assets	$16,864,879	Total current liabilities	$10,861,969
		Long-term debt	$6,688
		Capital stock	175,000
Fixed assets	18,194	Treasury stock	(16,000)
Other assets	18,969	Retained earnings	5,874,385
TOTAL ASSETS	$16,902,042	TOTAL LIABILITIES AND CAPITAL	$16,902,042

WORKING CAPITAL	
Current assets	$16,864,879
Current liabilities	−10,861,969
	$ 6,002,910

NET WORTH	
Capital stock	$ 175,000
Treasury stock	(16,000)
Retained earnings	5,874,385
	$ 6,033,385

As shown in the balance sheet exhibits in this chapter, the asset side on the left must always correspond to the liabilities and equity on the right. For example, consider an office building purchase. The value of the office (or asset) shown on the left would always be shown at cost. The mortgage, or liability, would be shown on the right. The difference between the two, or equity (cash paid), appears under liabilities. The total of the right column must always equal or "balance" with the total

Exhibit 5-13
Income Statement (Completed-Contract Method)

XYZ CONSTRUCTION CO., INC.
(COMPLETED-CONTRACT METHOD)
INCOME STATEMENT
FOR THE YEAR ENDED 12/31/91

REVENUES		
Completed contracts	$50,081,975	
Less cost of revenues	46,205,537	
Gross profit	3,876,438	
Expenses (G&A)	2,928,238	
	948,200	
Other income	149,698	
Other expenses	3,008	
Net profit before taxes	$ 1,094,890	
Provision for taxes	394,160	(36 percent)
Net profit after taxes	$ 700,730	
Retained earnings 12/31/90	$ 5,173,655	
Retained earnings 12/31/91	$ 5,874,385	

NOTE—Under 1986 Tax Reform Act, 90 percent of the $2,346,545 gross profit earned on uncompleted contracts (from the uncompleted jobs in progress schedule), or $2,111,890, also would be taxable as 1991 income because revenues exceeded the $10,000,000 three-year average.

asset values on the left. As the mortgage is reduced, the equity increases proportionately, as the following balance sheets illustrate:

OFFICE BUILDING—BALANCE SHEET
12/31/70

Assets		Liabilities	
Office building	$100,000	Mortgage	$ 90,000
		Equity	10,000
Total Assets	$100,000	Total Liabilities/Equity	$100,000

OFFICE BUILDING—BALANCE SHEET
12/31/91

Assets		Liabilities	
Office building	$100,000	Mortgage	$ 40,000
		Equity	60,000
Total Assets	$100,000	Total Liabilities/Equity	$100,000

Exhibit 5-14
Comparison of the Four Accounting Methods

Comparison of Accounting Methods for XYZ Construction Company, Inc.

Accounting Method	Year 1991 Net Profit After Taxes	Retained Earnings 12/31/91	Total Assets 12/31/91
Modified cash	$ 569,338	$6,134,658	$ 6,381,049
Straight accrual	3,497,762	8,671,417	16,902,042
Percentage-of-completion	2,202,519	8,458,717	17,211,646
Completed-contract	700,730	5,874,385	16,902,042
	Working Capital 12/31/91	**Net Worth 12/31/91**	**Net Worth-Working Capital**
Modified cash	$6,263,183	$6,293,658	$30,475
Straight accrual	8,799,942	8,830,417	30,475
Percentage-of-completion	8,587,242	8,617,717	30,475
Completed-contract	6,002,910	6,033,385	30,475

Although the office building in 1991 may have a market value of $300,000, it is always shown at cost. The notes to the statement could disclose that the fair market value (FMV) established by a recent appraisal is much higher. The following discussion explains each component of the balance sheet.

Current Assets. *Current assets* are cash and other holdings that can be converted to cash relatively quickly without interfering with normal business operations. "Quickly" typically means within one year, although this conversion period may be longer if the business operating cycle is longer than one year. Current assets include cash, cash equivalents, marketable securities, accounts and notes receivable, costs and estimated earnings in excess of billings, inventory, and prepaid expenses. These assets are defined below. Depending on the situation, an underwriter may classify and treat some of these assets as noncurrent assets.

Cash. *Cash* is a current asset when it is U.S. dollars or other forms of currency that have the characteristics of checking or demand deposits. It can be described as "cash in bank" or "cash on hand."

Cash Equivalents. *Cash equivalents* are short-term, highly liquid investments such as certificates of deposit, time deposits, money market certificates, and commercial paper. They have maturity dates of ninety days or less, and their value is fairly definite since they are so near maturity that a fluctuation in interest rates would only insignificantly affect their value. They are held for redemption within one year or as a temporary investment of working capital. Equity securities (stocks) are not considered cash equivalents.

Marketable Securities. *Marketable securities* are mostly stocks and bonds. Values of marketable securities can usually be quickly determined by checking the most recent bid prices on the stock or bond exchanges where they are traded. The less susceptible they are to wide fluctuations in price, the more stable and sound they are. The CPA will generally declare asset values at cost unless there is a permanent decrease in value. The value would be written down to market value, and the decrease reflected in the current year income statement. If the value is given only on the basis of cost, however, there may be a note to the statement giving the latest market values if the decrease in value is temporary and material.

Accounts Receivable. *Accounts receivable* are monies due from clients or accounts. Since accounts receivable are generally the largest current asset, anyone reviewing a financial statement should watch closely how promptly the receivables are turning over or being collected. Many companies prepare a monthly aging showing accounts that are current (i.e., with a debit balance usually less than 30 days old) and those in the 30-to-60, 60-to-90, and 90-to-120 days and older categories. An account with a balance that is 90 days old and older should be questioned and perhaps disallowed as a current asset, particularly if the account is in dispute. A contractor's *retainages*, or percentages of each billing withheld until the contract is fully completed, would not be included in this aging.

The CPA examines the collectibility of receivables and establishes an allowance or reserve for those that the company determines questionable. Wording on the balance sheet would usually describe this asset as an "account receivable, less allowance for doubtful accounts of X dollars." Once it has been decided that the account cannot be partly or totally collected, it will be written off the books as a bad debt. This write-off will then appear as an expense on the income statement, reducing both net income and the tax liability during the year in which it is written off.

Equitable Subrogation. If a contractor is declared in default, its accounts receivable relating to a bonded project inure to the surety's benefit as it arranges with another construction firm for completion of the remaining work. There is legal precedent establishing the surety's right to accounts receivable on a bonded project, which is often referred to as the *doctrine of equitable subrogation.*

Conflicts have occasionally arisen with a lender who has taken assignment of receivables as security for a loan and duly recorded this security interest in accordance with the Uniform Commercial Code

(UCC). Where this duality of interests exists, and the surety is called upon to complete a defaulted contract, costly litigation may result as each party attempts to perfect its right to these assets in the courts.

Despite well established case law, an appeals court in Florida recently upheld the lender's priority right over a surety to assigned receivables, only to be overturned by the Florida Supreme Court. Transamerica Insurance Co. *v.* Barnett Bank of Marion County, NA, Case #72, 531, was decided by the Supreme Court of Florida on March 16, 1989. The previous, overturned case was Case #524 50 2D 439 (Fla. 5th DCA 1988). This case was of great concern to the surety industry. If the Supreme Court had not reversed the lower court judgment, long-established legal precedents upholding the surety's right to accrued receivables would have been nullified. The cost of completing a defaulted contract could have risen significantly, particularly with a large accumulation of retained percentages. The lower court's decision would have established the lender's priority to these assets and would have denied the surety the remedy of defraying its cost to complete by not having the receivables available as part of the remaining unpaid contract balance due from the project owner. The loss to the surety would have been the difference between the contract balance and the cost to complete plus unpaid labor and material claimants.

Earned Estimates, Retainage. In addition to accounts receivable, the corresponding classification of earned estimates and retainage on uncompleted contracts may be found on the contractor's statement. Where this category is used, the amounts due on completed contracts are usually carried under the accounts receivable classification.

As described above, the "conversion to cash within one year rule" does not necessarily apply to retainages because a contractor's operating cycle can extend well beyond one year. Retainages can be over 120 days old and still be collected when the jobs they relate to are completed. On larger jobs, that may go on for more than one year, retainages can accumulate for much longer periods and still be treated as current assets. Conversely, when a general contractor or other prime contractor has withheld retainage from a subcontractor, and retainage extends beyond one year, the retainage is still treated as a current liability for the prime contractor.

Other receivables that are not part of normal operations usually represent such transactions as advances or loans to officers, employees, or affiliates or amounts due from the sale of fixed assets. While these items may be classified as current assets by the accounting profession, underwriters tend to reclassify most of the other receivables as noncurrent. However, when it can be established that some part of these receivables has been collected subsequent to the statement date, they will be treated as current.

Timing. Sureties must consider that a CPA will generally not complete and release a financial statement for perhaps 60 to 90 days after the fiscal year end. Many changes can occur during this period. While these changes may not be identified as "subsequent events" in the notes to the statement, they should be conveyed to the surety.

Notes Receivable. *Notes receivable*, like accounts receivable, also represent monies due from an account. Unlike accounts receivable, they are not carried as open accounts on the company's books, but are represented by a promissory note as evidence of the debt. Notes are usually interest-bearing instruments and can be payable on demand or at some future date.

If the term of the note is longer than one year, the CPA classifies whatever is due within the first twelve months as a current asset and the remainder as notes receivable, due after one year. This portion will be shown in other or noncurrent assets.

The underwriter usually classifies notes receivable as noncurrent except when they have been paid since the statement date. Thus, while a CPA may classify certain assets as current on the balance sheet according to GAAP, the underwriter may choose to treat them more conservatively by designating some to be noncurrent instead of allowing them to be included in the twelve-month evolution into cash. The notes will be further discussed in Chapter 6.

Costs in Excess of Billings. *Costs in excess of billings* or costs and estimated earnings in excess of billings are generally referred to as *underbillings*. They are current assets unique to construction accounting and are crucial in portraying the contractor's financial condition when statements are prepared on either a percentage-of-completion or a completed-contract basis.

Inventory. *Inventory* is ordinarily considered a current asset when it can be used on a project (i.e., converted to cash) within a year. Nevertheless, the extent to which inventory is viewed as liquid by a surety varies from business to business. For example, a general contractor who subcontracts a large portion of work would usually show very little, if any, building materials on hand (inventory). The exception to this situation occurs when a phase of the job is performed by the general contractor, who would then stock inventory for concrete foundations and finished carpentry, for example. On the other hand, an electrical, plumbing, or roofing subcontractor could show significantly more inventory than the general contractor. Cable, switch gears, pipes, shingles, and sheet metal, for example, would be found in warehouses or stored at job sites. To get a true financial picture in these cases, the surety should compare how much inventory is general as opposed to how much is purchased for a specific job or inventory work-in-progress.

General Inventory. It is important to make this distinction because general inventory is "less liquid" in the sense that its cash value may not be realized until well into the future. Since some materials may remain warehoused for months or years, eventually becoming obsolete, the surety might consider only a certain percentage of general inventory as a current asset.

Inventory Work-in-Progress. Materials purchased for a specific job are referred to as inventory work-in-progress. Because it will become part of the actual construction job, and thus part of the contractor's charges to the owner, it is considered in the same sense as an account receivable. In this case, the full value of the asset should be treated as current even though the materials may be stored on or off the job site and may not become part of the intended construction phase for days or weeks beyond the date of their arrival and storage. Inventory work-in-progress is viewed differently from general inventory by the surety underwriter, and the two are often classified separately on the balance sheet.

Asset Value of Inventory. A CPA usually states the *asset value of inventory* work-in-progress for a contractor on the basis of cost. The asset value of general inventory for a business is stated on the basis of cost or market value, whichever is lower. For example, if in anticipation of a general price increase for copper pipe, a plumbing contractor buys large quantities of copper pipe for the future and the price increases as expected, the market value would be higher than cost. In this case, cost would be shown as the asset value because it is lower than market value. If, however, the value of copper pipe decreased, the asset value would be stated on the basis of market value.

In manufacturing industries that need large quantities of raw materials, the ratio of inventory to other current assets becomes much higher. Here, inventory is divided into three categories: raw materials, goods in process, and finished goods. A general guideline for reviewers of financial statements is that a manufacturer's inventory should not exceed 100 percent of other current asset values or be more than 50 percent of total current assets.

The underwriter should also be aware of the importance of inventory turnover as it relates to cost of goods sold. The formula for computing inventory turnover is cost of goods sold divided by average inventory. The average is computed on the basis of beginning and ending inventory. If, for example, annual cost of goods sold was \$5,000,000 and the average value of inventory was \$2,500,000 (\$5,000,000 ÷ \$2,500,000 = 2), inventory turned over only twice a year, or every six months. This could indicate that sales were sluggish, inventory was too high or obsolete, and cash flow was severely strained.

On the other hand, an average value of inventory of only $833,000 would provide a much healthier turnover rate of six times a year, or every sixty days ($5,000,000 ÷ $833,000 = 6).

LIFO and FIFO. *LIFO* and *FIFO* are terms used to state the "costs of goods sold" on the income statement and in valuing inventory. LIFO, "last in, first out," means that costs are calculated using the most recent prices paid for the raw materials. Based on the premise that costs continue to rise, LIFO would produce a higher cost of goods sold, and earnings would thus be stated on a more conservative basis. FIFO, "first in, first out," means that costs are calculated using the older, and usually lower, costs of materials as first purchased. This method usually produces a lower cost of goods sold, thus showing greater earnings and tax liability than under LIFO.

In selecting the LIFO or FIFO method for valuing inventory, CPAs are often faced with a decision that favors either the credit or the tax picture, but not both. LIFO is appealing for a financially strong business with good credit because in showing reduced earnings, it produces a lower tax liability. Although LIFO shows lower earnings, credit analysts are usually more comfortable with the quantitative reliability of a LIFO-prepared statement.

On the other hand, because FIFO usually presents a stronger financial picture and is therefore better for credit purposes, a company may be willing to incur a greater tax liability if the trade-off is better credit. FIFO may also be a better way to value older inventories that are subject to spoilage or obsolescence.

Prepaid Expenses. *Prepaid expenses* are a current asset generated from such prepayments as insurance premiums, advertising service costs, payment of quarterly income tax estimates, and interest on loans. The company makes payment in advance for benefits to be received, together with payment of obligations not yet due.

Prepaid expenses are another item that may be treated differently by a CPA and an underwriter. Under GAAP, these payments are treated by CPAs as current assets on the theory that they will be used, or benefit will occur, within one year.

The underwriter classifies most prepayments as noncurrent assets because they are not considered liquid resources available for financing the cost of current construction and because it is unlikely that they would be canceled to obtain a refund for the unexpired portion of the benefit provided. The underwriter might consider prepaid income taxes as an exception because estimated quarterly tax payments offset accrued income tax liability. If quarterly prepayments exceed the actual tax liability, a company can apply for a refund of the overpayment.

Noncurrent Assets. *Noncurrent assets* include fixed assets and other assets.

Fixed Assets. *Fixed assets* consist of property, plant, and equipment that are part of normal business operations and are not intended for resale. Property, plant, and equipment includes land, buildings, machinery, furniture, and motor vehicles. Their asset value is declared on the basis of cost less depreciation, or "net book value."

Depreciation accounts for the anticipated decline in the value of an asset over its useful life through wear, tear, age, and obsolescence. Depreciation can be calculated on a straight-line basis in which a fixed percentage is deducted from the replacement cost every year. Depreciation can also be calculated on the basis of declining amounts per year in which the first year's depreciation is the greatest, and a lesser percentage is deducted in successive years. The notes to the financial statement should identify the method used to depreciate any item. (Land is never depreciated and is always carried at cost.) An example of straight line depreciation follows. A dump truck costing $30,000 new with an expected useful life of five years would be depreciated at a "straight line" rate of $6,000 per year until it is fully depreciated ($30,000 ÷ 5 = $6,000 per year).

This example would appear on the balance sheet under fixed assets at the end of the first two years as follows:

First Year

Truck (cost)	$ 30,000	
Less accumulated depreciation	6,000	$ 24,000

Second Year

Truck (cost)	$ 30,000	
Less accumulated depreciation	12,000	$ 18,000

Like inventory, the need for fixed assets varies from one contractor to another, and the surety must consider this fact when reviewing the amount of fixed assets as part of its credit decision. A general contractor may own a building but may not possess large quantities of rolling stock and heavy equipment. The electrical, HVAC, and plumbing contractor may need more equipment, such as trucks and generators, to operate. However, it is the grading, paving, utility, and bridge contractors that may need large and expensive quantities of heavy equipment. In the latter cases, the underwriter could face very high current and long-term debt service, which often creates an unbalanced financial condition. In this same context, if a contractor decides to lease equipment rather than buy it and the leased equipment contains a purchase option, certain accounting principles require that the leases be "capitalized." This lease would be included with the current and long-term lease payments, which are treated on the balance sheet in the same manner as payments due under a note for the purchase of the equipment.

Other Assets. Other assets resemble prepaid expenses, but the benefits or use derived usually extend well beyond twelve months. Other assets include organization, loan, and research and development costs. These costs are carried as an asset and are written off, or amortized, over a specified number of years until they finally disappear from the balance sheet. These assets have no physical existence and are commonly referred to as "intangible assets." As such, they are eliminated by the underwriter in analyzing tangible net worth. Goodwill is also considered an intangible asset, representing the difference between the price of an acquired company and the related value of net assets actually acquired.

The cash surrender value of whole life insurance policies (CSVLI) is also carried under the category of other assets. Because the policy is readily convertible to cash, many surety underwriters treat it as a current asset in their analysis. To correspond with this, any policy loans should be treated as current liabilities.

Current Liabilities. The second component on a balance sheet is *current liabilities*. Like current assets, current liabilities are any obligations due and payable within twelve months. The different kinds of current liabilities, described below, include notes payable, accounts payable, billings in excess of costs and estimated earnings, income taxes and accrued expenses.

Notes Payable. *Notes payable* include the current maturities of long-term debt, or those due within twelve months of the statement date, as well as all balances due on short-term working capital lines. It is important for the surety underwriter to determine how these obligations are secured and guaranteed. If any current assets have been pledged as collateral, the surety may request a letter from the lender agreeing to the exemptions of receivables from the loan agreement on bonded contracts. The principle of equitable subrogation would apply here regardless of any UCC filings of record against these assets by a lender. Contract balances not yet earned are also available to the surety in financing completion costs if defaults occur.

Notes payable to officers of a corporation, affiliates, or other parties may also exist. Depending on the size of these obligations, their effect on the ratio of current assets to current liabilities, the extent to which they impair working capital, and the desire of the note holders (payees), the underwriter may require these obligations to be subordinated to the interests of the surety. In so doing, the noteholder executes a subordination agreement on the surety's form, agreeing neither to accept nor to demand repayment without the surety's written consent.

Some subordination agreements (usually in the case of long-term notes when scheduled repayment is amortized on a monthly basis exceeding twelve months) permit repayment according to the terms of the note, while others allow no repayment of principal but may permit periodic payment of accrued interest. In any form of insolvency proceedings involving liquidation of company assets, the surety's rights of recovery would take precedence over those of the subordinated noteholder.

Once a note has been subordinated, the entire amount (when no principal payment is permitted) may be treated as noncurrent and carried "below the line" as a long-term liability in the surety underwriter's analysis of working capital *or as an increase in equity*. When payment of principal is allowed, the balance due beyond twelve months might also be treated as an increase in equity.

Two words of caution: First, it is not uncommon for subordination agreements to be breached, inadvertently or otherwise. A clear explanation by the underwriter to the parties involved of the exact meaning and intent of the agreement when it is drawn up does much to prevent misunderstandings or "mistakes." Second, any notes payable to suppliers of materials with whom normal selling terms would be on an open-account basis could signal cash flow or working capital problems and should be thoroughly investigated. This investigation may include a general trade survey conducted with other suppliers to determine the extent of the problem.

Accounts Payable. *Accounts payable* are amounts due on invoices from materials suppliers, leasing companies, and any other vendors. Invoices for operating and overhead costs are also accounts payable.

It is not uncommon for a company to prepare an aging of these accounts. It is useful in determining how promptly the company is meeting its obligations. These agings are set up in time categories similar to those used in accounts receivable aging.

General contractors who subcontract a good part of their work carry monies due subcontractors as a separate category of accounts payable. The current billings from the subcontractors and the retainages withheld from them on past requisitions are usually reported here in the same proportion as that withheld from the general contractor by the owner. Friction between the general contractor and the subcontractor may occur if, for example, an owner reduces retainage withheld under the general contract from 10 percent to 5 percent at 50 percent completion, and these reductions are not passed along to the subcontractors. The terms of the subcontract should clearly spell out how this situation will be addressed. Because contractors in specialty trades subcontract very little, amounts due their subcontractors would probably be carried in accounts payable.

Billings in Excess of Costs. *Billings in excess of costs* or billings in excess of costs and estimated earnings are generally referred to as *"overbillings."* This is the opposing construction accounting category to the underbilling asset, both of which will be examined more closely in the section on construction accounting.

Income Taxes. Taxes will also be examined in the construction accounting section under the discussion of deferred income taxes.

Accrued Expenses. *Accrued expenses* are all other current obligations owed but not yet paid, including salaries and bonuses accrued since the preceding pay period, interest accrued on notes payable, and payroll taxes withheld from employees' pay checks.

As illustrated in Exhibits 5-5 and 5-10, total current liabilities subtracted from current assets is commonly referred to as *working capital* or *net liquid assets*. To refine further the ability of the company to retire current debt quickly, inventory and prepaid expenses are eliminated from current assets to arrive at *net quick assets*. This is also referred to as the "acid test." If current liabilities exceed current assets, *deficit working capital* exists. Similarly, if total liabilities exceed total assets, but not total paid in capital, a *retained earnings deficit* exists. If total liabilities exceed total assets and paid in capital, there would be a *deficit net worth* or a state of *insolvency*.

Noncurrent Liabilities. *Noncurrent* or *long-term liabilities* include maturities of debt exceeding twelve months and loans against CSVLI unless the latter is treated as a current asset for underwriting purposes. Deferred taxes and subordinated notes payable may also be included as long-term liabilities, although the CPA may show them as current liabilities.

There is sometimes a long-term liability called *debentures* or *debenture bonds*. Debentures are formal promissory notes that mature well into the future. The notes are given to the "subscribers" or lenders as evidence of corporate debt; they specify the interest rates to be paid and the maturity dates. As with other unsecured promissory notes, debentures are backed only by the company's general credit.

In some cases these instruments are called *subordinated debentures*. Under specific covenants in the notes, they are subordinated to general creditors in the event of liquidation.

Equity or Net Worth. *Equity*, or *net worth*, is the third item on the balance sheet. The owner's interest in a business is owners' or stockholders' equity. It is composed of the value of capital stock issued plus any retained earnings (accumulation of net income minus dividends).

Capital Stock. In evaluating capital stock, it is instructive to examine the three basic forms of organization for a business, (1) sole proprietorships, (2) partnerships, and (3) corporations, in order to assess the potential financial liability of the owners or stockholders.

The Sole Proprietorship. In a *sole proprietorship*, one person owns the assets and is responsible for all liabilities. It is the least complex of the three forms of business organizations. The balance sheet follows the same concept as the "office building" illustration described earlier in that the assets and liabilities are business related.

The equity section of the balance sheet for a sole proprietorship would be described as proprietorship or owner's equity. This is the value the sole proprietor has in the business (assets minus liabilities equals the sole proprietor's interest).

General and Limited Partnerships. The *general partnership* is made up of two or more individuals. The partnership collectively owns all assets and owes all debts, and the residual net worth belongs to the partnership. The partnership agreement usually empowers one partner to commit the others on any type of contractual agreement. In a financial collapse, the general partners are jointly and severally liable for the partnership debts, and their individual assets are subject to levy by creditors.

A *limited partnership* affords greater protection to partners because the limited partners cannot be held liable for any more than their individual investment in the partnership. There must, however, be at least one general partner who is fully exposed and responsible for all liabilities. Limited partnerships were popular before the 1986 Tax Reform Act because they were used for buying into tax shelter contrivances involving everything from real estate and oil leases to cattle-feeding lots. The 1986 Tax Reform Act removed many of the attractive tax features of limited partnerships. The equity section of the balance sheet for a partnership would include no stock issued in a partnership accumulation of net income minus withdrawals by the partners.

The Corporation. A *corporation* is a legal entity, separate from its owners and employees. It owns all assets and owes all debt. Stockholders generally enjoy immunity from all corporate obligations. Its capital is created by two or more individuals making investments in the corporation through the purchase of capital stock. Initially, these incorporators apply either to the state in which they are domiciled or to any other state they choose for a corporate charter. They decide among themselves the classes of stock, the number of shares of each class to be issued and authorized, and the par value of each share. These factors become a part of the charter and may be changed only by a charter amendment, which is subject to state approval. The two most common classes of stock are common and preferred, with separate par values assigned to each. Par value can be any value agreed upon, with common stock usually being less per share than the preferred stock.

As an example of typical capital structure, assume that a corporation was chartered in Georgia in 1957. It was authorized to issue 1,000,000 shares of common stock at $5.00 par value and 10,000 shares of 5 percent preferred stock at $50 par value. Only 500,000 shares of common stock and 1,000 shares of preferred stock were initially issued. The day the company opened for business, stockholders' equity consisted of $2,500,000 cash for common stock and $50,000 for preferred stock. The balance sheet would appear as follows:

Assets		**Liabilities**	
Cash	$ 2,550,000	None	
		Stockholders' Equity	
		Common Stock $5.00 par value, authorized 1,000,000 shares, issued and outstanding 500,000 shares	$2,500,000
		5 Percent Preferred Stock $50.00 par value, authorized 10,000 shares, issued and outstanding 1,000 shares	50,000
Total Assets		**Total Liabilities/Equity**	
	$2,550,000		$2,550,000

There would still be 500,000 shares of authorized and unissued common stock and 9,000 shares of preferred stock available for future purchase by stockholders.

If, at a future date, 100,000 common shares were sold for $10 per share, or $1,000,000, $500,000 of this would be in excess of the par value ($5 par value x 100,000 = $500,000) and would be classified separately in the capital section under common stock as "capital in excess of par" or "paid in capital."

As the term implies, preferred stock takes preference over common in the payments of dividends and distribution of assets in the case of liquidation. In the preceding illustration, the preferred shareholders would be entitled to a fixed 5 percent of par dividend per share (or $2.50) when the board of directors declared dividends. Dividends must be paid to these shareholders before any dividends can be paid on the common shares. There are various types of preferred stock that may affect the amount and frequency of dividend payments.

Common stockholders have no fixed limit on the amount of dividends they may receive, assuming that sufficient earnings are available and the board of directors has declared them. The preferred dividends, however, must always be paid first. As the corporation prospers, higher dividends may be declared on the common stock and, conversely, when corporate fortunes wane, the common stock dividends will likely fall. While common shareholders take a greater risk in the years of flat earnings or operating losses, their rewards can be greater in times of prosperity.

In the corporate charter, the incorporators state which classes of stock will be voting and nonvoting, with voting stock having one vote per share. Voting control of a corporation can sometimes be a significant underwriting consideration. This is particularly the case with closely held corporations, where a limited number of privately owned shares of stock are available and control often rests with the older owners. It is important to know the continuity plans of a corporation and to whom the stock eventually will pass.

Retained Earnings. *Retained earnings* are earnings retained from the previous period plus net income during the current period, minus any dividends during the current period. Profits reflected on the income statement at the end of the fiscal year are added to the retained earnings balance from the preceding year, while income statement losses and dividends declared are deducted. In construction accounting, retained earnings are affected by which accounting method was selected for tax and financial reporting purposes.

A review by the surety underwriter of retained earnings over several years may be helpful in assessing the corporation's commitment to growth—an important issue in the surety's decision to extend credit. If despite profitable operations, excessive salaries, bonuses, or dividends are paid annually to the detriment of corporate growth, a surety might be less inclined to extend credit than it would to a company that accumulates earnings (i.e., shows corporate growth).

In addition to retained earnings, there are other capital transactions that affect net worth, such as the infusion of additional capital through stock purchases, payment of dividends, and repurchases of outstanding stock previously issued by the corporation. A reconciliation of net worth, or statement of stockholders' equity, would fully describe these changes.

The combination of capital stock and retained earnings, or corporate net worth, represents the stockholders' investment. As any astute investor knows, *return on investment (ROI)* should be maximized to the fullest extent. If ROI is insufficient for very long, it might be prudent for a contractor to liquidate and invest the capital in less risky ventures, thereby providing a higher yield with much less effort.

It is important to recognize the difference between a corporate division, subsidiary, and affiliate. A *division* is merely an internal designation and not a separate legal entity. A *subsidiary* is a separate corporate entity with stock that is owned wholly or partially by the parent corporation. An *affiliate* exists whenever one person either directly or indirectly owns or controls two or more business organizations (not necessarily corporations).

Income Statement

The *income statement* shows total sales or revenues, expenses, and profit or loss during the fiscal year. The income statement is also called the profit and loss (P&L) statement or the statement of earnings.

A *fiscal year* is an accounting period of twelve months starting at any time during the year. The selection of the fiscal year ending date depends on when operations are at their seasonal peak in order to make the organization attractive for credit purposes. Because this selection will usually create a greater tax liability for the organization, it is also acceptable to the IRS.

In addition to the fiscal year-end financial statement, interim statements may be prepared throughout the year to show the operating results for the number of months elapsed since the close of the preceding fiscal year. For example, a six-month interim statement for a November 30 fiscal year-end (FYE) would reflect revenues generated and costs incurred for the period from December through May.

Exhibits 5-2, 5-4, 5-7, and 5-13 show the income statements as presented for the four accounting methods. The text that follows shows how an organization sets up and calculates its revenues and costs in order to determine its net profit after taxes. This figure is then carried forward to retained earnings on the balance sheet.

To arrive at gross profit (gross margin), all revenues are reduced by the direct costs of the company's product, or *cost of revenues*. These direct costs for a manufacturer are the cost of goods sold, or raw materials purchased plus manufacturing labor costs and depreciation of manufacturing machinery. For a retailer or wholesaler, these costs would consist of the purchase price of finished goods held for sale. For a construction firm, the cost of revenues would include the cost of direct labor, materials, subcontractors, and *unallocated indirect costs*.

The following discussion explains how net profit is calculated. An organization would recognize its revenues for each of the four accounting methods in the following ways:

- In *cash-basis accounting,* revenues are recognized as cash, which is defined as all cash received during the accounting period.
- In *accrual-basis accounting*, revenues are defined as all billings during the accounting period.

- In *completed-contract accounting*, revenues are all receipts and accrued billings on completed jobs since their inception.
- In *percentage-of-completion accounting,* revenues are defined as all receipts from completed contract work, less those recognized in preceding accounting periods as uncompleted contracts, plus costs incurred and profits earned on uncompleted contracts, less those recognized in preceding accounting periods.

The *cost of revenues (direct costs)* for the four accounting methods would be recognized as follows and factored into the calculation of net profit.

- Cash—all direct cost cash expenditures
- Accrual—all direct cost cash expenditures plus accrued accounts payable for direct costs
- Completed Contract—all direct cost cash expenditures for completed contracts only plus corresponding accrued accounts payable for direct costs
- Percentage-of-Completion—all completed-contract direct costs paid and accrued, less those previously recognized in preceding periods, plus cash expenditures and corresponding accrued accounts payable for direct costs on uncompleted contracts less those previously recognized

General and administrative expenses are those expenses arising from general operating costs of a recurring nature, not specifically allocated as direct costs, reducing gross profit to net operating income (loss) and discussed under components to the financial statement.

Gross Profit – G&A Expenses
= Net Operating Profit (Loss)

Other income is income produced from nonoperating, and often nonrecurring, sources, including gain on the sale of fixed assets (assets sold for a price in excess of their depreciated or net book value) as well as interest earned on investments.

Other expenses are interest expense and losses on the sale of assets. By looking at cash flow trends, the levels of liquidity can determine the capital available from short-term investment (interest earned) and the weight of debt service (interest expense).

Note: G&A, other income, and other expenses can be recognized under all four accounting methods.

Net Operating Profit (Loss) + Other Income – Other Expenses
= Net Profit (Loss) Before Taxes

The prevailing federal and state income tax rates are applied to the net profit that is reported under the four accounting methods. Deferred taxes could arise from the temporary differences in depreciation, and the differences in income recognition.

Net Profit (Loss) Before Taxes – Provision for Income Taxes
= Net Profit (Loss) After Taxes

Statement of Retained Earnings

The *statement of retained earnings* presents changes in capital stock and retained earnings not reflected on the income statement. Examples of changes that can occur in retained earnings, besides changes in net income, are additional capitalization and the payment of dividends.

Statement of Cash Flows

A *statement of cash flows* provides information about the cash receipts and cash payments during the accounting period. Included is information about operating, investing, and financing activities during that period. As such, a statement of cash flows should assist those using the statement in assessing the following factors:

1. The ability to generate future positive cash flows to meet the company's obligations without the need for external financing
2. The differences between the amount of net income and the related net cash flow from operations
3. The investment and financing activities and the cash and noncash aspects of the company
4. The causes of the change in the amount of cash shown on the balance sheet at the beginning and end of the period

The statement of cash flows can use either the direct or indirect method.

Under the direct method, the income statement must be converted from the accrual basis to the cash basis. Changes in the balance sheet accounts that are related to items on the income statement must be considered. The accounts involved are all current assets or current liabilities.

Under the indirect method, certain adjustments are necessary to convert net income to cash flows from operating activities. First, changes that occurred in current accounts other than cash must be analyzed for their effects on cash. Then items such as depreciation that affected net income but not cash must be taken into account.[1]

Each method includes a reconciliation of net income and net cash flows from operating activities.

Notes to the Financial Statement

Notes to the financial statement describe (1) accounting methods the company uses for financial and tax reporting, (2) methods of depreciation of fixed assets, (3) schedules of notes payable, (4) details of overbillings and underbillings (for construction accounting only), (5) contingent liabilities, (6) subsequent events, (7) pending litigation, (8) loans to officers and affiliates, and (9) any other disclosures of material consequence to the users.

Supplemental Information

The schedules described in this section represent a great deal of information not usually included in the body of the CPA-prepared financial statement, but that the surety will find helpful. The well-prepared client should have the following schedules available.

Schedule of General and Administrative Expenses. This schedule itemizes general and administrative expenses (Exhibits 5-4 and 5-7) not included on the income statement. The surety uses this information to identify abnormal expenditures that may be inconsistent with the company's cost control and profit retention objectives. Examples of such expenses include excessive salaries, bonuses, and travel and entertainment expenses. A sizable bad debt can suggest that management has neglected to establish a sound credit policy or investigative procedures in screening product purchasers on open account selling terms.

Excessive legal costs can indicate that a firm is perhaps overly litigious or that it is involved in the costly defense of its failure to adequately fulfill contractual agreements.

Schedules of Accounts Receivable and Payable. While schedules of accounts receivable and payable do not ordinarily appear on an audited statement, they may occasionally appear on an unaudited or internally prepared statement. These schedules assist the surety who wants an aging of each account to determine (1) which receivables are not "turning over" or being collected in a timely manner and (2) which creditors are not being paid within their selling terms.

Schedule of Equipment. A schedule of equipment may appear on the statement of a manufacturer, contractor, or other organization that has invested a substantial amount of capital in the equipment needed to develop its product. A schedule of equipment would likely be part of the statement from highway, bridge, water and sewer, and grading contractors. These schedules should describe each piece of equipment, its original cost, the depreciation charged against it, and its resulting net book value.

Schedule of Inventory. For a manufacturer, the schedule of inventory provides information about (1) raw materials, (2) goods in process, and (3) finished goods. In reviewing this schedule, a surety would look at the relationship of raw materials and finished goods to goods in process as well as the relationship of inventory to other current assets. Very large quantities of raw materials and finished goods compared to the quantity of goods in process and/or a disproportionate ratio of inventory to other current assets might signal sluggish sales.

A contractor might prepare a schedule of inventory work-in-progress, which allocates the cost of materials purchased for contracts underway. The materials may be stored on or off the job sites, but not yet be recognized as costs incurred.

Schedule of Unallocated Indirect Costs. This schedule includes costs not allocated as direct job costs to specific contracts. Examples are shop expenses for components fabricated for units on jobs in progress and equipment repair charges.

Again, these schedules are not a part of the financial statement but may be furnished as supplements. The schedules of completed and uncompleted jobs for construction firms, however, are usually included as part of the financial statement. The schedules list the contracts completed since the preceding fiscal year end and give final contract prices and gross profits. For uncompleted contracts, this schedule details adjusted contract prices, billings, costs, earned profits, estimated costs to complete, and overbillings or underbillings. (See Exhibits 5-8 and 5-9.)

CONSTRUCTION ACCOUNTING

Construction contractors typically use the completed-contract or percentage-of-completion accounting methods for financial reporting and tax purposes. Both are extensions of accrual-basis accounting. They are used instead of cash-basis and straight accrual accounting because they more accurately reflect a contractor's financial condition by recognizing the fact that final project costs and revenues are estimates. These methods are explained and illustrated below along with other special construction accounting situations including Subchapter S corporations, pro forma statements, and regulatory financial reporting.

Completed-Contract Method

The completed-contract method reflects income actually earned on long-term contracts completed during an accounting period. The income statement therefore reflects only revenues from completed jobs, and the tax liability on profits earned from uncompleted work is deferred into future accounting periods.

The balance sheet, on the other hand, reflects all receivables and payables due and owing on both completed and uncompleted contracts. It indicates costs in excess of billings carried as a current asset and billings in excess of costs as a current liability. Neither of these classifications has an effect on profits earned on the work completed through the statement date on uncompleted jobs, and each merely anticipates that unbilled costs will eventually be billed and become accounts receivable. On the liability side, the contractor is charged with billing more than costs.

In order to generate tax revenues on uncompleted work more quickly, there has been strong sentiment in Congress to repeal Internal Revenue Code provisions that allow the use of the completed-contract method. The 1986 Tax Reform Act went a long way toward full repeal but was stopped by opposing congressional forces. The enacted reforms still allow use of the completed-contract method when total average revenues for the preceding three years are under $10 million. If this criterion cannot be met, 90 percent of earned profits on uncompleted jobs become taxable. This is called the *90-10 rule*. Tax law, however, does not permit a contractor to defer taxes completely until a job is completed and profit is recognized on the tax return. (See Alternative Minimum Tax (AMT) treatment in the next section.)

Percentage-of-Completion Method

The percentage-of-completion method is similar to the completed-contract method with the following exceptions:

1. The balance sheet carries cost and estimated earnings in excess of billings as a current asset and billings in excess of cost and estimated earnings as a current liability.
2. Costs plus earned profits on uncompleted jobs are reflected with those from completed jobs on the income statement. Including the costs and revenues from uncompleted jobs on the income statement usually presents the organization as being in a stronger financial position. A greater income tax liability, however, may also result.

The earned income or profit calculation must be considered first. It is determined by the *cost-to-cost ratio*; i.e., the percentage of costs incurred at the statement date compared to the total estimated costs of the job at completion. This percentage then is applied against the total revised estimated gross profit when the job is complete, thus showing the earned profit. Consider the following example:

A $2 million job is bid with a 10 percent gross profit, or $200,000, leaving $1,800,000 as the total estimated cost. Six months later,

$900,000 in costs, or 50 percent of the total estimated costs, have been incurred. This is the percentage factor applied against the $200,000 total estimated gross profit at completion, thus producing $100,000 earned profit at the statement date. This earned profit then is added to the $900,000 costs incurred to arrive at total earned revenue of $1 million. Billings on this job at six months are $980,000, or $20,000 less than the revenue. This difference would be expressed as cost and estimated earnings in excess of billings under current assets. The balance sheet would show the following:

Billings	$980,000	
Costs	–900,000	
Estimated Earnings	–100,000	
	$ 20,000	Underbilled

Suppose billings were $1,050,000, and costs and earnings were the same. Billings would then be in excess of costs and estimated earnings creating a current liability. This would be shown as follows:

Billings	$1,050,000	
Costs	–900,000	
Estimated Earnings	–100,000	
	$ 50,000	Overbilled

Construction costs can fluctuate. If, in the same example, the contractor was able to accomplish a savings through "buying out" materials at a better price, making total anticipated costs only $1,750,000, the result would be $250,000 in total estimated profit. Costs incurred would be the same, and billings at six months would be $1,200,000. This situation can be expressed in the following way:

Step 1—$900,000 (cost incurred) ÷ $1,750,000 (total costs) = 51.4 percent earned of the total estimated profit of $250,000, or $128,500 as earned income or profit.

This would appear on the balance sheet as follows:

Step 2—Billings ($1,200,000) in excess of costs ($900,000) and estimated earnings ($128,500) = $171,500 (Overbilled)

The following is the same project as it would appear on the income statement as earned revenue:

Costs	$ 900,000
Plus: Earned Profit	128,500
Total	$1,028,500
Less: Overbilling	171,500
Equals: Earned Revenue	$ 857,000

Percentage-of-completion is considered the most accurate way to portray a contractor's financial condition when a contract takes longer than 12 months to complete. It is therefore recommended for financial reporting purposes. As mentioned, the completed-contract and cash methods are more popular for tax reporting.

If a contractor uses the percentage-of-completion or cash methods for financial statement purposes and the completed-contract methods for tax purposes, the alternative minimum tax (AMT) requires that the company compute and pay tax at a 20 percent rate on the difference between taxable income on the financial statements and the tax return. Various complex tax computations are required to arrive at the amount of tax; but, in the long run, what AMT accomplishes is that only a small part of the tax due on uncompleted jobs is deferred. In essence, a prepayment of tax occurs because, in the year the job is completed, an AMT credit is allowed for the tax previously paid. This affects or reduces the actual tax currently due.

These examples have shown how profit is accounted for using different accounting methods. However, losses do occur, and once they become known, the entire estimated loss should be recognized in the current accounting period or fiscal year and should be charged against revenues for that year. This keeps income lower and therefore less taxes are paid. Using present value of money calculations, profits are worth more in a present year than in a future year.

Deferred Income Taxes

When the completed-contract method is used, it can generate a deferred tax liability. How to calculate deferred taxes is a controversial issue in the accounting profession. Some professionals prefer the *income statement approach* that uses generally accepted accounting principles (GAAP). In the past this method was the only one used, and it is the method applied to all examples in this chapter.

The introduction of Statement of Financial Standards (SFAS) 96 brought forward a new method, the *balance sheet approach.* In this method, deferred taxes are provided for virtually all differences between financial and tax bases of assets and liabilities, as opposed to just "temporary" or timing differences. Because of the controversy and complexity of implementing this method, the profession postponed the mandatory implementation until December 15, 1991. Both approaches are discussed below.

Income Statement Approach. Consider a contractor whose net income before taxes is $100,000 for financial statement purposes, but whose tax return shows only $20,000. The difference in income before taxes is comprised of "temporary" differences that will disappear with time. These differences result primarily from different fixed-asset depreciation methods and profit-recognition methods used for book and tax purposes. To compute deferred taxes, the prevailing tax rate—34 percent, for example—is applied to both the $100,000 and the $20,000. The resulting difference in tax is reported as deferred tax and is added to, or subtracted from, the previous year's deferred tax liability on the balance sheet. The $34,000 ($100,000 x 34 percent) tax would be the total tax expense on the financial statements.

Balance Sheet Approach. In the balance sheet approach to deferred taxes, virtually all actual differences between the financial and tax bases of assets and liabilities are considered, rather than just the temporary differences. In calculating the deferred tax, liabilities are based on the higher of regular tax or alternative minimum tax (AMT). In essence, current year rates are projected and applied to future years' differences. This projected tax is then totaled and reflected as a liability on the balance sheet.

The tax on the difference for one year is shown as a current liability. The rest, which is applicable to future years, is shown as a long-term liability. The adjustment, up or down, needed to bring the liability balance to actual is the amount shown on the income statement as current-year deferred tax. This means that both the income statement and the balance sheet will reflect the current-year actual tax computed and due, as well as the remaining computed deferred tax related to future years.

The treatment of deferred income taxes arising from temporary differences in income recognition has been a controversial subject for underwriters. The tax due could be a current or long-term liability. What might appear as deferred income today could disappear as officers' bonuses tomorrow. Because there are also other ways to avoid taxes, in the context of this text, all deferred tax liability arising from the differences in income recognition is treated as current.

If a contractor sustains a net operating loss (NOL), that loss can first be carried back as a reduction against taxes paid over the preceding three years; and the contractor can apply for a refund. This tax reporting loss can also be carried forward as a reduction to future tax reporting profits for the next fifteen years. When this is done, it should be stated in the notes to the financial statements. The underwriter may also consider it as an offset against deferred tax liability on the balance sheet for financial reporting although it has not been reflected as a reduction of the liability in the financial statements.

Underwriting Considerations

Consider some of the *percentage-of-completion* statement features of XYZ Construction Co., Inc., that would make the account attractive to all surety companies.

1. There are twice as many current assets as current liabilities, or a 2-to-1 current ratio. This is part of the healthy "balanced" condition for which a surety looks. The higher the ratio, the more assets to provide a cushion for unforeseen events that might affect the company's ability to meet obligations. Most sureties have established minimums they accept as a current ratio, with perhaps a 1.2-to-1 or 1.1-to-1 ratio being too low.

2. As shown earlier in Exhibit 5-6, net worth of $8,617,717, often referred to as "loss paying power," exceeds all current and long-term debt of $8,593,929. This is another feature that is of interest to sureties. In XYZ's case, there is a debt-to-equity ratio of almost 1-to-1:

$$\frac{\$8{,}617{,}717 \text{ (equity)}}{8{,}593{,}929 \text{ (debt)}} = \underset{\text{(debt)}}{1} : \underset{\text{(equity)}}{1.0027}$$

In many cases, however, debt exceeds equity, and the underwriter should carefully analyze this disparity. For example, while twice as much debt as equity might be acceptable, four or five times may be too much. Most sureties establish a maximum debt-to-equity relationship for underwriting purposes.

3. Sizable cash balances are carried with surplus cash invested in short-term marketable securities. This has been partly accomplished through overbillings to various owners, but it also indicates that receivables are being promptly collected, and profits are being realized on most of the jobs. Within reasonable limits, overbillings are healthy and common in the industry. When they exceed the total anticipated profits for the entire job, however, these billings might be considered excessive. When this occurs, it is sometimes referred to as *job borrow* or *plowback*.

4. Exhibit 5-6 shows that total accounts receivable and earned estimates and retainage exceed all accounts payable and due subcontractors by $4,497,735 ($4,604,902 + $5,916,091 – $2,604,198 – $3,419,060). This is another cushion and a potential hedge against unanticipated events such as falling behind in the collection of receivables.

5. As shown earlier in Exhibit 5-7, a gross profit margin of 7.4 percent was generated, which is respectable for a general contractor performing a large volume of work. G&A expenses appear to be well under control at 3.5 percent of total revenues, particularly where $682,460 was paid to three officers as salaries in addition to the $850,000 paid in bonuses. The $133,608 in interest earned indicates that the cash flow remained strong throughout the year, while the interest expense remained low.

6. Of major significance is the return on investment (ROI), which was an impressive 34.3 percent. This would be calculated as follows:

> Net profit after tax of $2,202,519 as of 12/31/91 divided by the net worth of $6,415,198 at 12/31/90 equals 34.3%. The $6,415,198 net worth for 12/31/90 was composed of $175,000 of capital stock minus $16,000 of treasury stock, and plus $6,256,198 of retained earnings.

Subchapter S Corporations

There are certain income tax advantages of a corporation changing from a regular or "C" corporation to an "S" corporation. As a result of the reduction in individual income tax rates under the 1986 Tax Reform Act, many contractors converted from the "C Corporation" tax filing status to the "Subchapter S" status under the Internal Revenue Code. In a *Subchapter S corporation*, every stockholder reports its respective net earnings on a personal income tax return. There is usually no corporate tax liability. The IRS has established a thirty-five-stockholder limitation, however, on Subchapter S corporations; and there can only be one class of capital stock issued.

When there is a conversion to a Subchapter S corporation, the corporate balance sheet and income statement no longer carry any provision for current or deferred taxes after the date of conversion. This increases retained earnings, thus creating a healthier financial picture from a credit perspective. A negative feature is that the individuals generally may have to make sizable withdrawals from the corporation in the form of higher salaries or bonuses to meet their increased personal tax liability because corporate earnings are now taxed to them. It is important for the surety underwriter to determine with reasonable accuracy the amount of these additional withdrawals. The CPA is frequently in a position to provide this estimate, particularly when the same accounting firm prepares the stockholder's personal tax returns as well as the corporation's Subchapter S return. Based on this estimate, underwriters may make an adjustment in the analysis of working capital to provide for these additional withdrawals.

When actual distributions of all profits are made to the stockholders of a Subchapter S corporation at the end of the year, working capital can be greatly impaired. As a result, it is a good idea for the surety to have an agreement with the contractor to limit distributions to normal salary and bonus levels. An additional amount could be allowed for the additional personal tax liability incurred using the Subchapter S over what would have been the case filing under a "C" corporation.

Pro Forma Statements

Pro forma statements are projected financial statements. Financial forecasting is often necessary for budgeting purposes. Therefore, the ability to project sales, costs, and capital requirements enables a firm to forecast operating results, cash flow, and increases in retained earnings through a given period. These projections can apply to the cumulative effect of monthly sales and cost projections based on historical trends, market conditions, and other factors on a single transaction.

If, for example, a firm planned to sell an asset for cash after the date of its latest FYE financial statement, against which the firm carried a sizable corresponding debt, a pro forma statement would forecast the effects of the sale on the financial condition at the time of the statement date. Assume that this asset had a book value of $300,000, a corresponding debt of $150,000, and was sold for $400,000, subject to a 40 percent capital gains tax. The effect of this sale would be to increase working capital and retained earnings by $210,000:

Net Worth		Working Capital	
$400,000	Sale	$400,000	Sale
–300,000	Book Value	–150,000	Debt
100,000	Capital Gain	250,000	
+150,000	Debt Removal	–40,000	Tax
250,000		$210,000	Increase
–40,000	40% Tax		
$210,000	Increase		

Regulatory Financial Reporting

Many organizations must periodically file financial qualifying reports with various governmental regulatory authorities for licenses to conduct business in the public sector. An independent CPA usually prepares these reports based on GAAP and gives a full opinion. The regulatory bodies promulgate financial standards for a particular line of business and monitor compliance with these standards. For construction firms, there is often a limit to which capital and other resources may be committed. This limit is usually translated into the single job size and aggregate work programs permitted.

Two such regulatory agencies are the Securities and Exchange Commission (SEC) and state, county, or local governments. The SEC is the federal agency that regulates all securities trading in the United States. It can grant, suspend, and revoke the registration of any security it finds to be financially unsound. To monitor the soundness of publicly traded securities, the SEC mandates the filing of 10Q (quarterly) and 10K (annual) reports, which disclose all material developments that take place in the corporate structure of regulated corporations from one period to the next.

State, county, and local governmental agencies also regulate financial reporting. Many of these agencies establish prequalification requirements for those bidding on public works projects. For instance, bidders on any public work project might be required to disclose their financial condition. The requirements of these agencies only vaguely resemble the far more exacting and extensive requirements for disclosure of the SEC.

Relying on either of these reports as the only underwriting source would be questionable. The SEC reports, however, provide valuable background and operating information to the surety.

Sureties are subject to regulation by the U.S. Treasury Department, which establishes the single job size they can bond on federal projects. These limits are based on the sureties' capital and surplus as stated in their most recent annual reports.

NONCONTRACT SURETY ACCOUNTING

Except for the methods used in construction accounting, the preceding basic accounting methods and principles, the three kinds of reports from independent CPAs, and the fundamental analytical approach to evaluating financial information can be applied to the underwriting of noncontract bonds, as well as contract bonds.

In establishing the financial standards required for the riskier noncontract undertakings, many surety underwriters use a multiple of net worth in excess of the bond penalty as their general underwriting criteria. For example, the standard for a $10,000 plaintiff's attachment bond may be ten times the bond penalty, or $100,000. Once the net worth test is met, other statement features would also be of underwriting interest, such as ratios, liquidity and profitability.

Because of the infinite variety of judicial, and license and permit bonds and the degree of risk associated with each, it is well beyond the scope of this chapter to further generalize on financial underwriting standards. This is particularly true since the application of these standards for bonding considerations may vary significantly from one surety to another. However, as a general underwriting practice, many sureties require collateral in the form of cash equivalents or irrevocable letters of credit. This collateral is used to support the larger and more hazardous credit or financial guarantee risks, despite the financial worth of the applicant in many cases.

Of the accounting methods discussed, the straight accrual method is most often used to generate the financial statements sureties require in noncontract underwriting.

In any statement, the source of the financial data, its format, the qualitative and quantitative substance of the content, and its ultimate reliability for underwriting purposes can vary radically from one presentation to another. Statements for noncontract risks can range from one prepared by a national accounting firm, with full opinion from an independent CPA for a Fortune 500 corporation, to one manually produced by a small proprietorship on the surety's license and permit or court bond application form, without income statements, schedules, and notes. In the latter case, the credit analyst must often rely on balance sheet "guesstimates" an independent accountant may or may not have constructed from a trial balance. These brief, and often highly questionable, financial disclosures allow the surety to form only a general opinion of the applicant's liquidity, solvency, and credit worthiness.

The size and nature of a noncontract risk dictates the depth and quality of financial information a surety requires. For example, the balance sheet prepared on the surety's LP&M application form for a $2,500 liquor license bond would hardly suffice for a $250,000 supersedeas or temporary restraining order bond. For these larger bonds, the surety should require a more substantial statement before considering the risk.

The financial information furnished for noncontract surety obligations can be as diverse as the applicants themselves. As a result, the noncontract surety underwriter must be aware of the differences in the quality of financial information and the variations in balance sheet composition characteristic of certain businesses. For instance, the underwriter must recognize that a substantial capital investment in inventory and fixed assets for a manufacturer or automobile dealer is typical. On the other hand, this kind of profile for a travel agency or other service-oriented company would be unusual and questionable.

INDEMNITORS' FINANCIAL STATEMENTS

Because the surety requires a guarantee from a third-party for indemnity to support a bonded principal, the worth of this agreement is measured in terms of the indemnitor's financial strength. Accordingly, a surety also reviews indemnitors' financial statements, which vary greatly in quality and substance, particularly those furnished by personal indemnitors. While an independent CPA occasionally prepares a personal statement, indemnitors often prepare their own statements on sureties' forms or forms that their banks use. A principal's bookkeeper often types a form. Even when prepared by a CPA, these statements are rarely audited so that, in general, the personal statement is not as reliable as those required of a bonded principal.

It is always desirable for the personal statement to include schedules of the assets and liabilities stated on the balance sheet. The schedules break down securities, real estate, corresponding debts, and other items. While some of these documents may be accepted at face value, the surety may choose to verify some of the larger assets and notes payable or require additional details and explanations.

When the indemnitor is a subsidiary or affiliate, the financial data supplied are usually more reliable than that on personal statements. It is also likely that these financial statements have been prepared by an independent CPA.

The surety may base an underwriting decision partly on the liquidity and fixed asset "borrowing power" of an indemnitor and may rely on the ability to indemnify in terms of the following:

1. Making funds available to the principal during periods of temporary cash flow interruptions
2. Responding to the principal's capital requirements as serious operating losses are being sustained
3. Salvage for the surety who may be incurring losses in the completion of a defaulted obligation

SUMMARY

This chapter introduced and discussed the basic accounting principles and the methods used to prepare financial statements.

It emphasized the importance of the source of the financial data and the credentials of the preparer in terms of how heavily a surety can rely on the financial information presented by an applicant.

While compilation statements may be suitable for internal purposes, they do not provide information that is suitable as a basis for making underwriting decisions. Most sureties require at least a review or audited statement before making a decision. Furthermore, they usually directly verify the applicant's principal assets and liabilities.

The chapter defined the components of the financial statement. Also identified were the differences in how a CPA and a surety underwriter might treat assets and liabilities in determining working capital and tangible net worth.

The completed-contract and percentage-of-completion accrual accounting methods were compared to the straight accrual and cash methods. The relevance of each in evaluating contract and noncontract risks was also discussed. Deferred income arising from the temporary differences in income recognition and depreciation methods were explained. Also discussed were the ways in which each method is treated for financial and tax reporting purposes.

Fundamental statement analysis provided the key factors in determining what was of interest and concern to the underwriter and the significance of each in arriving at a sound underwriting decision. In any analysis, the underwriter must be aware that some financial statements will be more reliable than others. Noncontract cases and statements from personal and corporate indemnitors will vary greatly in terms of reliability, and the risk assumed by the surety often corresponds to the level of reliability of a statement. The greater the risk, the more significant the financial support required of indemnitors.

While a financial statement may not tell the entire story in every case, it is still the most reliable gauge for the measurement of a company's capital and creditworthiness.

Chapter Note

1. James Don Edwards, Roger H. Hermanson, R.P. Salmonson, and Peter R. Kensicki. *Introduction to Accounting,* 2nd ed. (Malvern, PA: American Institute, 1991), pp. 126, 130.

CHAPTER 6

Financial Analysis

One of the keys to successful suretyship is the ability to distinguish between companies that are well managed, profitable, and financially sound and those that are not. A financial analysis is how the surety makes this distinction. This chapter discusses financial analysis, its purpose and importance, and the two levels of financial analysis, financial statements and analytical procedures.

PURPOSE AND IMPORTANCE OF FINANCIAL ANALYSIS

The main purpose of financial analysis is to develop a thorough understanding of a company's credit worthiness. The results of the analysis will show whether the principal is a good credit risk or a poor credit risk, thus determining whether or not the surety decides to stand behind the principal.

Financial analysis is a name for a variety of techniques for gathering the evidence for the credit decision. It is an evaluation of an organization's operating and financial data through the use of ratios, trends, industry peer comparisons, reasonableness tests, and related procedures.

Financial analysis is used primarily when the surety arrangement (or bonding situation) involves a financial guarantee or payment obligation. The evaluation of the company's credit capacity is vital in such cases. Examples of such bonds include tax obligations, export/import bonds, and contract surety.

Financial analysis is less useful in underwriting other kinds of bonds such as license and permit or fidelity bonds. In such cases, however, the analysis still helps the underwriter to become comfortable with the company's ability to continue as a going concern.

FINANCIAL STATEMENTS

A bond underwriter's primary source of information for a financial analysis is a firm's financial statements. An in-depth review of a company's financial statements clarifies the company's financial position; its key accounting policies, obligations, sales, and earnings; the quality of its financial reporting; and the accountant's understanding of the industry. In order to perform this analysis, the surety must not only understand financial reporting, but it must also require financial reporting with full disclosure.

It is the company's responsibility to provide a financial statement that accurately and clearly reflects its financial position. It is the surety's responsibility to distinguish between a properly prepared financial statement and one that is not. As discussed in Chapter 5, a proper financial statement is one that is prepared according to *generally accepted accounting principles* (GAAP). These principles require financial statements to disclose the following information:

- Balance sheet
- Income statement
- Statement of changes in owner's equity
- Statement of cash flows
- Notes to financial statements

Contract Surety

Construction contractors are among the primary users of surety credit. Example Contractor, Inc. is discussed in the Appendix to this chapter, which, as mentioned, illustrates proper reporting by construction contractors. The illustration also shows several additional schedules that are included with the contractor's financial statements. These schedules help the surety to assess the financial strength of a contractor and the soundness of its management. The following schedules are included:

- Summary of contract earnings
- Earnings (in detail) from contracts completed and in progress
- Unallocated indirect costs
- General and administrative expenses

Noncontract Surety

There are industries other than construction contractors who use surety credit. While the techniques of financial analysis may be similar in contract and noncontract surety underwriting, the surety typically requires industry-specific information to be disclosed on the financial statements for a noncontract surety arrangement. The following are examples of such industry-specific information:

- Coal and other mining industries may be required to disclose the reclamation status of each mine site.
- Airlines may be required to disclose passenger miles traveled by class.
- Hotels may be required to disclose occupancy and vacancy rates.

The surety would evaluate this information by comparing it to industry statistics in order to rank the principal in its industry according to its financial health.

Exhibit 6-1 shows the critical facts that are revealed to the surety if financial statements are properly prepared. The Appendix to this chapter shows the format in which GAAP statements should be prepared.

Notes to the Financial Statement

In addition to the income statement and balance sheet (explained in Chapter 5), the *notes to the financial statement* are a critical component of the financial analysis. The notes are important because the clarity of the notes heavily affects the credibility of the financial statement as a whole. Experienced surety underwriters can evaluate from the notes alone just how well the preparers of the report really understand both the company's business and the procedures of preparing financial reports.

Notes to financial statements should clearly show whether a company is on a cash or accrual basis. Contractors generally use the percentage-of-completion or the completed-contract methods of accrual accounting, and it is critical to know which method a contractor uses to make a proper analysis of the company's financial strength.

The notes must explain the procedures for allocating indirect construction costs to jobs, as well as the procedures for determining the amount of gross profit recognized on jobs in progress. A reader should be able to analyze from the notes the financial impact of over- and underbillings, which are particularly crucial in construction accounting.

Exhibit 6-1
Critical Facts Learned in Financial Analysis Process

- Accounting method used to determine income recognition
- Method of determining income recognition for tax purposes
- The extent of litigation or contingent liabilities
- Related-party transactions
  - Joint ventures
  - Stock repurchase agreements
  - Lease commitments
  - Claims and adjustments
  - Personal guarantees
  - Pension, profit sharing, and other employee-benefit plans
- The size of
  - Working capital (current assets less current liabilities)
  - Annual volume
- Other disclosures for contractors
  - Backlog
  - Over- and underbillings
  - Detailed job schedules that tie to the financial statements
  - Amount of unallocated indirect costs

The notes should also reveal the composition of the construction company, which is particularly important when it is consolidated or combined with other companies. The company may have other sources of cash, or its assets might be draining off into other ventures. Discerning the calculation method for current and deferred taxes is important for the surety to determine the nature and extent of any current and future tax liabilities.

Information about any company involvement in litigation that does not appear in the financial statements should be detailed in the notes. This includes a background description of the litigation as well as an assessment of the financial impact an adverse judgment will have on the company. A surety should also be able to determine the accounting procedures for claims from the notes.

In many instances, the notes will contain information that is critical to properly assessing the future well-being of a company. This information includes the costs of profit sharing and pension plans, the accounting methods used for valuing inventories or supplies that the company possesses, and the methods used for depreciating fixed assets.

The extent of related party transactions and the existence of any stock repurchase agreements should appear in the notes, including the composition of long-term debt and the nature of any lease commitments. The maturity schedule of long-term debt and the principal payment requirements are also critical items that warrant mentioning in the notes.

Opinion Letter

The extent to which a surety can rely on financial statements is a function of the extent of the CPA's involvement with the financial statements and the quality of the CPA's presentation.

Guidelines from the American Institute of Certified Public Accountants (AICPA) enable CPA firms to provide a wider range of financial reporting assistance to companies and individuals than ever before. Privately owned companies may choose from three different levels of service (or opinions): the audit, the review, and the compilation. Each offers a different degree of reliability in terms of the accuracy of a financial statement.

Audits. An *audit* provides the highest degree of assurance to the reader. The independent certified public accounting firm expresses an opinion about how closely the financial statements conform to GAAP, thus assuring the surety that the company's financial data have been tested. Only a CPA who is certified in a given state or territory can make this judgment.

When a CPA firm's report accompanies audited financial statements, it signifies a high degree of reliability that is recognized by analyzers of financial information. Before a CPA firm can issue an audit report, it must perform numerous audit procedures to test the reliability of the financial statements. There are tests to verify the assets, liabilities, revenues, and expenses shown in the financial statements. These tests are not performed in a review, which will be treated in the next section. For example, in auditing accounts receivable, a CPA firm independently communicates with the principal or client to verify that the amounts shown are correct and to determine that they are reasonably collectible. These procedures show the CPA firm that (1) significant assets are properly recorded, are the property of the company, and are reflected in the correct amount and account in the financial statements; and (2) significant obligations of the company have been recognized.

The auditors also analyze and evaluate the effectiveness of a company's accounting procedures and internal accounting controls. An effective internal control system captures all significant financial transactions and helps safeguard assets. If an effective system is in place, the auditor should be able to test it by analytically reviewing transactions. An effective system should also favorably affect the nature and extent of the required auditing procedures because the data in a good system require less checking than that in a poor system.

Finally, the auditing firm tests the financial statements to ensure that they properly reflect the amounts recorded in the accounts and records. The financial statements should contain all required disclosures and any other information needed to accurately reflect a company's financial position.

The result of this auditing process is the CPA firm's opinion attesting to the fairness of the financial statement presentation in conformity with generally accepted accounting principles. The value of this opinion is measured by the great extent to which sureties rely on audited financial statements. No other form of CPA involvement with financial statements provides the same degree of assurance.

Reviews. The purpose of a *review* is to identify unusual relationships or individual items in a company's financial profile. With this information, the CPA challenges a company's financial statements to determine whether or not they comply with GAAP principles.

Reviews of financial statements provide a significantly lower degree of assurance than audits. In a review the CPA firm interviews management and may perform some analytical procedures in order to state that it is not aware of any material changes that should be made for the financial statements to conform with GAAP. When the review is complete, the CPA firm issues a report briefly describing the nature and extent of the procedures performed and inquiries made of management. The report also states that the CPA firm did not perform an audit and cannot express a professional opinion.

The significant difference between an audit and a review is that, in a review, the CPA does not verify data with outside sources, evaluate internal control procedures, observe physical assets, test accounting records, or examine detailed support. A review is limited basically to inquiry of company management. An audit is based on independent tests of the company's financial statements. Nevertheless, a review does provide some degree of assurance, and many sureties find a review to be a cost-effective alternative to an audit. It is very different from compilation, in which the CPA provides no assurance.

Compilations. *Compilation* statements organize and present a firm's capital resources and obligations in a professional accounting format. They are useful management tools in monitoring operating trends and current financial condition. The CPA firm or public accountant assists in preparing the financial statements, but is not obliged to make inquiries unless it observes an obvious error or lack of disclosure. Therefore, the firm cannot assure the surety that the financial statements meet any of the professional standards.

A compilation provides little to no assurance because it has significant limitations. The CPA firm is not required to perform any specific tests or to make inquiries of management or analyses of statements unless there are obvious deficiencies in the statements. In preparing a compilation, the CPA firm has only the following obligations:

- To have sufficient knowledge of the accounting principles and practices of the industry in which the company operates
- To have a general understanding of the nature of the entity's business transactions, the form of its accounting records, the qualifications of its accounting personnel, the accounting basis on which the financial statements are to be presented, and the form and content of the financial statements
- To read the financial statements to ensure that (1) they are appropriate in form and clerically accurate, and (2) they appear to contain adequate disclosures as required by existing professional standards

Most sureties will not accept compiled financial statements for year-end statements, but may accept them for interim purposes. The compiled statements would probably require additional schedules to support items on the balance sheet and statement of income.

Analyzing the Quality of Financial Statements

In addition to the opinion of the CPA, the surety should independently assess the quality of the financial information. Although sureties are neither CPAs nor qualified to perform accounting or auditing tasks, they must be able to make reasonable judgments about the quality of financial data in order to justify their reliance on financial statements for the purpose of extending credit.

In evaluating financial information, the surety should watch for the following "red flags" that are a signal of poor quality or the CPA's lack of knowledge or industry experience:

1. *Late reporting.* Audited financial statements should be available within ninety days of the end of the fiscal year. Late reports are often a sign that there are problems with the underlying records or that there are significant disputes between the contractor and the CPA or discrepancies which need to be resolved. The audited financial statement should be issued and in the hands of the surety not later than ten days after the date of the CPA's opinion letter.
2. *Errors in the statement, footnotes, or supporting schedules.* There is no such thing as an inconsequential error in a CPA-prepared statement. Sureties rely heavily on the expertise of the CPA to perform the work with due diligence. Where there are obvious errors, there are often more substantial ones that remain hidden.

3. *Inadequate footnote disclosure.* Footnotes are the primary responsibility of management, but the CPA has a duty to see that they are accurate and complete.
4. *Lack of appropriate or properly prepared supporting schedules.* This might mean that the principal or contractor is trying to hide unfavorable information about the business.
5. *Changes in the reporting entities, accounting policies, or the CPA.* Changes in entities or accounting policies interfere with the ability to track performance. These changes can mask the full impact of negative financial developments. A change in CPAs is a major event that must be carefully evaluated. It may be a positive change if the new CPA firm has greater knowledge and experience in the company's industry. It may also be a signal that there is a disagreement between the contractor and the CPA, who knows best about accounting presentation or disclosure issues.

ANALYTICAL PROCEDURES

The analytical procedures for financial analysis include numerous quantitative techniques used to evaluate the creditworthiness of a company. The techniques include working capital and net worth, ratio analysis, trend analysis, and gross profit analysis for construction contractors.

Working Capital and Net Worth

Every company has a business transaction cycle that represents the cycle of converting company resources to the sale of goods or services. This cycle is called the *operating cycle;* it changes constantly as the company's resources are consumed and replenished. The length of the operating cycle of most companies can be measured in days, weeks, or months. However, many companies may have operating cycles in excess of a year or longer. For example, a contractor may take two years to complete a project. When the surety analyzes a company's financial position, it is important to evaluate this operating cycle. The two indicators used to evaluate the cycle are working capital and net worth.

Working capital is the difference between current assets and current liabilities. *Current assets* are cash and other assets that are expected to be converted into cash within one year, or the average length of the operating cycle, whichever is greater. *Current liabilities* are those obligations that will be paid or liquidated in the same period.

Working capital measures the short-term aspects of the operating cycle, and creditors use it to evaluate the company's ability to furnish cash in the current year.

Net worth, or *net equity*, is the difference between assets and liabilities. It represents the investment and retained earnings in the company. Net worth is sometimes referred to as *long-term liquidity* because it measures the company's ability to produce profits over the long run, or the long-term aspects of the operating cycle. Net worth also indicates the company's ability to sustain losses.

Analysts often use working capital and net worth as benchmarks to determine the level of *credit capacity*, i.e., the safest level of credit that can be extended, on the basis of the belief that these factors represent the company's *loss paying power*. Depending on the analyst, various multipliers may be used to establish a level of credit capacity. For example, a multiplier of 10 times working capital or 5 times net worth may determine a subsequent year's working line of bonding credit, i.e., the new amount for which the principal may be bonded.

Although working capital and net worth are reliable measures of a company's operating capacity, they should not be the only techniques used to analyze creditworthiness because both indicators are greatly affected by the accounting methods or the quality of financial reporting, as mentioned in the section on financial statements.

Ratio Analysis

Ratio analysis is a mathematical technique for assessing a company's current financial posture using information from the financial statements.

This section discusses each ratio, illustrates its calculation, and describes its importance to creditors. (The illustrations are based on the discussion of Example Contractor, Inc. in the Appendix to this chapter.) Ratio analysis is better understood by grouping the different ratios into three areas of performance measurement: solvency, efficiency, and profitability.

Solvency Ratios. *Solvency ratios* measure the ability to meet obligations as they become due, even though some obligations arising from current operations may be settled a number of years in the future. The six ratios in this category are (1) quick ratio, (2) current ratio, (3) current liabilities to net worth, (4) current liabilities to inventory, (5) total liabilities to net worth, and (6) fixed assets to net worth.

Quick Ratio (Acid Test). The *quick* or *acid-test ratio* is an indication of the company's ability to cover current obligations. It reveals the protection afforded short-term creditors in cash and near-cash assets and is obtained by dividing cash, plus marketable securities and current receivables, by current liabilities. Example Contractor yields a 1.2 ratio:

$$\frac{\text{(Cash + marketable securities + receivables)}}{\text{(Current liabilities)}} =$$

$$\frac{(\$507{,}540 + \$289{,}000 + \$688{,}245 + \$1{,}000{,}608 + \$32{,}356)}{(\$2{,}094{,}196)} = 1.2$$

Any time the ratio is greater than 1.0, it indicates a liquid condition. Like the current ratio, the quality of the assets included in the acid-test ratio should be evaluated. For example, an experienced analyst would not include retention receivable or retention payable for construction contracts because these obligations usually take longer to collect or pay and are not considered cash. As a result, the quick or acid-test ratio for Example Contractor would be recalculated at 0.7:

$$\frac{(\$507{,}540 + \$289{,}000 + \$688{,}245 + \$32{,}356)}{(\$2{,}094{,}196)} = 0.7$$

Current Ratio. The *current ratio* expresses the relationship between current assets and current liabilities. It compares the amount of current assets with which payments can be made to the amount of current liabilities requiring payment. This ratio is computed as total current assets divided by total current liabilities. For Example Contractor, the current ratio is 1.4:

$$\frac{\text{Current assets}}{\text{Current liabilities}} = \frac{\$2{,}863{,}085}{\$2{,}094{,}196} = 1.4$$

The higher the ratio, the more capable the company is of meeting its current obligations.

An experienced analyst would assess the reliability of the current ratio through a comprehensive review of items such as the following:

- Classification issues: simply reclassifying liabilities as noncurrent instead of current has a direct effect on the ratio.
- The qualities of the assets: For example, will receivables be collected? How rapidly? Will receivables from officers or other related parties ever be converted into cash? Should they be reclassified as noncurrent?
- Certain management decisions, while good for the company, may increase footings on both sides of the balance sheet, effectively flattening the ratio.

Current-Liabilities-to-Net Worth Ratio. The *current-liabilities-to-net worth ratio* expresses the relationship of current liabilities (current debts) to equity. The current-liabilities-to-net worth ratio recognizes that as net worth increases in relation to "creditors' equity," the risk assumed by the current creditors decreases. Therefore, the company is more capable of protecting the creditors because it can absorb losses. For Example Contractor, the ratio yields 2.58 times:

$$\frac{\text{Current liabilities}}{\text{Net worth}} = \frac{\$2{,}094{,}196}{\$808{,}727} \times 100 = 258\%$$

The higher the ratio, the more risk creditors assume. The lower the ratio, the greater the borrowing capacity and long-term financial stability. An extremely low ratio can also indicate a poorly leveraged condition that might be caused by under-aggressive financial policies.

Current-Liabilities-to-Inventory Ratio. The *current-liabilities-to-inventory ratio* is determined by dividing current liabilities by inventory. This division indicates the extent to which a business relies on funds from the disposal of unsold inventories to meet its debts. If large increases in sales occur at the same time that there are proportional increases in inventory, this may create a significant increase in current liabilities if the growth is not monitored properly. This ratio is dependent on the nature of a company's transaction cycle. The nature of manufacturing is based on the conversion of inventory to sales. However, a construction contractor's transaction cycle is based on the completion of a project and is not dependent on the conversion of inventory to sales. For Example Contractor, current liabilities are 36.23 times greater than inventory:

$$\frac{\text{Current liabilities}}{\text{Inventory}} \times 100 = \text{Current liability to inventory ratio}$$

$$\frac{\$2{,}094{,}196}{\$57{,}803} \times 100 = 3{,}623\%$$

Without an evaluation of the company's business cycle, this ratio would indicate that Example Contractor has a problem when compared with its industry, as shown later in Exhibit 6-3. This, however, is not the case because Example Contractor's inventory is composed of supplies and does not directly relate to the operating cycle.

Total-Liabilities-to-Net Worth Ratio. Total liabilities are all current and long-term liabilities. The *total-liabilities-to-net worth ratio* measures the extent to which "creditors' equity" in the assets of the business exceeds that of the net worth or owners' equity. The higher the ratio, the more risk the creditors are assuming. It is computed by dividing total liabilities (total debts) by net worth. For Example Contractor, this ratio is 2.86:

$$\frac{\text{Total liabilities}}{\text{Net worth}} = \frac{(\$2{,}094{,}196 + \$217{,}604)}{\$808{,}727} \times 100 = 286\%$$

Fixed-Assets-to-Net Worth Ratio. The *fixed-assets-to-net worth ratio* expresses the relationship of net fixed assets (total fixed assets less accumulated depreciation) to net worth. Fixed assets are identified on Example Contractor's balance sheet as property and equipment, less accumulated depreciation. They total $248,298. Example Contractor has a net worth of $808,727. A ratio of 30.7 percent results from the following calculation:

$$\frac{\text{Fixed assets}}{\text{Net worth}} \times 100 = \text{Fixed-assets-to-net worth ratio}$$

$$\frac{\$248{,}298}{\$808{,}727} \times 100 = 30.7\%$$

This ratio measures the degree to which an owner's equity has been invested in capital or fixed assets. The lower the ratio, the smaller the investment in fixed assets compared to net worth, and the greater the proportion of capital available to support current operations. This ratio varies according to the industry. For example, a highway contractor generally requires more large pieces of earth-moving equipment (fixed assets) than would a general building contractor. As a result, the ratio for the highway contractor would probably be higher than the ratio for a general building contractor. The analyst also should consider the relationships between cost and accumulated depreciation, an indication of the average age of the assets. The age of assets could affect efficiency and maintenance cost, or it could indicate substantial market value over book value.

Efficiency Ratios. *Efficiency ratios* measure how efficient an operation or business is. Examples are measuring efficiency in collecting outstanding accounts receivable and in the use of inventory and working capital. The five efficiency measures include (1) collection period, (2) net sales to inventory, (3) assets to sales, (4) sales to net working capital, and (5) accounts payable to sales.

Collection Period Ratio. The *collection period ratio* is calculated by dividing accounts receivable by sales and multiplying the results by 365 days. The quality or receivables of an organization can be ascertained by comparing the result with comparable industry data. The collection period for Example Contractor is 53.8 times, calculated as follows:

$$\frac{\text{Accounts receivable}}{\text{Sales}} \times 365 \text{ days} = \text{Collection period ratio}$$

$$\frac{\$1{,}721{,}209}{\$11{,}683{,}190} \times 365 \text{ days} = 53.8 \text{ times}$$

Net Sales-to-Inventory Ratio. The *net sales-to-inventory ratio* is determined by dividing annual net sales by inventory. The transaction or operating cycle of the business must be understood to properly evaluate this ratio.

For inventory-oriented businesses, the ability to control inventory properly is important to management because generally, inventory is costly to store, may deteriorate or become obsolete, and may be insufficient to meet demand adequately. This ratio gives an indication of how quickly inventory is being turned over and its impact on the flow of funds into the organization. The ratio can vary significantly between different lines of business and with regard to the timing for this measure. A contractor's maintaining large amounts of inventory may be reasonable if the contractor is gathering materials and supplies for a project. Contractors differ significantly in this ratio because of their specialties. Even though low turnover figures typically mean that inventories are high relative to sales, if turnover is too high, this might indicate that insufficient inventory is on hand to operate efficiently. The net sales-to-inventory ratio for Example Contractor is determined to be 202.1 times, calculated as follows:

$$\frac{\text{Net sales}}{\text{Inventory}} = \text{Net sales-to-inventory ratio}$$

$$\frac{\$11{,}683{,}190}{\$57{,}803} = 202.1 \text{ times}$$

This would normally indicate a problem if Example Contractor's operating cycle was not understood.

Assets-to-Sales Ratio. The *assets -to-sales ratio* is determined by dividing total assets by annual net sales. This ratio is useful in evaluating sales with the total investment that is necessary to produce those sales. While the results may vary significantly industry to industry and specialty to specialty, a comparison with the industry median can assist in determining whether a business is overtrading or undertrading (not obtaining enough sales to justify the invested assets). The ratio of 26.7 percent for Example Contractor is calculated as follows:

$$\frac{\text{Assets}}{\text{Sales}} \times 100 = \text{Assets-to-sales ratio}$$

$$\frac{\$3{,}120{,}527}{\$11{,}683{,}190} \times 100 = 26.7\%$$

Sales-to-Net Working Capital Ratio. The *sales-to-net working capital ratio* compares sales (revenues) to working capital. It measures how working capital is used in the business and how many times more revenue is generated from that underlying capital. For Example Contractor, the ratio is 15.2:

$$\frac{\text{Sales}}{\text{Net working capital}} = \frac{\$11{,}683{,}190}{(\$2{,}863{,}085 - \$2{,}094{,}196)} = 15.2 \text{ times}$$

A desirable ratio may be near the norm for the particular industry being examined. A ratio that is too high may indicate that the company is doing too much work for its available working capital, making it highly sensitive to a cash flow interruption. A ratio that is too low may indicate an inefficient use of working capital, possibly due to poor market conditions or a poor marketing program.

Accounts Payable-to-Sales Ratio. The *accounts payable-to-sales ratio* is determined by dividing accounts payable by annual net sales. This ratio is useful in determining how well a company is paying its suppliers in relation to the sales being generated. A growing percentage trend, or one significantly larger than the industry norm or median, can mean that the suppliers are being used to help finance current operations. Short-term creditors are particularly interested in this ratio since it may signal possible difficulties in paying accounts that are due to be paid. The accounts payable-to-sales ratio for Example Contractor is as follows:

$$\frac{\text{Accounts payable}}{\text{Sales}} \times 100 = \text{Accounts payable-to-sales ratio}$$

$$\frac{\$1{,}552{,}086}{\$11{,}683{,}190} \times 100 = 13.3\%$$

Profitability Ratios. *Profitability ratios* are measures used to determine the ability of an operation or business to generate profits. Three commonly used profitability ratios are (1) return on sales, (2) return on assets, and (3) return on net worth.

Return on Sales Ratio. The *return on sales ratio* is sometimes called the *net-profit* or *net-earnings ratio*. Like the return-on-net worth ratio, it measures the company's profitability. It is obtained by dividing earnings (net profit after taxes) by sales (revenue).

For Example Contractor, earnings represent 0.9 percent of revenue:

$$\frac{\text{Net profit after taxes}}{\text{Sales}} \times 100 = \text{Return on sales ratio}$$

$$\frac{\$109{,}640}{\$11{,}683{,}190} \times 100 = 0.9\%$$

For every dollar of revenue, the company is making 0.94 cents after expenses and taxes. The higher the ratio, the more profitable the company.

A sophisticated analyst should also review the Statement of Earnings to evaluate the source of net profits. For example, nonoperating sources of income such as gains or losses on the sale of fixed assets, interest income and expenses, and writedown of investments may overshadow operating sources of income and therefore distort the return on sales ratio.

Return on Assets Ratio. The *return on assets ratio* is derived by dividing net profit after taxes by total assets. The result is a good indicator of profitability for a business. Operating profits are compared to the assets which are available to earn a return. Companies or contractors using their assets properly and efficiently will obtain a relatively high rate of return, while those businesses not as efficiently operated will have a lower rate of return. The result for Example Contractor for this ratio is determined to be a 3.5 percent return as follows:

$$\frac{\text{Net profit after taxes}}{\text{Total assets}} \times 100 = \text{Return on assets ratio}$$

$$\frac{\$109{,}640}{\$3{,}120{,}527} \times 100 = 3.5\%$$

Return-on-Net Worth Ratio. The *return-on-net worth ratio* is also called the *profit-to-net worth ratio* or *earning power*. It measures the rate of return on the investment (equity) in the business and is often looked at as an overall evaluation of profitability. This ratio is obtained by dividing earnings (net profit after taxes) by net worth (ending equity). For Example Contractor, the return on equity is 13.5 percent:

$$\frac{\text{Earnings}}{\text{Net worth}} \times 100 = \text{Return on net worth ratio}$$

$$\frac{\$\ 109{,}640}{\$\ 808{,}727} \times 100 = 13.5\%$$

For Example Contractors, this ratio indicates that the company is making 13.5 percent on its investment of $808,727.

A high ratio generally indicates positive performance, although too high a ratio could indicate too little investment. A low ratio may indicate poor performance, conservative management, or a mature company that has accumulated a significant amount of wealth relative to its established volume level.

Conclusions From Ratio Analysis. The ratios for Example Contractor show that it is a relatively strong company. The return on net worth of 13.5 percent indicates a good return on investment (above current interest rates) and that the company is profitable. The sales-to-net working capital ratio indicates that the company has not overextended its capacity to achieve the present level of profitability.

It is important for a creditor to recognize that a single ratio cannot be used to fully evaluate a company's financial strength. The use of several ratios is the most effective approach to analyzing a company's financial position.

Example Contractor Compared With the Industry

The ratios just discussed give any underwriter a basis for comparing a company's performance with that of its industry. This comparison would show how a company ranks with its peers, thus giving the underwriter another perspective from which to evaluate the company.

Sureties use statistics about industry norms published by organizations such as Dun & Bradstreet (D&B) and Robert Morris Associates (RMA) to assess companies' relative financial conditions. Sureties should be cautious when comparing ratios to industry norms because each organization uses different calculations in developing its ratios and statistics.

The D&B and RMA studies use statistical comparisons for selected *Standard Industrial Classification Codes (SIC Codes)* of comparable size. Each ratio has three values presented for comparisons: upper quartile, median, and lower quartile.

Although "median" and "quartile" are everyday terms for statisticians, their meaning may not be clear to others. In fact, each ratio is calculated individually for every company in the industry sample. The individual ratios then are arranged in order of size, that is, "listed" from highest to lowest. For certain ratios, there may be differences of opinion about what is a "strong" or "weak" value. The figure that falls in the middle is the *median* for the ratio in that sample. The figure that falls above halfway between the median and the highest ratio is the *upper quartile*. The figure that falls below halfway between the median and the lowest ratio is the *lower quartile*. Each median, then, is the typical ratio for all businesses in the sample. The upper and lower quartile values typify the experience of firms in the top and bottom fourths of the sample.

Values falling between the upper and lower quartile represent the middle 50 percent of all the companies that are sampled, and this range is sometimes referred to as the *safety zone*. These values are graphically represented in Exhibit 6-2. Ratio values greater than the upper and less than the lower quartiles begin to approach "unusual" values.

Dun & Bradstreet's Industry Norms & Key Business Ratios are based on a computerized financial statement file of more than 1 million companies in more than 800 lines of business. The statistics are

Exhibit 6-2
Graphical Representation of a Sample

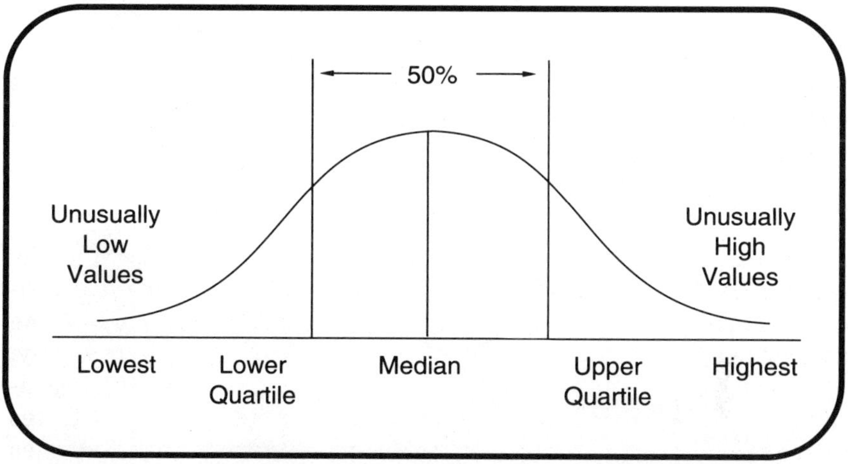

presented for a sample of companies in each business classification, as defined by two- and four-digit SIC Codes.

Exhibit 6-3 compares the ratios computed for Example Contractor with ratios compiled by D&B for a sample of contractors in similar fields of construction. The sample used for comparison includes SIC Code 1542, nonresidential construction contractors. For the industry sample, three ratios or values are presented, representing the beginning of the upper quartile, the median, and the beginning of the lower quartile.

Other Ratios

Numerous organizations compile and publish industry ratio statistics. Not all emphasize the same ratios. Robert Morris Associates (RMA), mentioned previously, is one of the better known organizations publishing industry ratio statistics.

In addition to these ratios, comparative industry statistics are developed for the balance sheet and income statement ratios. These statistics or percentages are often called *percentile ratios* or *common-size statistics* for the balance sheet and income statement. *Balance sheet ratios* are calculated by dividing items on the balance sheet by total assets; income statement ratios are calculated by dividing several measures of earnings by contract revenues. The balance sheet ratios are most useful in analyzing how a company uses its assets and how its debt is structured. Exhibit 6-4 shows a comparison of balance sheet and income statement ratios calculated for Example Contractor with those calculated from RMA financial statement data.[1]

Exhibit 6-3
Comparison of Example Contractor to Key Business Ratios for the Construction Industry

Ratio	Example Contractor	Industry Ratio*
Solvency		
1. Quick Ratio (Times)	1.2	1.5 UQ 1.2 Med 1.0 LQ
2. Current Ratio (Times)	1.4	1.9 UQ 1.5 Med 1.3 LQ
3. Current Liabilities to Net Worth (Percent)	258	83.2 UQ 156.2 Med 257.6 LQ
4. Current Liabilities to Inventory (Percent)	3623	138.6 UQ 340.2 Med 616.7 LQ
5. Total Liabilities to Net Worth (Percent)	286	96.2 UQ 174.5 Med 286.1 LQ
6. Fixed Assets to Net Worth (Percent)	30.7	10.0 UQ 19.1 Med 37.9 LQ
Efficiency		
1. Collection Period (Days)	53.8	38.6 UQ 54.1 Med 73.7 LQ
2. Sales to Inventory (Times)	202.1	293.5 UQ 120.7 Med 33.3 LQ
3. Assets to Sales (Percent)	30.7	24.4 UQ 31.7 Med 43.2 LQ
4. Sales to Net Working Capital (Times)	15.2	19.1 UQ 11.5 Med 6.6 LQ
5. Accounts Payable to Sales (Percent)	13.3	6.9 UQ 10.7 Med 14.9 LQ
Profitability		
1. Return on Sales (Percent)	.9	3.5 UQ 1.6 Med 0.6 LQ
2. Return on Assets (Percent)	3.5	8.5 UQ 4.3 Med 1.6 LQ
3. Return on Net Worth (Percent)	13.5	23.0 UQ 12.8 Med 5.0 LQ

UQ = Upper Quartile; Med = Median; LQ = Lower Quartile
*Dun's Analytical Services, "Industry Norms & Key Business Ratios," Three-Year Edition 1990-91, Agriculture, Mining, Construction, Transportation, Communication, Utilities

Exhibit 6-4
Comparison of Example Contractor, Inc.
Financial Statement Ratios with RMA Ratios

	RMA Commercial Construction	Example Contractor, Inc. 12/31/X9
Assets		
Cash & marketable securities	19.0	25.5
Accounts receivable		
current & other	39.3	23.1
retainage	7.0	32.1
Inventory	3.2	1.9
Under billings	4.7	8.1
Other current	4.1	1.1
Total current	77.3	91.8
Fixed assets (net)	13.9	8.0
Joint venture and investments	1.6	0.0
Other	7.1	.2
	100.0	100.0
Liabilities		
Notes payable—short-term	5.8	0.0
Accounts payable	29.1	28.5
Retainers payable	2.8	21.3
Income tax payable	1.6	0.7
Over billings	5.6	9.1
Current portion long-term debt	2.6	1.2
Other current & accruals	6.7	6.3
Total current	54.3	67.1
Long-term debt	7.7	7.0
Deferred taxes	2.0	0.0
Other non-current	1.2	0.0
Net worth	34.8	25.9
	100.0	100.0
Statement of Earnings Ratios		
Contract revenues	100.0	100.0
Cost of construction	84.9	94.2
Gross profit	15.1	5.8
Operating expenses	12.8	4.5
Other income	-0.2	-0.2
Earnings before taxes	2.5	1.4

Based on Robert Morris Associates, *Annual Statement Studies*, 1988 for SIC Code 1541 and 1542 using comparative historical data for contractors with revenue between $1 million and $50 million. Actual data is reproduced from fiscal year ending 3/31/88. Reprinted with permission, copyright Robert Morris Associates 1991.

Trend Analysis

While ratio analysis gives a financial picture of a company at a given point in time, trend analysis looks for patterns of movement in one variable, say performance, that follow the changes in some other variable over time.

Trend analysis reviews the same facts regarding a single company over a period of time, thus comparing the company's current financial position to its past positions. The analyst or underwriter develops a performance profile for the company, determines trends, and finds explanations or causal factors for deviation from the median.

Trend analysis is most valuable when two or more ratios are compared over the same period. Exhibit 6-5 shows that there may be a relationship between a current ratio and turns in equity. The turns in equity ratio compares sales to net equity. In the example, the company's working capital appears to be directly affected by increases in sales volume. As volume (turns in equity) goes up, working capital goes down, which means there is an inverse relationship between the two variables.

Financial Analysis of Construction Contractors

This discussion focuses on the special techniques applied to the financial analysis of a construction contractor. Special attention is given to gross profit analysis and the analysis of a contractor's estimating skills. These areas are critical in determining the contractor's creditworthiness.

Construction Contractors—What Makes Them Different? The contractor's business is different from other businesses because the transaction cycle, or operating cycle, is longer than that of other businesses. This difference makes it more difficult to evaluate the risk associated with financial statements. The analysis of working capital and net worth, as discussed previously, is usually not enough to fully analyze a contractor's credit capacity.

When a construction contractor sells a project, the transaction will typically last an average of nine to twelve months, and sometimes up to three or four years. A contractor does not know what the job's final revenue and cost until the job is completed, although these amounts can be estimated. In order to reflect this condition in a financial statement, the contractor typically uses the percentage-of-completion method under which the amount of earnings included in the income statement is based on an estimate of the monetary outcome of contracts (or jobs) in progress. These estimates make the financial evaluation of a contractor different from those for other industries. Therefore, since

Exhibit 6-5
Trend Analysis

	19X9	19X8	19X7	19X6	19X5
Current ratio	1.37	1.35	1.23	1.56	1.18
Turns in equity	14.4	15.4	16.8	12.4	15.4

Exhibit 6-6
Gross Profit Analysis from Statement of Earnings
(Thousands of Dollars)

	Contractor A	Contractor B
Job revenue	$20,000	$20,000
Job cost	18,000	18,000
Gross profit	2,000	2,000
G&A expenses	1,000	1,000
Pre-tax earnings	$1,000	$1,000
Equity	$2,000	$2,000
Gross profit rate	10%	10%

a contractor's financial statement is based largely on estimates, the surety must evaluate the contractor's estimating skills in order to correctly evaluate a contractor's financial position. The following sections demonstrate how different estimates would be evaluated.

Overall Risk Assessment. Exhibit 6-6 shows two contractors, A and B, who are both earning gross profit at the rate of 10 percent according to their statements of earnings prepared on a percentage-of-completion method. Their balance sheets reflect the same amounts of equity.

Further analysis of these contractors is illustrated in Exhibit 6-7, which shows information from financial statements prepared according to the format of Example Contractor. This exhibit shows that 95 percent of Contractor A's gross profit is attributable to completed contracts, and 5 percent is based on estimates. On the other hand, only 5 percent of Contractor B's gross profit is attributable to completed work, while the remaining 95 percent of Contractor B's gross profit is based on estimates. The implications of this analysis on the comparative quality of the contractors' equity are that only 5 percent of Contractor A's equity is subject to estimation, while 95 percent of Contractor B's equity is subject to estimation.

Exhibit 6-8 presents an abbreviated gross profit analysis for Contractor C. This example illustrates even more clearly the creditor's

Exhibit 6-7
Gross Profit Analysis from Summary of Construction Activity
(Thousands of Dollars)

	Contractor A			Contractor B		
	Completed	In Progress *	Total	Completed	In Progress *	Total
Job revenue	$19,000	$1,000	$20,000	$1,000	$19,000	$20,000
Job cost	17,100	900	18,000	900	17,100	18,000
Gross profit	$ 1,900	$ 100	$ 2,000	$ 100	$ 1,900	$ 2,000
G&A expenses			1,000			1,000
Pre-tax earnings			$ 1,000			$ 1,000
Equity			$ 2,000			$ 2,000
Percent of gross profit subject to estimating			5%			95%
Percent of equity subject to estimating			5%			95%

*Subject to the estimating process

Exhibit 6-8
Gross Profit Analysis from Summary of Construction Activity (Thousands of Dollars)

	Contractor C		
	Completed	In Progress *	Total
Job revenue	$10,000	$10,000	$20,000
Job cost	12,000	6,000	18,000
Gross profit	($2,000)	$4,000	$2,000
Gross profit rate	(20%)	40%	10%

*Subject to the estimating process

need to look beyond the gross profit rate in assessing the quality of reported earnings and equity.

Although Contractor C's statement of earnings shows a gross profit rate of 10 percent, there is a 20 percent loss on all completed contracts. This fact makes it difficult to believe that the contractor will realize the anticipated gross profit rate of 40 percent on the jobs still in progress.

Analysis of Estimating Skills. As suggested in the foregoing discussion, the contractor's estimating skills are critical to the creditor. The more evidence there is of the contractor's competence in estimating, the more confidence the creditor will have in the contractor's estimated gross profit figures for work in progress.

The creditor looks to the schedule of contracts completed (Schedule 1a in the Appendix) for the information needed to assess the contractor's estimating skills. A properly prepared schedule of completed contracts presents total revenue, cost, and gross profit for each job at the end of the prior reporting period and during the reporting period in which the work is completed. In reviewing these schedules, the creditor looks for evidence of two distinct estimating skills:

- The contractor's ability to "take off" plans and specifications and estimate jobs accurately. This ability can be tested by the consistency of gross profit rates realized during the life cycle of the job and by looking at the percentage of jobs on which losses were sustained.
- The field force's ability to estimate job progress compared with the original performance plan and the cost required to complete the job. This skill can be tested by comparing the gross profit rate realized when the job is completed with the rate of gross profit anticipated on jobs at interim periods and by

reviewing the number of jobs on which losses occurred but were not recognized until the final period.

While a review of these skills may identify estimating problems, additional research may disclose that the problems have actually arisen in the construction process or that difficulties in construction and estimating have contributed to the inconsistency in gross profit.

Exhibit 6-9 shows abbreviated schedules of contracts completed for Contractors D and E to illustrate how a creditor could assess and compare their estimating skills. This assessment would lead to the following conclusions:

- Contractor D's schedule of contracts completed demonstrates both types of estimating skills. There are no job losses reflected in the first three columns, "Job Totals at Completion"; and the interim gross profit rates derived from the second three columns, "Job Totals from Prior Years," were achieved when the jobs were complete, as shown by the third set of columns, "Job Totals for Year of Reporting."
- Contractor E's schedule of contracts completed suggests the opposite. The contractor experienced losses on 40 percent of the jobs completed. However, the gross profit rates on the job losses were thought to be positive at the end of the prior period. This indicates that neither of the job losses was recognized by estimators, superintendents, or the company president until the jobs were complete. This may also indicate that the company is trying to hide loss jobs by not recognizing loss in prior periods when they became evident.

The preceding analysis underscores the importance of preparing job schedules in the format presented by Example Contractor because they properly support the financial statements and highlight key information.

Assessment of Contracts in Progress. Part of the creditor's financial analysis of a contractor is an *assessment of contracts in progress*. The creditor's or underwriter's conclusions about a contractor's estimating ability as drawn from the schedule of contracts completed affects overall confidence in the schedule for contracts in progress (Appendix, Schedule 1b). For each job, this schedule summarizes contract price, revenue, cost, gross profit, and progress billings to date and for the reporting period. Comparing billings to date with revenue to date shows overbillings and underbillings, which affect the various categories on a balance sheet. Further review of gross profit on each job reveals any unusual profit recognition during the period.

Backlog Comparisons. *Backlog comparisons* are performed by anyone who analyzes a contractor's financial strength. The schedule of

Exhibit 6-9
Abbreviated Schedules of Completed Contract Schedule:
Contractors D and E

Contractor D

Job Number	Job Totals at Completion: Revenue	Cost	Gross Profit	Job Totals from Prior Years: Revenue	Cost	Gross Profit	Job Totals for Year of Reporting: Revenue	Cost	Gross Profit
1	$1,000	$ 900	$100	$ 500	$ 450	$ 50	$ 500	$ 450	$ 50
2	540	486	54	180	162	18	360	324	36
5	800	720	80	450	405	45	350	315	35
7	700	630	70	300	270	30	400	360	40
13	1,200	1,080	120	800	720	80	400	360	40
Total	$4,240	$3,816	$424	$2,230	$2,007	$223	$2,010	$1,809	$201
			10%			10%			10%

Contractor E

Job Number	Job Totals at Completion: Revenue	Cost	Gross Profit	Job Totals from Prior Years: Revenue	Cost	Gross Profit	Job Totals for Year of Reporting: Revenue	Cost	Gross Profit
1	$1,000	$ 900	$100	$ 500	$ 450	$ 50	$ 500	$ 450	$ 50
2	540	560	(20)	180	162	18	360	398	(38)
5	800	920	(120)	450	405	45	350	515	(165)
7	700	630	70	300	270	30	400	360	40
13	1,200	1,080	120	800	720	80	400	360	40
Total	$4,240	$4,090	$150	$2,230	$2,007	$223	$2,010	$2,083	$ (73)
			3.5%			10%			(3.6%)

contracts in progress presents, in the last three columns of Appendix, Schedule 1b, financial data on the contractor's future workload. By subtracting revenue recognized to date from the contract price, the contractor can calculate the backlog remaining on jobs in progress. Subtracting the estimated cost to complete the work from the backlog discloses the remaining gross profit to be realized on jobs still in progress.

The creditor is interested in knowing what portion of the selling, general, and administrative expense anticipated for the next fiscal year will be covered by the anticipated gross profit indicated in the future workload (backlog) portion of the contracts-in-progress schedule. The amount of anticipated selling, general, and administrative expense may be determined from the contractor's cash budget. Alternatively, the creditor may base an estimate of future expenses on the selling, administrative, and general expense schedule (Appendix, Schedule 2).

Schedule of Indirect Construction Cost. Another schedule used in the gross profit analysis for a contractor is the *schedule of indirect construction cost* (Appendix, Schedule 1c). This schedule tells the creditor the amount of indirect cost that was under- or over-allocated to jobs during the reporting period. It presents the actual amount spent by line item and the total effect of the offsetting costs charged to jobs during the year by major category, such as shop and yard, equipment, vehicles, and benefits.

The indirect-cost schedule in the Appendix (Schedule 1c) is appropriate for a general building contractor. It should be noted, however, that for a contractor whose equipment cost makes up a large part of the cost mix, this presentation may not be adequate. An additional schedule may be needed to analyze the effect, for example, of idle equipment or the appropriateness of hourly rates charged to jobs compared with the actual ownership cost of equipment in use. This indirect cost schedule may be the most significant indicator of the contractor's understanding of the business and management skill.

SUMMARY

This chapter addressed the issue of how a CPA, analyst, or underwriter evaluates the financial statements of a principal. It focused on the analysis of financial statements and the use of analytical procedures as a means to this end.

The primary financial statements required for an in-depth and complete analysis are the balance sheet, income statement, statement of changes in owner's equity, statement of cash flows, and the notes to financial statements.

Statements audited and prepared by a CPA offer the most reliable financial information. Audits give the highest degree of assurance since they are prepared using GAAP by a CPA certified in the state of domicile. Certain tests are performed to verify the assets, liabilities, revenues, and expenses shown in the financial statements.

Reviews provide less reliability than audited statements but more than compilations. In a review, a CPA neither verifies balances with outside sources nor evaluates internal control procedures. Compilations provide little to no assurance that the financial information provided is reliable. No specific tests are performed unless there are obvious deficiencies.

In addition to how the statement is prepared, the surety also looks for other factors that affect the quality and reliability of a financial statement. Slow reporting; errors in the statement; inadequate footnote disclosure; lack of appropriate or properly prepared supporting schedules; and changes in the reporting entities, accounting policies, or the CPA should cause the surety underwriter to be concerned about the quality of a financial statement.

Analytical procedures may be used in conjunction with a financial statement to evaluate the financial soundness of a company. These procedures include analyzing working capital and net worth, ratio analysis, trend analysis, and gross profit analysis for construction contractors.

In ratio analysis, once the ratios are determined, they are compared with others from similar businesses so that the surety can see where the potential principal falls in his class of business. Statistics used for this comparison are prepared by Dun & Bradstreet (D&B) and Robert Morris Associates (RMA). Values falling between the upper and lower quartile of similar types of companies can be considered to be in the "safety zone" for underwriting purposes.

Trend analysis shows a company's performance over a period of years, which can help the surety identify weak areas in finance and/or operations.

The gross profit analysis for construction contractors focuses on the estimating skills of the contractor and the field force's ability to estimate job progress. The surety also looks at backlog and indirect construction costs in assessing the financial soundness of a contractor. Because of the complexity of each of the financial examination processes discussed in this chapter, and because of the risks associated with surety underwriting, the chapter concluded with the idea that it takes extensive experience to become proficient in identifying well-managed, profitable, and financially sound companies.

Chapter Note

1. RMA has provided the following interpretation of Statement Studies figures:

   RMA recommends that Statement Studies data be regarded only as general guidelines and not as absolute industry norms. There are several reasons why the data may not be fully representative of a given industry:

   (1) The financial statements used in the *Statement Studies* are not selected by any random or statistically reliable method. RMA member banks voluntarily submit the raw data they have available each year provided that the companies' total assets are less than $250 million, except for contractors' statements which have no upper size limit.

   (2) Many companies have varied product lines; however, the *Statement Studies* categorize them by their primary product Standard Industrial Classification (SIC) number only.

   (3) Some of our industry samples are rather small in relation to the total number of firms in a given industry. A relatively small sample can increase the chances that some of our composites do not fully represent an industry.

   (4) There is the chance that an extreme statement can be present in a sample, causing a disproportionate influence on the industry composite. This is particularly true in a relatively small sample.

   (5) Companies within the same industry may differ in their method of operations, which in turn can directly influence their financial statements. Since they are included in our sample, too, these statements can significantly affect our composite calculations.

   (6) Other considerations that can result in variations among different companies engaged in the same general line of business are different labor markets; geographical location; different accounting methods; quality of products handled; sources and methods of financing; and terms of sale.

   For these reasons, RMA does not recommend the Statement Studies *figures be considered as absolute norms for a given industry. Rather, the figures should be used only as general guidelines and in addition to the other methods of financial analysis. RMA makes no claim as to the representativeness of the figures printed in this book.*

APPENDIX

Example Contractor, Inc.

Financial Statements and Additional Information

For the Years Ended December 31, 19X9 and 19X8

PREFACE

Example Contractor, Inc. represents a suggested financial presentation for construction companies. The presentation illustrates the disclosure requested by members of the surety and banking industries and represents the best features of current reporting and disclosure practices based on generally accepted accounting principles in effect in October, 1990.

Example Contractor, Inc. incorporates the disclosure requirements set forth in the AICPA's *Statement of Position on Accounting for Performance of Construction Type and Certain Production Type Contracts (SOP)* (81-1), and the *Audit and Accounting Guide for Construction Contractors*, as well as changes since the issuance of the SOP and Audit Guide. While it is not possible to present illustrations of every set of circumstances that the auditor might encounter in a contractor's financial statement, the example encompasses the most frequently encountered reporting and disclosure requirements for a contractor.

The additional information contains contract schedules completed and in progress, details of indirect construction costs and selling, and administrative and general expenses that are frequently requested by the surety and bankers industries, the primary users of contractor financial statements.

This version of Example Contractor, Inc. incorporates changes in generally accepted accounting principles and income tax law which occurred during the last several years, specifically:

- Statement of Financial Accounting Standards No. 95—"Statement of Cash Flows."
- Statement of Financial Accounting Standards No. 96—"Accounting for Income Taxes."
- Federal Income Tax changes of 1986, 1987, 1988, 1989, and 1990.
- Statement on Auditing Standards 58—Reports on Audited Financial Statements.

CONTENTS

REPORT OF INDEPENDENT CERTIFIED PUBLIC ACCOUNTANTS

Board of Directors and Stockholder
EXAMPLE CONTRACTOR, INC.
Metropolis, U.S.A.

We have audited the accompanying balance sheets of Example Contractor, Inc. as of December 31, 19X9 and 19X8, and the related statements of earnings and retained earnings, and cash flows for the years then ended. These financial statements are the responsibility of the company's management. Our responsibility is to express an opinion on these financial statements based on our audits.

We conducted our audits in accordance with generally accepted auditing standards. Those standards require that we plan and perform the audit to obtain reasonable assurance about whether the financial statements are free of material misstatement. An audit includes examining, on a test basis, evidence supporting the amounts and disclosures in the financial statements. An audit also includes assessing the accounting principles used and significant estimates made by management, as well as evaluating the overall financial statement presentation. We believe that our audits provide a reasonable basis for our opinion.

In our opinion, the financial statements referred to above present fairly, in all material respects, the financial position of Example Contractor, Inc. as of December 31, 19X9 and 19X8, and the results of its operations and cash flows for the years then ended in conformity with generally accepted accounting principles.

As discussed in Note E to the financial statements, the company changed its method of accounting for income taxes.

Certified Public Accountants
February 24, 19Y0

EXAMPLE CONTRACTOR, INC.
BALANCE SHEETS
December 31,

ASSETS

	19X9	19X8
CURRENT ASSETS		
Cash	$ 507,540	$ 329,414
Marketable securities, at cost	289,000	153,000
Receivables (Note B)	1,721,209	1,539,338
Unbilled amounts on completed contracts (Note A-1)	80,467	
Costs and estimated earnings in excess of billings on contracts in progress (Notes A-1 and C)	173,011	145,456
Inventories (Note A-6)	57,803	57,546
Prepaid expenses and other	34,055	29,996
TOTAL CURRENT ASSETS	2,863,085	2,254,750
PROPERTY AND EQUIPMENT, at cost (Notes A-3 and D)		
Land	35,000	35,000
Buildings and improvements	103,000	103,000
Construction equipment and vehicles	370,998	418,318
Office furniture and equipment	51,283	51,283
	560,281	607,601
Less accumulated depreciation	(311,983)	(255,637)
	248,298	351,964
OTHER ASSETS	9,144	8,025
	$3,120,527	$2,614,739

LIABILITIES AND STOCKHOLDERS' EQUITY

	19X9	19X8
CURRENT LIABILITIES		
Current maturities of long-term debt (Note D)	$ 36,530	$ 33,088
Accrued payroll, payroll taxes, fringe benefits, and amounts withheld from employees	196,760	103,076
Accounts payable		
Current	888,168	757,927
Retention	663,918	471,064
Accrued costs on completed contracts (Note A-1)	52,810	
Billings in excess of costs and estimated earnings on contracts in progress (Notes A-1 and C)	233,633	185,435
Income taxes (Notes A-4 and E)		
Currently payable	16,777	107,063
Deferred	5,600	4,000
TOTAL CURRENT LIABILITIES	2,094,196	1,661,653
LONG-TERM DEBT (Note D)	217,604	253,999
COMMITMENTS AND CONTINGENCIES (Note F)		
STOCKHOLDERS' EQUITY		
Common stock, par value of $1.00 a share; authorized 500,000 shares, issued and outstanding 50,000 shares	50,000	50,000
Retained earnings	758,727	649,087
	808,727	699,087
	$3,120,527	$2,614,739

See Report of Independent Certified Public Accountants and Notes to Financial Statements.

EXAMPLE CONTRACTOR, INC.
STATEMENTS OF EARNINGS AND RETAINED EARNINGS
Years ended December 31,

	19X9	19X8
EARNINGS FROM CONSTRUCTION (Notes A-1, C and Schedule 1)		
Revenues earned	$11,683,190	$10,748,327
Cost of construction	11,002,186	10,104,083
Gross profit	681,004	644,244
SELLING, ADMINISTRATIVE AND GENERAL EXPENSES (Schedule 2)	533,296	508,877
EARNINGS FROM OPERATIONS	147,708	135,367
OTHER INCOME (EXPENSES)		
Interest income	27,451	22,454
Other income	10,421	12,329
Gain on sale of fixed assets	12,560	254
Interest expense	(37,651)	(42,851)
Other expense	(2,349)	(2,662)
	10,432	(10,476)
EARNINGS BEFORE INCOME TAXES	158,140	124,891
INCOME TAXES (Notes A-4 and E)	48,500	22,700
NET EARNINGS	109,640	102,191
RETAINED EARNINGS, beginning of year	649,087	546,896
RETAINED EARNINGS, end of year	$ 758,727	$ 649,087

See Report of Independent Certified Public Accountants and Notes to Financial Statements.

EXAMPLE CONTRACTOR, INC.
STATEMENTS OF CASH FLOWS (DIRECT)
Years ended December 31,

	19X9	19X8
INCREASE (DECREASE) IN CASH AND CASH EQUIVALENTS		
CASH FLOWS FROM OPERATING ACTIVITIES		
Cash collected on contracts	$11,420,852	$10,592,293
Cash paid to suppliers and employees	(11,056,699)	(10,257,310)
Interest received	18,595	12,304
Interest paid	(28,795)	(32,701)
Income taxes paid	(146,620)	(127,387)
Cash paid to settle lawsuit for contract claims settlement		(26,453)
Net cash provided by operating activities	207,333	160,746
CASH FLOWS FROM INVESTING ACTIVITIES		
Proceeds from sale of construction equipment	40,000	6,500
Addition to equipment and vehicles	(35,000)	(128,450)
Increase in other assets	(1,119)	(2,310)
Net cash provided (used) in investing activities	3,881	(124,260)
CASH FLOWS FROM FINANCING ACTIVITIES		
Principal payments on long-term debt	(33,088)	(49,854)
Proceeds from refinancing of long-term debt		96,000
Net cash provided by financing activities	(33,088)	46,146
NET INCREASE IN CASH AND CASH EQUIVALENTS	178,126	82,632
CASH AND CASH EQUIVALENTS, beginning of year	329,414	246,782
CASH AND CASH EQUIVALENTS, end of year	507,540	329,414

EXAMPLE CONTRACTOR, INC.
STATEMENTS OF CASH FLOWS (DIRECT)
(continued)
Years ended December 31,

	19X9	19X8
RECONCILIATION OF NET EARNINGS TO NET CASH PROVIDED BY OPERATING ACTIVITIES		
NET EARNINGS	$109,640	$102,191
ADJUSTMENTS TO RECONCILE NET INCOME TO NET CASH PROVIDED BY OPERATING ACTIVITIES		
Depreciation	111,226	112,023
Gain on sale of equipment	(12,560)	(254)
Deferred taxes	1,600	(173,400)
Change in:		
Marketable securities	(136,000)	(53,000)
Receivables	(181,871)	(201,034)
Underbillings and unbilled amounts	(108,022)	13,466
Prepaid expenses and other	(4,316)	(5,417)
Accounts payable and other liabilities	416,914	303,627
Overbillings and accrued costs	101,008	46,877
Income taxes	(90,286)	15,667
	121,162	(58,555)
Net cash provided by operating activities	$207,333	$160,746

See Report of Independent Certified Public Accountants and Notes to Financial Statements.

EXAMPLE CONTRACTOR, INC.
NOTES TO FINANCIAL STATEMENTS
Years ended December 31, 19X9 and 19X8

NOTE A - SUMMARY OF SIGNIFICANT ACCOUNTING POLICIES

Example Contractor, Inc. is a general building contractor of commercial and light industrial buildings under long-term contracts. Example Contractor, Inc. operates primarily in the Southeast and Midwest.

A summary of the significant accounting policies applied in the preparation of the accompanying financial statements follows:

1. *Method of Accounting for Long-Term Construction Contracts*

   The accompanying financial statements have been prepared using the percentage-of-completion method of accounting and, therefore, take into account the cost and estimated earnings and revenue to date on contracts not yet completed.

   The amount of revenue recognized at the financial statement date is that portion of the total contract price that cost incurred to date bears to anticipated final total cost, based on current estimates of cost to complete. The amount of revenue recognized is not related to the progress billings to customers.

   Contract costs include all direct labor and related payroll benefits, materials, subcontractor costs and indirect cost allocations.

   As long-term contracts extend over one or more years, revisions in cost and earnings estimated during the course of the work are reflected in the accounting period in which the facts which require the revision become known.

   At the time a loss on a contract becomes known, the entire amount of the estimated ultimate loss is recognized in the financial statements.

   Contracts which are substantially complete are considered closed for financial statement purposes. Any accrued billings or costs related to these contracts are carried in the balance sheet as "Unbilled Amounts on Completed Contracts" and "Accrued Costs on Completed Contracts," respectively.

   The current asset, "Costs and Estimated Earnings in Excess of Billings on Contracts in Progress," represents revenues recognized in excess of amounts billed (underbillings) and the current liability, "Billings in Excess of Costs and Estimated Earnings on Contracts in Progress," represents billings in excess of revenues recognized (overbillings).

2. *Operating Cycle*

   Assets and liabilities related to long-term contracts are included in current assets and current liabilities in the accompanying balance sheets, as they will be liquidated in the normal course of contract completion, although this may require more than one year.

3. *Property, Equipment, and Depreciation*

   Property and equipment is carried at cost and is being depreciated principally on the straight-line method over the estimated useful lives of the related assets.

4. *Income Taxes*

   Deferred income taxes are provided for temporary differences in reporting income for financial statements and tax purposes arising from differences in the methods of accounting for depreciation. For tax purposes, contracts are reported on the "Percentage-of-Completion Method" as set forth in the 1986 Tax Act.

5. *Allocation of Indirect Construction Costs*

   Indirect construction cost is allocated to contracts as follows:

   Project Management—These costs are charged to contracts based on actual time on a per hour basis.

   Shop, Yard and Small Tools—These costs are charged to contracts based on a percentage of labor costs incurred by trade.

   Construction, Equipment and Vehicles—These costs are charged to contracts based on hours used.

   Payroll Benefits—These include payroll taxes, pension, welfare, vacation, group health, life and disability insurance, and workers compensation and liability insurance and are charged to contracts based on actual labor costs incurred.

   The difference between actual expenditures for indirect construction costs and the amounts allocated is charged to operations for the current year.

6. *Inventories*

   Inventories are stated at the lower of cost (first-in, first-out method) or market.

7. *Cash Equivalents*

   For purposes of the statements of cash flows, the company considers all highly liquid debt instruments purchased with a maturity of three months or less to be cash equivalents.

NOTE B - RECEIVABLES

Receivables at December 31, consist of the following:

	19X9	19X8
Contract receivables		
Current	$ 688,245	$ 823,015
Retention	1,000,608	697,967
	1,688,853	1,520,982
Other Receivables	32,356	18,356
	$1,721,209	$1,539,338

Contract receivables at December 31, 19X9 include $125,431 due from the majority stockholder on a contract in progress. This contract is for $690,000 of which the Company has reflected revenues of approximately $455,000 and gross profit of approximately $28,000 during the year ended December 31, 19X9. The Company collected $60,000 of this receivable during January 19Y0. In addition, the Company collected approximately $850,000 of the remaining receivables through February 24, 19Y0.

Other receivables contain advances to the stockholders in the amount of $15,000 and $9,000 for the year ended December 31, 19X9 and 19X8, respectively.

Current contract receivables at December 31, 19X9 are aged as follows:

0–30 days	$540,427
31–60 days	94,018
61–90 days	25,000
Over 90 days	28,800
	$688,245

NOTE C - CONTRACTS IN PROGRESS

Contract amounts, accumulated costs, estimated earnings and the related billings to date on contracts in progress at December 31, 19X9 are as follows (see Schedule 1):

	Contract Amount	Contract Revenue	Contract Cost	Gross Profit
Total construction activity	$22,079,799	$11,683,190	$11,002,186	$681,004
Contracts completed during the year (Schedule 1a)	(13,299,589)	(6,479,484)	(6,155,432)	(324,052)
Overallocated indirect construction cost			3,199	(3,199)
Callbacks and adjustments		(8,244)	(14,984)	6,740
Activity during the year on contracts in progress		5,195,462	4,834,969	360,493
Activity in prior years on contracts in progress		567,566	526,417	41,149
Contracts in progress December 31, 19X9 (Schedule 1b)	$ 8,780,210	5,763,028	$ 5,361,386	$401,642
Less progress billings to December 31, 19X9		5,823,650		
		$ (60,622)		

Included in the accompanying balance sheets are the following captions:

Costs and estimated earnings in excess of billings on contracts in progress	$ 173,011
Billings in excess of costs and estimated earnings on contracts in progress	(233,633)
	$ (60,622)

NOTE C - CONTRACTS IN PROGRESS (continued)

Contract amounts, accumulated costs, estimated earnings and the related billings to date on contracts in progress at December 31, 19X8, are as follows (see Schedule 1):

	Contract Amount	Contract Revenue	Contract Cost	Gross Profit
Total construction activity	$18,030,382	$10,748,327	$10,104,083	$644,244
Contracts completed during the year	(8,481,763)	(3,354,892)	(3,156,282)	(198,610)
Overallocated indirect construction cost			1,268	(1,268)
Callbacks and adjustments		(5,764)	(14,113)	8,349
Activity during the year on contracts in progress		7,387,671	6,934,956	452,715
Activity in prior years on contracts in progress		178,451	166,381	12,070
Contracts in progress December 31, 19X8	$ 9,548,619	7,606,101	$ 7,101,337	$464,785
Less progress billings to December 31, 19X8		8,070,886		
		$ (39,979)		

Included in the accompanying balance sheets are the following captions:

Costs and estimated earnings in excess of billings on contracts in progress	$ 145,456
Billings in excess of costs and estimated earnings on contracts in progress	(185,435)
	$ (39,979)

NOTE D - LONG-TERM DEBT AND LINE OF CREDIT

Long-term debt at December 31, consists of the following:

	19X9	19X8
Notes payable to bank, collateralized by construction equipment and vehicles with a carrying value of $192,600, due in monthly installments of $3,802 including interest of 9.75% through September, 19Y3	$142,969	$172,923
Mortgage note payable to bank, collateralized by land and building, with a carrying value of $104,600 due in monthly installments of $1,354 including interest at 11.75% through November, 19Z3.	111,165	114,164
	254,134	287,087
Less current maturities	36,530	33,088
Long-term debt	$217,604	$253,999

Aggregate maturities of long-term debt for the five years following December 31, 19X9 are as follows:

19Y0	$ 36,530
19Y1	44,525
19Y2	36,660
19Y3	5,381
19Y4	6,051
	$130,147

The Company has available an unsecured line of credit with a bank for $1,000,000. At December 31, 19X9 and 19X8, the line of credit was unused. Under the terms of this agreement, interest is charged at the prime rate plus 1%. This agreement is renewable annually on February 28.

NOTE E - INCOME TAXES

In 19X8, the Company adopted Statement of Financial Accounting Standards No. 96, Accounting for Income Taxes. Deferred tax liabilities represent the tax effects, based on current tax law, of future taxable amounts attributable to events that have been recognized in the financial statements. The cumulative effect of the change in accounting for income taxes results in a deferred tax benefit of $14,600 and is included in 19X8 provision.

During 19X8, the company was required to change its method of reporting long-term contracts from the completed contract method to the "Percentage-of-Completion Method" as set forth in the 1986 Tax Act.

The provision for income taxes as of December 31, consists of:

	19X9	19X8
Current income taxes payable		
Federal	$38,400	$179,000
State	8,500	31,700
	46,900	210,700
Deferred income taxes (benefit)	1,600	(173,400)
	48,500	37,300
Cumulative Effect of Change in Accounting for Income Taxes		(14,600)
	$48,500	$ 22,700

NOTE F - COMMITMENTS AND CONTINGENCIES

The Company is involved in various litigation with claims totaling approximately $310,000 relating to the failure of a subcontractor, to the Company, to pay its suppliers. In the opinion of management and counsel, the outcome of these claims will not have a material effect on the financial position of the Company

NOTE G - BACKLOG

Following is a reconciliation of the approximate backlog of signed contracts as of December 31,

	19X9	19X8
Balance as of January 1,	$ 4,300,000	$ 4,800,000
New contracts and change orders during the year	10,500,000	10,200,000
	14,800,000	15,000,000
Less contracts completed	11,700,000	10,700,000
Balance December 31,	$ 3,100,000	$ 4,300,000

In addition, between January 1, 19Y0 and February 24, 19Y0, the Company entered into contracts approximating $3,400,000.

ADDITIONAL INFORMATION

REPORT OF INDEPENDENT CERTIFIED PUBLIC ACCOUNTANTS ON ADDITIONAL INFORMATION

EXAMPLE CONTRACTOR, INC.
Metropolis, U.S.A.

Our audits were made for the purpose of forming an opinion on the basic financial statements taken as a whole of Example Contractor, Inc. for the years ended December 31, 19X9 and 19X8, which are presented in the preceding section of this report. The following additional information is presented for purposes of additional analysis. Such information has been subjected to the audit procedures applied in the audits of the basic financial statements, and, in our opinion, is fairly stated in all material respects in relation to the basic financial statements taken as a whole.

February 24, 19Y0

Schedule 1

EXAMPLE CONTRACTOR, INC.
SUMMARY OF EARNINGS FROM CONSTRUCTION

	Year ended December 31, 19X9			
	Revenue Earned	Cost of Construction	Gross Profit	GP %
Contracts Completed (Schedule 1a)	$ 6,479,484	$ 6,155,432	$324,052	5.00%
Contracts in Progress (Schedule 1b)	5,195,462	4,834,969	360,493	6.94%
Over Allocated indirect Construction Cost (Schedule 1c)		(3,199)	3,199	
Callbacks and adjustments on prior closed contracts	8,244	14,984	(6,740)	
	$11,683,190	$11,002,186	$681,004	5.83%

	Year ended December 31, 19X8			
	Revenue Earned	Cost of Construction	Gross Profit	GP %
Contracts Completed	$ 3,354,892	$ 3,156,282	$198,610	5.92%
Contracts in Progress	7,387,671	6,934,956	452,715	6.13%
Over Allocated indirect Construction Cost (Schedule 1c)		(1,268)	1,268	
Callbacks and adjustments on prior closed contracts	5,764	14,113	(8,349)	
	$10,748,327	$10,104,083	$644,244	5.99%

See Report of Independent Certified Public Accountants on Additional Information.

Example Contractor, Inc.
Contracts Completed
Year Ended December 31, 19X9

Schedule 1a

Contract	Contract Totals						Prior to January 1,19X9			
	Final Contract	Unbilled Conract	Final Cost	Accrued Cost to Complete	Gross Profit	GP %	Revenue Earned	Cost of Construction	Gross Profit	GP %
X807	$ 1,121,344	$	$ 1,046,139	$	$ 75,205	6.71%	$1,050,083	$ 975,782	$ 74,300	7.08%
X808	1,675,000		1,573,141		101,859	6.08%	1,263,788	1,185,621	78,167	6.19%
X809	1,698,000		1,752,378		(54,378)	-3.20%	1,395,201	1,357,592	37,609	2.70%
X811	2,346,770		2,199,854		146,916	6.26%	1,795,020	1,675,763	119,257	6.64%
X818	987,600		920,186		67,414	6.83%	848,310	787,864	60,446	7.13%
X901	1,678,450	21,344	1,576,322	15,838	102,128	6.08%	144,292	134,826	9,466	6.56%
X904	2,654,000	33,446	2,483,709	22,643	170,291	6.42%	63,023	58,765	4,258	6.76%
Jobs under $100,000	1,138,425	25,677	1,012,242	14,329	126,183	11.08%	260,389	232,325	28,064	10.78%
	$ 13,299,589	$80,467	$12,563,971	$52,810	$735,618	5.53%	$6,820,105	$6,408,538	$411,567	6.03%

Note C

Schedule 1a, Continued

Contract	Revenue Earned	Cost of Construction	Gross Profit	GP %
	Year Ended December 31, 19X9			
X807	$ 71,261	$ 70,356	$ 905	1.27%
X808	411,213	387,520	23,692	5.76%
X809	302,799	394,786	(91,987)	–30.38%
X811	551,750	524,091	27,659	5.01%
X818	139,290	132,322	6,968	5.00%
X901	1,534,158	1,441,496	92,662	6.04%
X904	2,590,977	2,424,944	166,033	6.41%
Jobs under $100,000	878,036	779,917	98,119	11.17%
	$6,479,484	$6,155,432	$324,052	5.00%

Schedule 1

Note C

See Report of Independent Certified Public Accountants on Additional Information

Example Contractor, Inc.
Contracts in Progress
Year Ended December 31, 19X9

Schedule 1b

				Contract to Date						
Job No.	Current Contract	Estimated Gross Profit	Percent Complete	Earned Revenue	Cost to Date	Gross Profit	GP %	Progress Billings	Under Billings	(Over) Billings
X811	$2,733,300	$164,041	87%	$2,377,180	$2,234,512	$142,668	6.00%	$2,525,800	$	$(148,620)
X903	1,375,500	83,152	89%	1,218,207	1,144,564	73,643	6.05%	1,219,500		(1,293)
X905	690,000	43,169	66%	454,597	426,155	28,442	6.26%	492,500		(37,903)
X909	2,245,630	135,149	23%	514,734	483,756	30,978	6.02%	366,900	147,834	
X910	322,500	24,873	59%	190,323	175,644	14,679	7.71%	195,500		(5,177)
Jobs under $100,000	1,413,280	155,957	71%	1,007,987	896,755	111,232	11.04%	1,023,450	25,177	(40,640)
	$8,780,210	$606,341	66%	$5,763,028	$5,361,386	$401,642	6.97%	$5,823,650	$173,011	$(233,633)
	Note C			Note C					Note C	

Contracts awarded after December 31, 19X9 but before February 24, 19Y0

Y001	$1,455,656	$ 87,339
Y002	877,650	70,212
Y003	89,775	7,182
Y006	966,750	58,005
	$3,389,831	$222,738

Schedule 1b, Continued

Job No.	Year Ended December 31, 19X9			Backlog		
	Revenue Earned	Cost of Construction	Gross Profit	Revenue Remaining	Cost to Complete	Estimated Gross Profit
X811	$1,809,614	$1,708,095	$101,519	356,120	$ 334,747	$ 21,373
X903	1,218,207	1,144,564	73,643	157,293	147,784	9,509
X905	454,597	426,155	28,442	235,403	220,676	14,727
X909	514,734	483,756	30,978	1,730,896	1,626,725	104,171
X910	190,323	175,644	14,679	132,177	121,983	10,194
Jobs under $100,000	1,007,987	896,755	111,232	405,293	360,568	44,725
	$5,195,462	$4,834,969	$360,493	$3,017,182	$2,812,483	$204,699
	Schedule 1					
	Note C					
Y001				$1,455,656	$1,368,317	$ 87,339
Y002				877,650	807,438	70,212
Y003				89,775	82,593	7,182
Y006				966,750	908,745	58,005
				$3,389,831	$3,167,093	$222,738

See Report of Independent Certified Public Accountants on Additional Information

Schedule 1c

EXAMPLE CONTRACTOR, INC.
INDIRECT CONSTRUCTION COSTS
Years ended December 31,

	19X9	19X8
PROJECT MANAGEMENT COSTS		
Salaries and benefits	$ 316,087	$ 297,415
Printing and supplies	13,410	12,609
Travel and auto expense	12,690	11,951
Other costs	3,900	4,107
	346,087	326,082
Project management allocated	(329,218)	(296,341)
Under (over) allocated	16,869	29,741
SHOP AND YARD		
Labor and benefits	32,916	29,610
Depreciation	4,110	4,060
Small tools and supplies	16,408	15,290
Repairs and maintenance	2,916	2,804
Insurance	2,800	2,600
Personal property taxes	4,755	4,450
Other	2,112	2,260
	66,017	61,074
Shop and yard allocated	(68,212)	(65,209)
Under (over) allocated	(2,195)	(4,135)
CONSTRUCTION EQUIPMENT AND VEHICLES		
Repairs and maintenance	9,410	8,255
Depreciation	74,136	76,923
Fuel	4,210	4,066
Insurance	5,901	5,285
Taxes & licenses—other	2,210	2,086
	95,867	96,615
Construction equipment and vehicles allocated	(86,534)	(90,083)
Under (over) allocated	9,333	6,532

See Report of Independent Certified Public Accountants on Additional Information.

Schedule 1c (continued)

	19X9	19X8
PAYROLL BENEFITS		
FICA	$139,061	$135,608
Federal U.C.	8,216	8,044
State U.C.	51,400	49,460
Workers compensation and liability insurance	208,903	197,416
Association Fees	8,916	8,466
Pension	132,408	129,255
Health and welfare	139,212	130,066
Training and other	31,680	29,400
Other	10,855	9,722
	730,651	697,437
Payroll Benefits allocated	(757,857)	(730,843)
Net under (over) allocated	(27,206)	(33,406)
Net indirect construction costs	$ (3,199)	$ (1,268)

See Report of Independent Certified Public Accountants on Additional Information.

Schedule 2

EXAMPLE CONTRACTOR, INC.
SELLING, ADMINISTRATIVE AND GENERAL EXPENSES
Years ended December 31,

	19X9	19X8
SELLING EXPENSES		
Estimating salaries and benefits	$ 80,600	$ 74,200
Advertising and promotion	26,577	23,218
Dues, subscriptions and association fees	7,689	6,114
Other selling expense	4,216	4,409
	119,082	107,941
ADMINISTRATIVE AND GENERAL EXPENSES		
Administrative and office salaries and benefits	286,602	278,732
Office supplies and expense	19,608	18,955
Vehicle and travel expense	13,122	12,915
Telephone	3,287	3,066
Data processing	18,212	18,009
Professional services	25,800	24,900
Insurance	7,600	7,200
Depreciation	32,980	31,040
Miscellaneous	7,003	6,119
	414,214	400,936
	$533,296	$508,877

See Report of Independent Certified Public Accountants on Additional Information.

Index

A

B

C

D

E

F

G

H

I

J

L

M

N

O